QBasic® Made Easy

QBasic®

Don Inman
Bob Albrecht

Osborne **McGraw-Hill**

Berkeley   New York   St. Louis   San Francisco
Auckland   Bogotá   Hamburg   London   Madrid
Mexico City   Milan   Montreal   New Delhi   Panama City
Paris   São Paulo   Singapore   Sydney
Tokyo   Toronto

Osborne **McGraw-Hill**
2600 Tenth Street
Berkeley, California 94710
U.S.A.

Osborne **McGraw-Hill** offers software for sale. For information on software, translations, or book distributors outside of the U.S.A., please write to Osborne **McGraw-Hill** at the above address.

This book is printed on recycled paper.

QBasic® Made Easy

 234567890 DOC 9987654321

ISBN 0-07-881698-X

CONTENTS
AT A GLANCE

CONTENTS

INTRODUCTION

BASIC is the most popular programming language in the world. Today, various versions of BASIC are running on more than 50 million computers. BASIC is widely used because it is easy to learn and use, yet extremely powerful.

QBasic, the newest version of BASIC from Microsoft, Inc., is designed to be used by the absolute beginner, as well as by the advanced programmer. Its features facilitate structured programming, making programs more efficient and easier to understand.

You can accomplish all the tasks of creating, editing, running, and saving your programs within the QBasic programming environment with its easy-to-use menu system. A complete on-line help system is available as you write your programs. In very little time a beginner can write simple yet powerful programs.

ABOUT THIS BOOK

The material in this book is organized so that a beginner to QBasic can make a natural learning progression. The text is sprinkled with many program examples that are interesting, fun, and useful. New concepts are introduced within the context of executable programs, and each program is thoroughly explained.

It is assumed that you have a working knowledge of your computer's disk operating system (DOS). It is also assumed that you have the QBasic files from the distribution disk, which are available on a hard disk, a 5 1/4-inch floppy disk, or a 3 1/2-inch diskette.

The book opens with discussions and explorations of the QBasic programming environment. In the opening chapter, you learn how the screen is divided into windows. You use the Immediate window to execute some simple QBasic statements and see some immediate results. After using these statements for direct execution, you learn to use the same statements in small, simple programs written in the View window.

You then write programs using QBasic statements that calculate numeric results and manipulate string information. The concept of assigning values to simple variables is presented, along with information on formatting printed results. After you learn how to use variables, you are introduced to QBasic control structures that are used for making decisions and controlling program flow.

Since everyone is not a perfect programmer or a perfect typist, the book introduces editing and debugging techniques before delving into the advanced programming features of QBasic. This information allows you to correct and refine the programs you write.

Many of the features that you will need to write programs quickly are already a part of QBasic. These include many useful programmed functions, ready for use. In addition, you are shown how to write functions of your own, called user-defined functions.

A complete chapter is devoted to the use of FUNCTION and SUB procedures that enable you to write programs in modules that perform specific functions. These procedures allow you to break long programs into small blocks, each block performing its own task.

Various ways are shown to enter data, both individual items and complete blocks of items. You are shown how to use arrays to manipulate blocks of related data that share a common name. The use of arrays leads naturally into discussions and demonstrations of data files. A complete chapter is devoted to sequential files and another to random-access files.

The final chapter in the book contains a "backpack" of many routines that you can use again and again.

CONVENTIONS USED IN THIS BOOK

Several conventions are used throughout this book to assist you in distinguishing between narrative text and items that have special meanings. Special items may be cautions, reminders, notes, introduction of technical terms, and items that you should type.

For example, when you are asked to enter data, you will see the word "Type" followed by a colon and the data to be typed (in boldface characters). On subsequent lines there may be instructions to press one or more keys. These lines are printed as a block, separate from the narrative text, and appear as in the following example:

Type: **BEEP**
and press ENTER

In some instances, you will be asked to press two keys in combination. Key combinations are indicated by a hyphen (-) between the two keys, as shown here:

Press: CTRL-BREAK

In some instances, you will be asked to press two or more keys in succession. A sequence of keypresses is shown with a comma between the keys, as follows:

Press: ALT, R, ENTER

When new terms are introduced, they are printed in italics. For example,

The *View window* is used for entering programs.

The text following such an italicized term will explain its meaning and use.

Program messages or parts of the program screen that appear in text are printed in monospace font (similar to their appearance on the screen) to distinguish them from the narrative text, as shown here:

```
CLS
LoRate = .0882
INPUT kwh
PRINT kwh * LoRate
```

This book also uses graphic notations to emphasize specific material or concepts. The word *note, caution,* or *remember* (lowercase and in italics) follows the special notation, as shown here:

Figures, programs, and tables are set off from the narrative text by box enclosures.

THE CONVENIENCE DISK
FOR *QBASIC MADE EASY*

You'll be able to take any program in this book and modify it to suit your own particular needs. As you progress through the book, you will find that the programs get longer and longer. It is tough on your fingers and your patience to enter them from the keyboard. The convenience disk for *QBasic Made Easy* provides these programs, making your work much easier.

We refer to this disk as the "convenience disk" for still another reason: it has a READ.ME file that gives you brief descriptions of all the programs in the book and their specific locations.

We want to make this clear: as the authors, we encourage you to use these programs. Use them in any way you want; we just want you to enjoy and learn. That's why we set so low a price on the disk (just $9.95), and why we don't worry about our copyright.

As the authors, we thank you for buying and using our book.

—Don Inman and Bob Albrecht

To order:

The disk is $9.95 (plus 70¢ sales tax if you're a California resident). Please print your name and address on your order, as well as the number of disks you want and the size (5 1/4-inch or 3 1/2-inch). Enclose a check or money order for the proper amount.

Mail this information to:

The Mail Order Emporium
530 Hilmar St.
Santa Clara, CA 95050

Please allow 3 to 6 weeks for delivery. Osborne/McGraw-Hill assumes NO responsibility for this offer. This is solely an offer of the authors, Don Inman and Bob Albrecht, and not of Osborne/McGraw-Hill.

GETTING STARTED

You can learn to read and understand QBasic. You can learn to express yourself in QBasic and use it to make the computer do what you want it to do, the way you want it done. By using this book, you can learn to read, understand, and write QBasic programs.

This chapter gets you started. It introduces the latest version of Microsoft BASIC, called QBasic. In this chapter, you will explore the QBasic environment with its windows and menus. In particular, you will learn how to

- Use QBasic's windows, menus, and dialog boxes

- Access a menu

- Select an item from a menu

- Follow instructions that appear in the display screen

- Move between the Edit and Immediate windows

- Execute immediate statements in the Immediate window

- Move between the Edit window and Output screen

- Exit gracefully from QBasic

You will learn how to load QBasic into your computer, explore the QBasic environment, and begin using QBasic to tell the computer what to do and how to do it.

LEARNING A BIT ABOUT QBASIC

QBasic is a computer language, a language that you use to communicate with a computer. Compared to human languages such as English, Spanish, or Japanese, a computer language is simple. QBasic has a small *vocabulary* (list of words it knows), and a *syntax* (rules of grammar that it follows).

A *program* is a set of instructions, a plan for doing something. You may have already used or created programs, such as:

A recipe for baking cookies
Instructions for opening a combination lock
Directions on how to get to someone's house
Instructions for assembling a model or a toy

A *QBasic program* is a set of instructions that tells the computer what to do and how to do it in the language that the computer understands—QBasic. The program follows the rules of QBasic and makes the computer do what you want it to do. You will begin learning about programs in the next chapter.

Microsoft has provided an easy-to-use environment for you to learn how to use the QBasic language. It uses a system of menus for selecting things that you want to do. The display screen is divided into areas called *windows*. You perform different actions in each type of window. When QBasic needs information from you, it displays special boxed areas, called *dialog boxes*, that indicate what type of information is needed.

QBasic is compatible with Microsoft GW-BASIC and IBM BASICA but is easier to use and much more powerful. It accepts command selections from either a mouse or the keyboard.

A DOLLOP OF DOS

QBasic runs under the Microsoft Disk Operating System (MS-DOS) that is provided on tens of millions of IBM-compatible computers. The authors assume that you have some knowledge of the Microsoft Disk Operating

System or of PC-DOS, the version of MS-DOS licensed to IBM. This book uses the term DOS to refer to MS-DOS, PC-DOS, or any other compatible disk operating system.

This book assumes that you know how to use the following DOS commands:

DIR	The DIRectory command lists the names of all the files on a disk
DISKCOPY	Copies everything on a disk to another disk
FORMAT	Formats a disk. A new, never-before-used disk must be formatted before it can be used. A previously used disk may be recycled, but do so with caution; formatting erases previously stored information from the disk
COPY	Copies named files or groups of named files

The book also assumes that you are using DOS and QBasic from a floppy disk in drive A or from a hard disk in drive C.

When you load DOS into your computer from drive A, you see the famous DOS *A prompt* (A>) and a blinking cursor (_), as shown here:

```
A>_
```

In this case, disk drive A is your default disk drive. Information is read from, or written to, drive A (the default drive) unless you designate another disk drive.

If your system has a hard disk drive, then you are probably using DOS from your hard disk. You see a C prompt (C>) and a blinking cursor, perhaps as shown here:

```
C>_
```

or

```
C:\>_
```

In this case, your hard disk is the default disk drive. Information is read from, or written to, the hard disk drive (the default drive) unless you designate another drive.

QBasic is either on a floppy disk or on the hard disk. You should use the DOS DIR command to search the floppy or hard disk in order to locate the QBASIC.EXE file. Look for the following file name in the display or print-out of the disk directory: QBASIC.EXE.

EXPLORING THE QBASIC ENVIRONMENT

Now it is time to begin using QBasic. The disk drive used to load QBasic depends on the disk drive where the QBASIC.EXE file is located. If you are using QBasic from a floppy disk on drive A, you should use drive A for the demonstration programs. You would probably use drive C if you copied the original QBasic files to your hard disk.

Loading QBasic

If you are loading QBasic from a floppy disk, insert your QBasic disk into drive A. If you are loading QBasic from a hard disk, you may use a floppy disk in drive A as a data disk to load and save programs created from QBasic.

At the DOS prompt, do the following:

Type: **QBasic**
and press ENTER

You may also load QBasic by entering the file name in any combination of upper- and lowercase letters. For example: **qbasic**, **QBASIC**, or even **QbAsIc**. However, if you omit a letter, type the letters out of order, or type an incorrect letter, you will get a response from the computer similar to this:

```
A>QBasix              (or C>QBasix for a hard disk)
Bad command or file name
```

If that happens, just try again:

Type: **QBasic**
and press ENTER

The prompt and your command on the screen will look like this:

```
A>QBasic              (or C>QBasic for a hard disk)
```

When the command has been entered correctly, the light on drive A comes on as the QBasic file is loaded. If you are using drive C, there may be no light, but you will probably hear a whirring sound as the file is loaded.

When the file has been loaded from whichever drive you are using, you see QBasic's opening screen, as shown in Figure 1-1. In the middle of the screen is a rectangular area with a welcome message and copyright notice. Near the bottom of the rectangle, QBasic displays two choices:

```
< Press ENTER to see the Survival Guide >
< Press ESC to clear this dialog box >
```

Do not press any key yet. This rectangle is an example of a QBasic dialog box. Dialog boxes contain instructions, information, or choices for you to make before proceeding. You will learn about other dialog boxes as you encounter them. This particular one provides two choices near the bottom of the box.

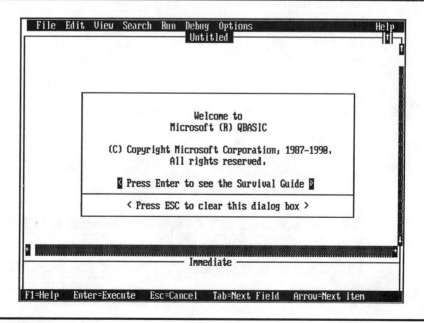

FIGURE 1-1.   Opening screen

The first choice, which is highlighted, says, "Press ENTER to see the Survival Guide." Do not press ENTER at this time. You can investigate the Survival Guide later by reloading QBasic and choosing the first option in the dialog box. Some of the information in the QBasic Survival Guide is given in Appendix A, "The QBasic Survival Guide."

The second choice says, "Press ESC to clear this dialog box." To begin your exploration of QBasic, clear the opening dialog box, as follows:

Press: ESC

When you press ESC, the screen shown in Figure 1-2 appears. This *Control Center* is the place in the QBasic environment where you control most of the actions that you want QBasic to perform. When you are working in other parts of the environment, you can return to the Control Center by pressing the ESC key.

 If you are using a mouse with QBasic, you can select menus, dialog boxes, and other choices by moving the mouse pointer to the appropriate item and clicking on the item. The mouse pointer appears on the screen as a solid rectangle.

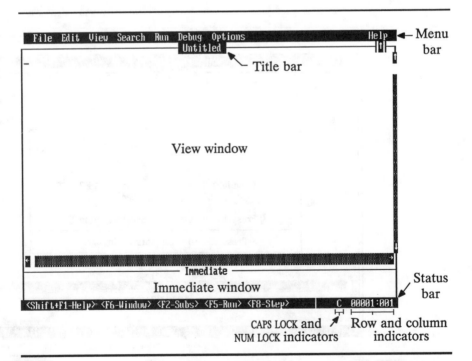

FIGURE 1-2. QBasic Control Center

Let your eyes roam about the screen. Notice the following:

- Across the top of the screen is the *menu bar.* Within it are the names of QBasic menus that you can access:

- The screen is divided into two windows—a large window near the top and a small window near the bottom.

- The large, upper window is the *View window.* At the top of this window, near the center of the screen, is the *title bar,* which now reads "Untitled."

- The smaller, narrow window near the bottom of the screen is the *Immediate window.* The word "Immediate" appears in the top center part of this window.

- The line across the bottom of the screen is the *status bar.* When you activate a menu or a dialog box or leave this screen, the status bar changes. It usually contains a description of where you are, what a given menu option will do, or how to get help, as shown here:

Browsing the Menu Bar

QBasic is like a well-designed learning center with many interesting places to browse, play, create, design, contemplate, or do whatever else you want to do with your computer.

You should begin by highlighting a menu name in the menu bar by pressing the ALT key:

Press: ALT

Notice that the word "File" and the first letter of all the other menu names in the menu bar are highlighted. Notice also that the status bar at the bottom of the screen has changed, as shown by the screen in Figure 1-3.

Compare the screen in Figure 1-3 with the one in Figure 1-2. Note the word "File" in the menu bar; also note the status bar in the two figures.

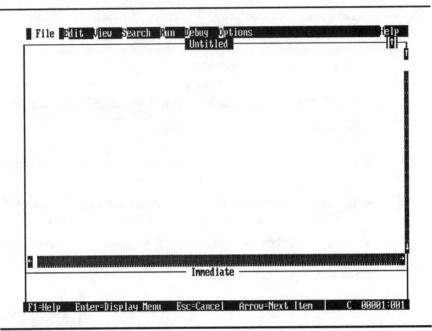

FIGURE 1-3. File highlighted on menu bar

Press: ALT

again, and the screen shown in Figure 1-2 reappears.

Press: ALT

again so that the word "File" is highlighted, as shown in Figure 1-3.

Press: ESC

The highlight is now turned off, and you're back at the Control Center shown in Figure 1-2. Practice using ALT and ESC to turn on and off the highlighting in the menu bar.

If File is not now highlighted,

Press: ALT

so that the menu bar appears as in Figure 1-3. Now,

Press: the right arrow (→) key

to move the highlight to the right from the File menu item to the Edit menu item, as shown here:

Press the → key again to move the highlight to the right from the Edit menu item to the View menu item:

Repeat the → keypresses until the highlight is on the Help menu item at the extreme right of the menu bar:

Then press the → key one more time. The highlight returns to the File item.

As you have just seen, pressing the → key moves the highlight one item to the right in the menu bar. You can also use the left arrow key (←) to move the highlight one item at a time to the left across the menu bar. Practice highlighting items on the menu bar by pressing ← and →.

No matter which item in the menu bar is highlighted, you can return to the QBasic Control Center with nothing highlighted by pressing the ESC key. You can also use the ALT key to turn off the highlight on the menu bar.

Selecting a Menu

The items on the menu bar are the names of the menus. Each menu contains a list of options that you can choose from to tell the computer what to do. You can browse the menus as easily as you browsed the menu bar and look at each menu briefly. First,

Press: ESC

to make sure that you are in the QBasic Control Center with no item highlighted in the menu bar. Then,

Press: ALT

to highlight the File item. When the File item is highlighted,

Press: ENTER

to select the File menu. The File menu appears in the View window, below its name in the menu bar, as shown by the screen in Figure 1-4.

 If you are using a mouse with QBasic, you can select menus, dialog boxes, and other choices by moving the mouse pointer to the appropriate item and clicking on the item. The mouse pointer appears on the screen as a solid rectangle. To see the File menu shown in Figure 1-4, you would move the mouse until its pointer was on the File item on the menu bar and then press the left mouse button.

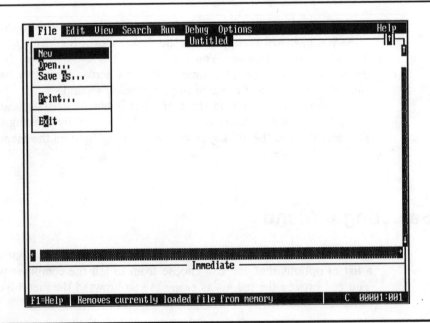

FIGURE 1-4. File menu

You can see that the File menu has five choices. The first choice, New, is highlighted. The other items on this menu are Open..., Save As..., Print..., and Exit. For now, just look. You'll learn how to select menu items in Chapter 2, "Tiny Programs." Some items on the menu are followed by ellipses (...); others are not. Items with no ellipses are executed immediately when you select them. Items with ellipses are not executed immediately; they require further information, which is requested by display dialog boxes. Notice that the status bar describes the action of the highlighted item, New.

You can return to the QBasic Control Center from the File menu by pressing ESC.

The File menu is one of eight menus that you can select by moving the highlight across the menu bar. An easy way to browse all of the menus is to first select the File menu (press ALT and then press ENTER) and then press the → key to display other menus in the menu bar. Each time you press the → key you will see the next menu. Browse the menus and just look for now.
Begin browsing the menus from the Control Center:

Press: ALT
and then press ENTER

to select the File menu shown previously in Figure 1-4.

Throughout this book, a series of keypresses, such as the preceding two, will use this shortcut notation:

Press: ALT, ENTER

Then,

Press: →

to move from the File menu to the Edit menu shown in Figure 1-5. The Edit menu has six choices, the first of which is highlighted in the menu bar and described in the status bar. You will use Cut, Copy, Paste, and Clear in Chapter 6, "Editing and Dynamic Debugging." You will use New SUB... and New FUNCTION... in Chapter 8, "FUNCTION and SUB Procedures."

Press: →

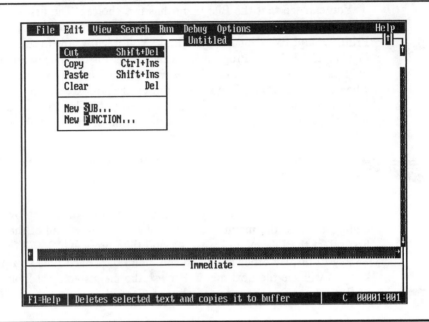

FIGURE 1-5. Edit menu

again to move from the Edit menu to the View menu, which displays the options Index, Contents, Topic:, Using Help, and About. . . . Notice that the first item in the View menu is highlighted in the menu bar and described in the status bar.

Press: →

again to move from menu to menu until the last item on the menu bar, Help, is displayed. The Help menu has four items: Index, Context, Topic:, and Help on Help. You can use these selections when you run into trouble and need on-line help.

If you press → when the Help menu is displayed, the Help menu is erased and the File menu reappears. You can also use the ← key to browse the menus. Pressing ← displays the menu to the left of the current menu. When you have finished browsing, press ESC to go back to the Control Center.

If you want to move to a specific menu on the menu bar, you can do it quickly from the keyboard by holding down the ALT key and then pressing the highlighted letter of the menu you want, as shown in Table 1-1. This book will indicate such a key combination in this way:

Press: ALT-F

Desired Menu	Press
File menu	ALT-F
Edit menu	ALT-E
View menu	ALT-V
Search menu	ALT-S
Run menu	ALT-R
Debug menu	ALT-D
Options menu	ALT-O
Help menu	ALT-H

TABLE 1-1.   Shortcut Keys for Accessing Menus

EXPLORING WINDOWS

Make sure that you are in the Control Center with the blinking cursor in the upper-left corner of the View window (shown in Figure 1-2). You can move the cursor back and forth between the View window and the Immediate window by pressing F6. With the cursor in the View window,

Press: F6

The cursor moves to the Immediate window, as shown here:

Press: F6

again, and the cursor moves back to the View window.

Press: F6

once more to move it to the Immediate window.

Using the Immediate Window

When the cursor is in the Immediate window, you can enter QBasic statements. *Statements* are combinations of words called *keywords* that QBasic understands. When you type a QBasic statement in the Immediate window and press ENTER, the computer obeys the statement immediately. For example, BEEP is a keyword that you can use as an immediate QBasic statement. It tells the computer to make a beeping sound.

Be sure that the cursor is in the Immediate window; then

Type: **BEEP**
and press ENTER

The computer beeps and the Immediate window looks like this:

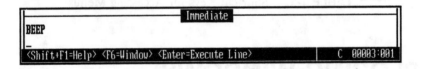

Notice that the cursor has moved to the line below the BEEP keyword, ready for another direct statement.

Suppose you make a typing mistake or type a word that is not a valid QBasic statement. For example, on the line below the previous immediate statement (BEEP), do this:

Type: **BLEEP**
and press ENTER

When you press the ENTER key, a Syntax error dialog box appears on the screen, as shown in Figure 1-6. The Syntax error dialog box has two options: OK and Help. The brackets enclosing the left choice (OK) are highlighted and the cursor is blinking under the letter O of OK. This tells you that the OK choice is now active.

Press: TAB

to move to the next choice in the dialog box (Help). The second choice is now active.

Press: TAB

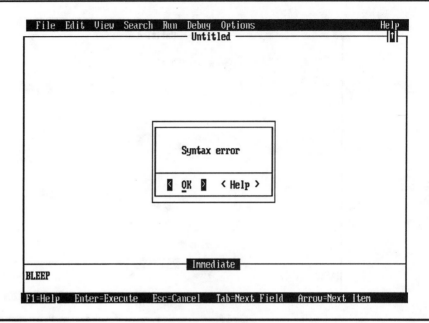

```
 File  Edit  View  Search  Run  Debug  Options              Help
─────────────────────── Untitled ─────────────────────────┤↑│
│                                                              │
│                                                              │
│                                                              │
│                   ┌──────────────────────┐                   │
│                   │                      │                   │
│                   │     Syntax error     │                   │
│                   │                      │                   │
│                   │  ◄ OK ►    < Help >  │                   │
│                   │                      │                   │
│                   └──────────────────────┘                   │
│                                                              │
│                        ─ Immediate ─                         │
│BLEEP                                                         │
 F1=Help   Enter=Execute   Esc=Cancel   Tab=Next Field   Arrow=Next Item
```

FIGURE 1-6. Syntax error dialog box

again to move back to the first choice (OK) and make it active. Selecting this choice means that you want to clear the syntax box. Do so now:

Press: ENTER

The Syntax error dialog box disappears, and the display is like the one shown in Figure 1-7. Notice that the cursor is positioned at the invalid QBasic statement (under the letter B). You can correct the error by moving the cursor with the → key to the offending letter L in BLEEP and pressing the DEL key. This deletes the letter L and moves the letters to the right of it one place left to make the word BEEP.

Press: ENTER

and you hear the BEEP again.

 You can use the arrow keys and DEL or BACKSPACE to correct mistakes and make changes within a window. Use the TAB key to move the cursor between options in a dialog box.

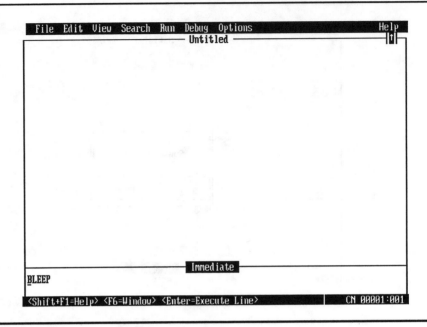

FIGURE 1-7. Syntax error dialog box removed

USING THE OUTPUT SCREEN FROM THE IMMEDIATE WINDOW You use the View window to enter QBasic programs made up of QBasic statements. You use the Immediate window to enter immediate QBasic statements. When a QBasic statement that produces visible output is executed, the output is shown on the *Output screen.*

CLEARING THE OUTPUT SCREEN If the cursor is not in the Immediate window now, press F6 to move it there. You can clear the Output screen by executing a direct CLS statement. The CLS statement clears any previous text from the Output screen. The QBasic prompt, "Press any key to continue," appears whenever QBasic finishes executing an immediate statement or a program that affects output to the screen.

Type: **CLS**
and press ENTER

The QBasic Control Center screen disappears and you see the Output screen. It is blank except for one line at the bottom, shown here:

```
Press any key to continue
```

Press any key (the SPACEBAR is a good choice) to return to the Control Center screen with the CLS statement and cursor in the Immediate window. Notice that the cursor now appears on the line below CLS, ready for a new direct statement:

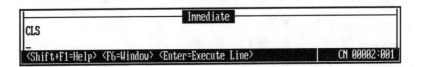

CLEARING THE IMMEDIATE WINDOW   Only two lines normally show in the Immediate window—the last line executed and the current input line. The BEEP statement given earlier has scrolled out of the window. You can scroll previous immediate statements back into the window by pressing ↑.

Press: ↑

once to move the cursor under the letter C of CLS, as shown here:

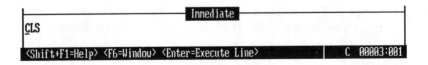

Press: ↑

a second time to scroll the previous statement back into the Immediate window. The BEEP statement, which was corrected from BLEEP, comes back into the window, as shown here:

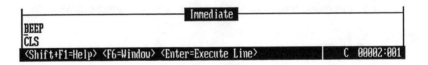

Press: ↑

again to scroll another statement back into the Immediate window. The two BEEP statements (the original one and the corrected one) now show in the window:

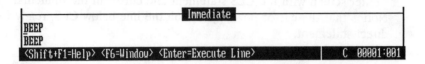

Since BEEP was the first immediate statement entered, nothing will happen when you press ↑ again. Try it. You can use ↓ to scroll in the reverse direction. Experiment with ↓ also.

Now, erase all the statements in the Immediate window:

Press: ↑

until both BEEP statements show in the Immediate window.

Press: CTRL-Y

which erases everything on the first line. The other lines scroll up so that the second BEEP and the CLS statement show in the Immediate window. The cursor now lies under the B of the second BEEP statement:

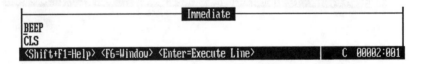

Press: CTRL-Y

again. The line with the second BEEP is erased, and the previously entered CLS statement scrolls to the top line in the Immediate window.

Press: CTRL-Y

once more, and the CLS statement is erased; the Immediate window is now clear.

Printing the Date and Time

When you first turned on your computer, you probably entered the current date and time. You can print the current date and time from QBasic by using the PRINT keyword followed by the QBasic keyword DATE$ or TIME$. You use PRINT in immediate statements to print something on the Output screen. DATE$ returns the computer's date, and TIME$ returns the computer's time.

You have cleared the Immediate window, and you should also clear the Output screen. To do so,

  Type: **CLS**
  and press ENTER

Press any key to return to the Control Center and the Immediate window. Then

  Type: **PRINT DATE$**
  and press ENTER

The Output screen appears with the date at the top:

01-03-1991

The prompt "Press any key to continue" is displayed at the bottom of the Output screen.

 Even mouse users must press a key to return to the View window.

The date is printed in the form 01-03-1991, representing the date January 3, 1991. Of course, if you misspell PRINT or DATE$, the Syntax error dialog box appears. In that case, press ENTER to return to the Immediate window for corrections.

When you return to the Immediate window, you will see that the previous immediate statements have scrolled upward and that the cursor appears on the line below the last statement, ready for another statement.

  Type: **PRINT TIME$**
  and press ENTER

Because the Output screen was not cleared after the previous PRINT statement, the time is printed below the date, as shown by the screen in Figure 1-8. The prompt to continue appears at the bottom of the Output screen. Press any key to return to the Immediate window.

Other Statements in the Immediate Window

Try the following immediate statements in the Immediate window.

Type: **CLS**
and press ENTER

This clears the Output screen. Return to the Immediate window and enter the current date and then the current time. The following examples use a fictitious date and time. You should enter the current date and time. First enter the date as follows:

Type: **DATE$ = "1-4-91"**
and press ENTER

This changes the computer's date but prints no output.

Type: **TIME$ = "11:30"**
and press ENTER

This changes the computer's time but prints no output. Next, print the new date and time on the same line of the Output screen:

Type: **PRINT DATE$, TIME$**
and press ENTER

The Output screen is shown in Figure 1-9. The comma used in the PRINT statement tells the computer to print the values in *standard print positions*. In this example, the value of DATE$ was printed in the first standard print position; the value of TIME$ was printed in the second standard print

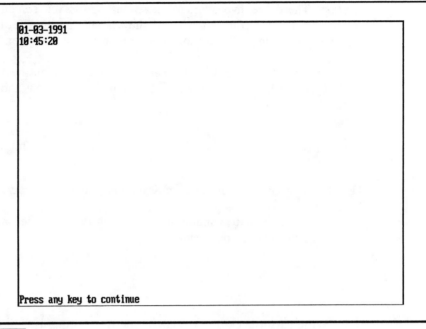

FIGURE 1-8. Date and time printed

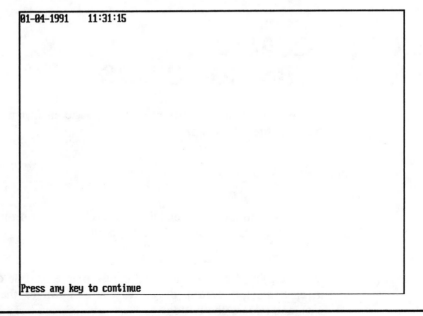

FIGURE 1-9. Date and time printed on one line

position. There are five standard positions across the screen. Position 1 begins at column 1 (the left edge of the screen), position 2 at column 15, position 3 at column 29, position 4 at column 43, and position 5 at column 57.

You can use the F4 key to move back and forth between the View window and the Output screen or between the Immediate window and the Output screen at any time:

Press: F4

The "Press any key to continue" message disappears, and you return to the Immediate window.

Clear the Immediate window now by using CTRL-Y, as before. When the Immediate window has been cleared,

Press: F6

to move the cursor back to the View window.

EXITING QBASIC
AND RETURNING TO DOS

This concludes your first explorations of the QBasic environment. To leave QBasic, activate the File menu:

Press: ALT-F

Then use the ↓ key to move the highlight to the last item on the File menu, Exit. Press ENTER to exit QBasic and return to DOS.

 If you are using a mouse, move the mouse pointer to File on the menu bar, click the left button, drag the pointer down to the last choice (Exit), and release the button.

SUMMARY

After reading the brief overview of QBasic and DOS at the beginning of this chapter, you learned to load QBasic and began your explorations. The QBasic environment includes the QBasic Control Center (where statements and programs are entered) and the Output screen (where printed output is displayed).

You explored the menu bar at the top of the Control Center, and you learned how to access any of the menus on the menu bar by pressing ALT and the first letter of the desired menu.

The Control Center is divided into two windows: the View window (where QBasic programs are entered), and the Immediate window (where QBasic immediate statements are entered). You moved the cursor back and forth between the two windows with the F6 key. You learned to enter statements in the Immediate window and see immediate results on the Output screen. You moved back and forth between the Immediate window and the Output screen by using the F6 key.

Last, you learned to leave QBasic and go back to DOS by selecting the Exit option from the File menu.

TINY PROGRAMS

In this chapter, you will learn to understand and use simple QBasic programs. A program is a set of instructions that tells the computer what to do and how to do it. You will learn how to enter a program into the computer's memory, run the program, save the program to a disk, and print a copy of a program to your printer.

A QBASIC PROGRAM

As you learned in Chapter 1, "Getting Started," you can use the Immediate window for testing QBasic statements. You learned to use

CLS	To clear the Output screen
BEEP	To beep the computer's speaker
PRINT	To print information on the Output screen
DATE$	To get or change the computer's date
TIME$	To get or change the computer's time

The programs in this chapter use all of these QBasic keywords. You will also use some new keywords.

Load QBasic into your computer's memory; then press the ESC key to clear the Welcome to QBasic dialog box. The screen shown in Figure 2-1 appears. You are now in the View window. You use the Immediate window to enter an instruction that the computer will execute as soon as you press ENTER. You use the View window, however, to enter a QBasic program; once entered, such a program can be run or saved for recall and later use.

Entering the Program

It is important to clear the screen before printing any information on the QBasic Output screen. Therefore, one of the first statements you use in a program is CLS (CLear Screen). You used an immediate BEEP statement in Chapter 1, "Getting Started," to give a short beep on the computer's speaker. You will now write a program that uses CLS and BEEP.

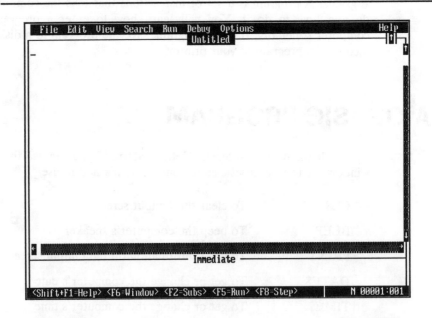

FIGURE 2-1. Control Center screen

You may type your programs in uppercase, lowercase, or mixed upper- and lowercase. When you press the ENTER key (after typing a program line), QBasic automatically formats the line. Sometimes there will be no changes from the way you typed it. However, suppose you typed the first statement in lowercase letters, as **cls**.

QBasic uses all uppercase letters for its keywords (CLS is a keyword). Therefore, when you press ENTER, cls is changed to

CLS

Enter the following two-line program in the View window:

Type: **CLS**
and press ENTER
Then type: **BEEP**
and press ENTER

This program is very simple. It clears the Output screen and sounds a beep. The program, shown here, has two program lines.

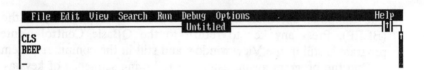

In Chapter 1, you used statements such as CLS, PRINT DATE$, PRINT TIME$, and BEEP as immediate statements in the Immediate window. You type an immediate statement and press ENTER. No formatting is done in the Immediate window; the computer executes the statement immediately. However, when you type a statement in the View window, it is not executed immediately when you press ENTER. Instead, it is stored in the computer's memory as it is entered. After entering all lines of your program, you can tell the computer to run (execute) the entire program.

Running the Program

As you type your program in the View window, it is stored in the computer's memory, ready to use. To execute the program, use the Run menu. To see the Run menu:

Press: ALT, R   (two keystrokes)

The Run menu, with the Start choice highlighted, appears.

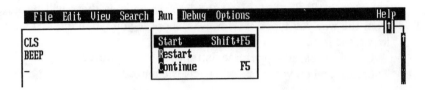

Sometimes a menu covers part of your program. If that happens, don't worry; it won't affect the program's execution. To start the program from the first program line, select Start by pressing ENTER while Start is highlighted.

When you press ENTER, the computer runs the program. The Output screen is cleared, and a beep comes forth from the computer's speaker. The program ends, with the following message at the bottom of the Output screen:

```
Press any key to continue
```

The computer executed the program from the top (CLS) to the bottom (BEEP). Press any key to return to the QBasic Control Center. Your program is still in the View window and still in the computer's memory.

Run the program again, using the following sequence of keys as a shortcut:

Press: ALT, R, ENTER   (three keystrokes)

 This book indicates a series of keystrokes to be pressed in order by using commas between the key labels, as in ALT, R, ENTER.

Again you see the Output screen, clear except for the message "Press any key to continue" at the bottom of the screen. Press a key to return to the View window.

Erasing the Old Program

You can use the File menu to clear the program from memory and from the View window so that you can then enter a new program. First, pull down the File menu:

Press: ALT, F

This selects the File menu, as shown by the screen in Figure 2-2. While the New option is highlighted,

    Press: ENTER

When you press ENTER, the File menu disappears and the following dialog box appears in the View window:

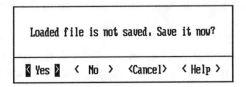

Whenever you have a program in the View window that hasn't been saved, QBasic displays this dialog box before it lets you use the New or Open...

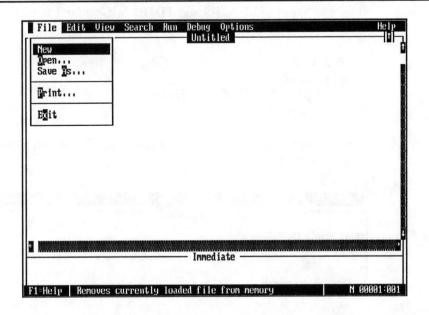

FIGURE 2-2.   File menu with New option highlighted

selection from the File menu. Notice that the Yes option is highlighted at the bottom of the dialog box.

 Do not press ENTER yet.

If you press ENTER while the Yes option is highlighted, the program in the View window will be saved. Don't save this program yet.

Press: TAB (to move the highlight from the Yes option to the No option) and press ENTER

When you press ENTER with the No button highlighted, the program is not saved. The two-line program is erased from memory, and the View window is cleared for a new program.

A NEW PROGRAM

Since you have used DATE$ and TIME$ in Chapter 1 from the Immediate window, use them now in a program.

Type: **CLS**
and press ENTER
Then type: **PRINT DATE$, TIME$**
and press ENTER

Now, enter your first name on the third line. The screen should now look something like this:

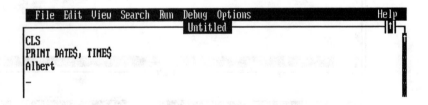

 Albert is used as the first name in the demonstration. You may use Albert's name or your own first name.

Running the New Program

As you type your program in the View window, it is stored in the computer's memory, ready to use. To execute the program, use the Run menu. To see the Run menu:

Press: ALT, R

The Run menu, with the Start choice highlighted, appears:

While the Start option is highlighted,

Press: ENTER

When you press ENTER, the program does not run. Instead, a Syntax error dialog box appears in the View window, as shown in Figure 2-3. Notice that the word "Albert" (or your first name) is highlighted. QBasic is telling you that the syntax error was caused by this word.

QBasic has a limited vocabulary. It does not know the word "Albert." "Albert" creates a syntax error when you use it in this way, as does any other word that QBasic does not know.

When the Syntax error dialog box appears, press the ENTER key. The dialog box disappears, and the cursor blinks under the first letter of the word in the program that caused the error.

Press: CTRL-Y

to delete the word in error. The line disappears, as shown here:

```
 File  Edit  View  Search  Run  Debug  Options                    Help
├──────────────────────────── Untitled ───────────────────────────────┤
CLS
PRINT DATE$, TIME$
─
```

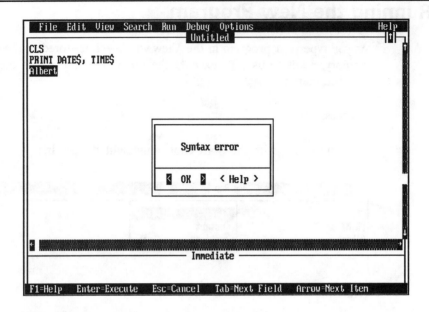

FIGURE 2-3. Syntax error at Albert

CTRL-Y deletes a complete program line. Therefore, the word "Albert" is deleted. The cursor is now at the beginning of the line, ready for a new statement.

If you want to print your name, you must use a PRINT statement and enclose your name in double quotation marks, as follows:

Type: **PRINT "Albert"**   (use your name if you want)
and press ENTER

You now have

```
CLS
PRINT DATE$, TIME$
PRINT "Albert"

-
```

You may also want to add a beep to signify the end of the program.

Type: **BEEP**
and press ENTER

Your program should now look like this:

```
CLS
PRINT DATE$, TIME$
PRINT "Albert"
BEEP
_
```

Press: ALT, R, ENTER

to run the program. Then the Output screen appears, showing the information that you asked to be printed:

```
01-05-1991      08:30:15
Albert
```

Of course, a beep sounds at the end of the program, and the prompt "Press any key to continue" is displayed at the bottom of the Output screen, as described in Chapter 1. Press a key to display the Control Center showing your program. Study each command. Each line is executed in the order that it appears in the program, from top to bottom, as shown in Table 2-1.

In this program, the lines are executed in the order in which they are written from top to bottom. In more complex programs that you will use later, you may use other statements to change the sequential execution order.

Order	Statement	Purpose
1	CLS	Clears the Output screen
2	PRINT DATE$, TIME$	Prints the computer's date and time on the Output screen, each in a different print area (called a print field)
3	PRINT "Albert"	Prints the information contained in quotation marks on the Output screen
4	BEEP	Makes a beeping sound from the computer's speaker

TABLE 2-1.   Statements in First Program

The computer continually updates the date and time. The PRINT statement in the second line of the program prints the computer's current date and time. The date and time displayed when you run the program will probably be different than that shown in the example.

The information enclosed in double quotation marks in the third line of the program is a *string*, sometimes referred to as a *string constant*. The PRINT statement in this line tells the computer to print on the Output screen whatever is enclosed in quotation marks. Even though the computer didn't recognize the word "Albert" on the first try, it will print the word when it is part of a string, enclosed in double quotation marks. Strings are discussed in more detail in Chapter 4, "String Manipulations."

 You can use the F4 key to toggle back and forth between the Control Center and the Output screen.

Press: F4

to see the Output screen. Notice that the prompt, "Press any key to continue," is not on the Output screen now. It is displayed only following the completion of a program run.

Press: F4

several times to toggle back and forth between the Output screen and the Control Center screen.

Saving the Program

To save a program, you must give it a name, called a *file name*. A file name can have up to eight characters (letters and numbers). The first character must be a letter. Name this program ALBERT01. Later, there might be programs called ALBERT02, ALBERT03, and so on.

 This book assumes that you are using disk drive A. That is, you began with DOS in drive A and then loaded QBasic at the DOS command line, as follows:

```
A>QBasic
```

In this case, disk drive A is the default disk drive. It is used unless you specify another drive. If you have a hard disk, perhaps you are working from it (you see C> instead of A>). If so, your hard disk is the default disk drive.

You have entered your first program, and it is stored in memory. Memory storage is temporary. If you want to keep a permanent copy of the program, you must save it to a disk file. You can save the program from the File menu, using your file name ALBERT01. To do this,

    Press: ALT, F

The File menu drops down over your program. Don't worry about this; your program remains in memory, unaffected by the menu. The first choice, New, is highlighted on the File menu. This is not the choice you want. Use the ↓ key to move the highlight to Save As. . . . If you overshoot the Save As option, use ↑ to move the highlight to Save As. . ., as shown here:

When you have highlighted Save As. . ., press ENTER to select it. You can also use the quick way to access Save As. . . :

    Press: ALT, F, A   (you do not have to press ENTER)

Regardless of the method you use to select Save As. . ., the File menu disappears, and you see the Save As dialog box shown in Figure 2-4.

The Save As dialog box contains two smaller boxes, labeled File Name and Dirs/Drives, and three options at the bottom, labeled OK, Cancel, and Help. The cursor is blinking in the File Name box, waiting for you to enter a name for your program. Do not enter the file name yet. The Dirs/Drives box contains the list of disk drives available for saving your program. In Figure 2-4, you are within a subdirectory named QBasic in the current hard disk

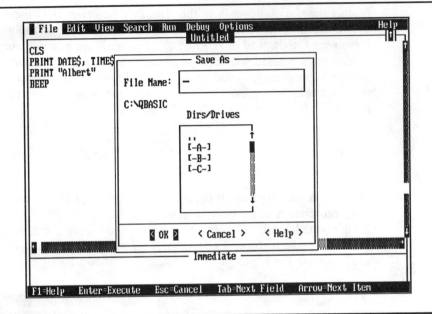

FIGURE 2-4. Save As dialog box

drive C. In this example, disk drives A, B, and C are available for saving the program. The double dot (..) selection in the Dirs/Drives box accesses the next higher directory (the root directory) of the currently active disk drive (drive C).

SELECTING A DRIVE AND ENTERING A FILE NAME   This discussion assumes that you are using a data disk in drive A to save your programs. Press the TAB key to move the cursor from the File Name box to the Dirs/Drives box. Then press the ↓ key until you have highlighted the drive you want. For example, if you want to save the program to a disk in drive A, press the ↓ key until you have highlighted drive A. Then press the ENTER key.

When you press ENTER, the highlight moves back up to the file name box, with *.BAS in the box, as shown in Figure 2-5. Notice that the disk drive now active (A:\) is now displayed under File Name. This indicates that the file will be saved to drive A. Use the file name ALBERT01 for this program. Ignore the name *.BAS, which disappears as soon as you start typing. The characters .BAS are called the *file name extension* (the three letters are an abbreviation of BASIC). QBasic automatically appends this extension to a program's file name unless you specify a different extension (limited to three letters). To enter your file name,

Type: **ALBERT01**

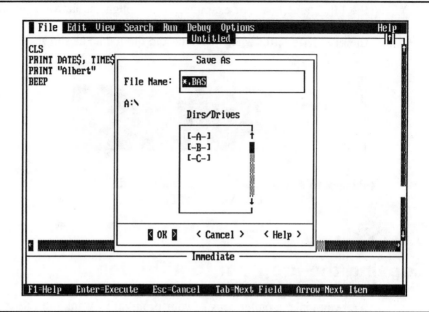

═══ **FIGURE 2-5.**   Ready for file name

Before you press ENTER, check the file name for accuracy, making sure that you typed a zero (0) rather than a capital letter O.

When you are sure that the file name is correct,

Press: ENTER

When you press ENTER, the Save As dialog box disappears, and the program is written to the disk that you selected. You have now saved the program under the file name ALBERT01, and its name now appears at the top of the View window with a .BAS extension, as shown here:

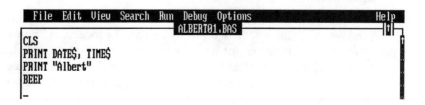

ANOTHER WAY TO SAVE A PROGRAM   You can save a program to any disk drive from the Save As dialog box by designating the desired drive in the File Name box. For example, even though the active drive may be drive C, you can save program ALBERT01 to a disk in disk drive B, by including the disk drive letter when you type the file name, as shown here:

Be sure to include a colon (:) between the disk drive designation (B) and the name of the program (ALBERT01).

Copying the Program to a Printer

You can make a paper copy of your program by using the File menu to print the program on your printer. First access the File menu:

Press: ALT, F

Then use ↓ to move the cursor to the Print. . . option.

Press: ENTER

A dialog box appears, as shown by the screen in Figure 2-6. You have three choices for printing:

• Selected Text, when active, prints any text in the View window that you have highlighted. You will learn to do this later. For now, this is not the right choice.

• Current Window, when active, prints all text that is currently in the View window. In Chapter 8, "FUNCTION and SUB Procedures," you will create programs that have one or more program blocks that do not show in the View window. You would use the View menu to access the window containing the part of the program you wanted to print. For now, ignore this choice.

• Entire Program is preceded by a black marker (♦) in parentheses. You *do* want to print the entire program; this is the choice you want.

FIGURE 2-6.   Print dialog box

Be sure that your printer is on line; then press ENTER while the Entire Program choice is active. The dialog box disappears, and the computer prints a copy of your program. The program remains in the View window. Leave it there for the next section.

Adding or Deleting Program Lines

Add a "Happy Birthday" greeting to your program, as follows. Move the cursor to the B of BEEP in the last line.

```
CLS
PRINT DATE$, TIME$
PRINT "Albert"
BEEP
```

Press ENTER. This pushes the BEEP statement down one line and opens a blank line. Move the cursor to the first position of the blank line:

```
CLS
PRINT DATE$, TIME$
PRINT "Albert"

BEEP
```

Next, type the following line, but don't press ENTER. As you type the line, it is entered into memory.

Type: **PRINT "Happy Birthday"**

The cursor appears after the last double quotation mark.

You could now access the Run menu and run the program without pressing the ENTER key after typing the new statement. If you do press ENTER, a blank line will appear before the BEEP statement:

```
CLS
PRINT DATE$, TIME$
PRINT "Albert"
PRINT "Happy Birthday"

BEEP
```

You don't need a blank line. To delete it,

Press: DEL

The program now looks like this:

```
CLS
PRINT DATE$, TIME$
PRINT "Albert"
PRINT "Happy Birthday"
BEEP
```

RUNNING THE PROGRAM WITH ADDED LINES   To access the Run menu,

Press: ALT, R, ENTER

This prints the following lines on the Output screen:

```
01-10-1991    10:31:22
Albert
Happy Birthday
```

The message "Press any key to continue" appears at the bottom of the Output screen.

All of the desired information is crowded into the top three lines. You may want to print a blank line between your name and the "Happy Birthday" message. To do so, press any key to go back to the View window; then move the cursor to the beginning of the line that prints "Happy Birthday."

```
PRINT "Happy Birthday"
```

Press ENTER and a blank line appears above the PRINT statement. Move the cursor to the beginning of the blank line. Then,

> Type: **PRINT**   (do not press ENTER)

The program is now modified, as shown here:

```
CLS
PRINT DATE$, TIME$
PRINT "Albert"
PRINT_
PRINT "Happy Birthday"
BEEP
```

To run the modified program,

> Press: ALT, R, ENTER

The Output screen shows the following information:

```
01-10-1991    10:32:32
Albert

Happy Birthday
```

Whenever you use the keyword PRINT as a statement by itself, it causes a carriage return and line feed. In this case, the PRINT statement prints a blank line before the "Happy Birthday" message.

SAVING THE MODIFIED PROGRAM You saved your first program as ALBERT01.BAS. You have just finished modifiying it, thus creating a new program. You have not saved it yet. To do so, access the File menu and select the Save As... option. The Save As dialog box appears with the old file name, ALBERT01.BAS, in the File Name box. You can change the 1 in the file name to a 2 in order to save this version of the program as ALBERT02, as shown in the Save As dialog box of Figure 2-7. Alternatively, you can type the new name ALBERT02; the old name disappears when you start typing the new name.

Loading a New Program

You have used the New option on the File menu to prepare the View window for entering a new program, the Start option on the Run menu to run a program from memory, the Print... option on the File menu to copy a program from memory to the printer, and the Save As... option on the File

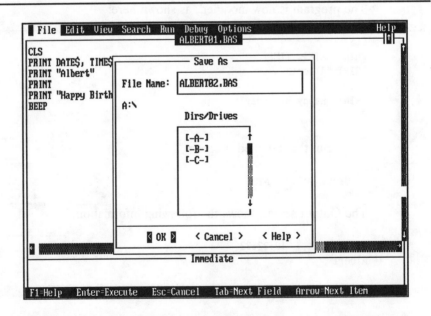

FIGURE 2-7. Saving the new program

menu to save a program from memory to a disk. You will now learn how to load a program from a disk into memory.

You can now load the file ALBERT01.BAS from the disk to which it was saved.

Press: ALT, F   (to activate the File menu)

Press the ↓ key until the highlight is on the Open. . . option; then press ENTER. In this demonstration, the program was saved to drive A, which is still active. Therefore, the Open dialog box appears, as shown in Figure 2-8. The list of files on your disk may also contain other file names, including those that were on the original QBasic disk. Notice that the active drive (A) is indicated just below File Name. If you are using a different active drive, your dialog box will be different. In that case, press the TAB key to select the Dirs/Drives box, and press the ↓ key to select the desired drive. Then press ENTER. The cursor returns to the File Name box.

The files shown on the selected disk have a .BAS extension and are listed in the box labeled Files.

Press: TAB

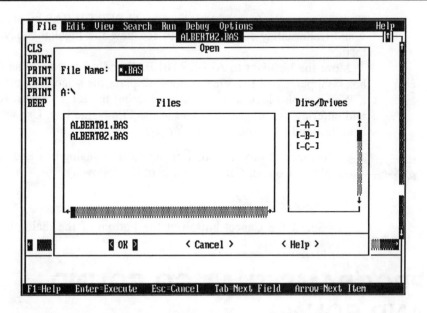

FIGURE 2-8. Opening a file

to move the cursor to the Files box. Then,

Press: ↓

once to highlight ALBERT01.BAS, as shown here:

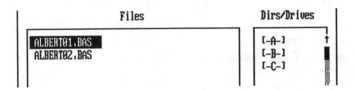

Press the ↓ key again to move the highlight to ALBERT02.BAS.

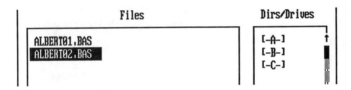

You can move the highlight back up to ALBERT01.BAS by pressing ↑. Press ↓ and ↑ alternately several times to see how the highlight moves back and forth.

Move the highlight to ALBERT01.BAS and press ENTER. The Open dialog box disappears and the View window displays the selected program.

You can also load a program by ignoring the file names in the Files box and entering the program's name in the File Name box. Use whichever way is easiest and most comfortable for you.

To cancel a program load or any QBasic dialog box and return to the QBasic Control Center, do one of the following:

- Press ESC.
- Select the Cancel button at the bottom of the dialog box and press ENTER.

PROGRAMS THAT GO ROUND AND ROUND

So far, you have used programs that run from the first statement to the last statement in sequential order. The programs have stopped after executing the last statement. Now you will see some programs that are never ending; they go round and round, perform the same action over and over. The programs will not stop until you use the CTRL and BREAK keys to stop the action.

Looping in SCREEN 0

You have been using the default Output screen mode, SCREEN 0, called the *text mode*. SCREEN 0 is normally used for programs that output text rather than graphics. When first loaded, QBasic automatically selects SCREEN 0 as the Output screen mode.

If you have a program in the View window, access the File menu and select the New option to get a clear View window. If you are starting a new session, load QBasic and press ESC to get the clear View window. Then enter the following program. Indent the SOUND statement in the DO...LOOP by typing two spaces to its left.

```
CLS
DO
  SOUND 1000 * RND + 40, 10 * RND
LOOP
```

When the program has been entered,

Press: ALT, R, ENTER

in order to run the program. The program goes around and around in the DO...LOOP. The Output screen is cleared, and a series of sounds emanates from the computer's speaker. Music from outer space? It's not very melodic, so when you tire of it, stop the program:

Press: CTRL-BREAK

This displays the View window, which shows your program and stops the music. There is no information sent to the Output screen so it is blank while the program is running.

Now that you have the program in the View window,

Press: ALT, F, A

to access the File menu and select the Save As... option. When the Save As dialog box appears, save the program under the name SOUND01.BAS.

The DO...LOOP is a fundamental structure of QBasic. In this program, the SOUND statement between the keyword DO and the keyword LOOP is executed over and over until you interrupt the program. Notice that the line inside the DO...LOOP is indented. This makes the DO...LOOP easier to read and understand.

The SOUND statement specifies the frequency in cycles per second (also referred to as Hertz, abbreviated as Hz). The duration is specified in clock ticks (18.2 clock ticks in a second). The SOUND statement uses the following values of frequency and duration:

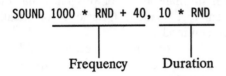

RND is a built-in QBasic *function* that returns a number greater than 0 but less than 1.

$$0 < RND < 1$$

To get the desired frequency, this value is multiplied by 1000, and 40 is added to the result. Therefore, the range of frequencies is

$$40 < 1000 * RND + 40 < 1040$$

To get the duration, another random value is multiplied by 10. Therefore, the range of durations is

$$0 < 10 * RND < 10$$

Table 2-2 shows sample values of RND, 10 * RND and 1000 * RND +40 and the frequencies and durations used in the SOUND statement. Since SOUND uses only integer values, the actual frequencies used are in the range of 40 to 1039. The duration values are 0 through 9. The frequency is in cycles per second (Hertz, or Hz), and the duration is in clock ticks. There are 18.2 clock ticks in one second. Therefore, the sounds last less than a half second.

a.	**RND**	**1000 * RND + 40**	**Frequency**
	.7055475	745.5475	745
	.533424	573.424	573
	.5795186	619.5186	619
	.2895625	329.5625	329
	.301948	341.948	341
	.7747401	814.7401	814
	$1.401764E{-}02$	54.01764	54
	.7607236	800.7236	800
	.81449	854.49	854
	.7090379	749.0379	749
b.	**RND**	**10 * RND**	**Duration**
	$4.535276E{-}02$	0.4535276	0
	.4140327	4.140327	4
	.8626193	8.626193	8
	.79048	7.9048	7
	.3735362	3.735362	3
	.9619532	9.619532	9
	.8714458	8.714458	8
	$5.623686E{-}2$	0.5623686	0
	.9495566	9.495566	9
	.3640187	3.640187	3

TABLE 2-2. (*a*) Sample Random Values for SOUND Frequency and (*b*) Sample Random Values for SOUND Duration

OTHER WAYS TO WRITE THE PROGRAM   You could write this QBasic program in many ways. Although it is not necessary, QBasic can use line numbers or line labels. You could write the program as follows:

```
CLS
LoopTop:
  SOUND 1000 * RND + 40, 10 * RND
GOTO LoopTop
```

The line label (LoopTop:) is used in place of DO. Notice that a colon follows the label. This enables QBasic to locate a label in a program. The program uses a GOTO statement (GOTO LoopTop) in place of LOOP. No colon is used after the reference to the label in the GOTO statement. The DO . . . LOOP used in program SOUND01 is simpler and easier to read than one that requires a search for labels; therefore, it is preferred over a GOTO loop. When you are using programming languages that do not have the DO . . . LOOP structure, you may have to use GOTO, as in the following example.

 If you have used GW-BASIC or BASICA (or almost any other BASIC versions), you must use a *line number* at the beginning of each line.

```
10 CLS
20 SOUND 1000 * RND + 40, 10 * RND
30 GOTO 20
```

You can load and run this GW-BASIC program in QBasic.

You will find yourself using the DO . . . LOOP frequently in your programs. The DO . . . LOOP allows you to make programs "loop back" and repeat so that parts of programs are executed several times. In future chapters, you will learn to introduce conditions in a DO . . . LOOP that allow you to exit from the loop when the specified condition is true.

LOOPING WITH COLOR   The following program uses a DO . . . LOOP to change the color used to print a word on the screen, assuming you are using a color monitor.

```
CLS
DO
  COLOR 16 * RND
  PRINT "Albert ";
LOOP
```

The COLOR statement inside the DO . . . LOOP produces colors randomly with numbers 0 through 15. The PRINT statement prints the word "Albert" followed by a blank space. The semicolon at the end of the PRINT statement tells the computer to stay on the same line after printing Albert's name. Therefore, as long as there is room, Albert's name is printed over and over on the same line. When the line is full, the printing continues on the next line. When the screen is full, the information on the screen is pushed up one line (scrolling) to make room for more.

Enter this program by activating the File menu (ALT, F; then choose New), and type the program in the View window. Run it from the Run menu (ALT, R; then choose Start). The word "Albert" is printed in many colors. When the screen fills, the program continues going round the DO ... LOOP, printing on the bottom line, thus pushing up previous lines (scrolling). This goes on until you interrupt the program:

Press: CTRL-BREAK

This returns you to the View window, which now shows the program in its normal colors. The only change is that the location where the interrupt took place is highlighted in bright white letters.

To see the Output screen in its final state, press F4. Press F4 again when you are ready to return to the View window; then save the program from the File menu as COLORS01.BAS.

The first line of the program (CLS) clears the screen. The COLOR statement inside the DO ... LOOP specifies only one number, the foreground color. Therefore, the background color remains the same throughout the program. If you want to change the background color, you add a comma and a second number that specifies the background color:

```
COLOR ForegroundColorNumber, BackgroundColorNumber
```

You can use the foreground and background colors shown in Table 2-3 when you are using the text screen mode (SCREEN 0).

TIMER LOOP   You have previously used TIME$ to print or change the computer's time. QBasic also has a TIMER *function*. The TIMER function returns the number of seconds that have passed since midnight. At midnight, the value of TIMER is 0. At high noon, the value of TIMER is 43200. At one minute before midnight, the value of TIMER is 86340. The following program prints the current value of TIMER on the Output screen within a DO ... LOOP. You can watch the value of TIMER being continually updated. The value is printed in hundredths of seconds.

```
CLS
DO
  LOCATE 12, 36
  PRINT TIMER
LOOP
```

Color Number	Background Color	Foreground Color
0	Black	Black
1	Blue	Blue
2	Green	Green
3	Cyan	Cyan
4	Red	Red
5	Magenta	Magenta
6	Brown	Brown
7	White	White
8	—	Gray
9	—	Light blue
10	—	Light green
11	—	Light cyan
12	—	Light red
13	—	Light magenta
14	—	Yellow
15	—	Bright white

TABLE 2-3. SCREEN 0 Background and Foreground Colors

Enter the program and run it. Watch the value of TIMER change at the center of the screen. The value is always printed at the same location because of the *LOCATE statement* in the DO...LOOP. This statement specifies the row and column where the first character of the value of TIMER is to be printed, as shown here:

```
LOCATE 12, 36
```

Row   Column

The PRINT statement prints the value of TIMER on each pass through the loop. When you have seen enough time go by, interrupt the program with CTRL-BREAK. Save the program from the File menu as TIMER01.BAS.

The TIMER function is useful for timing computer actions and providing delays that you may want to use in programs.

Looping in SCREEN 1

The SCREEN 1 statement sets a *graphics mode* for the Output screen. When you specify SCREEN 1, you can use many graphics statements that cannot be used in SCREEN 0, the text mode. The next program gives you a graphics preview, setting colorful points in a random way on the Output screen. The program also produces random sounds.

```
SCREEN 1: CLS
COLOR 0, 1
DO
  PSET (319 * RND, 199 * RND), 4 * RND
  SOUND 3000 * RND + 40, 5
LOOP
```

 You can use more that one statement on a line if you separate the statements by a colon, as in the first line of this program.

Enter the program after accessing the New option on the File menu. Then run it from Start on the Run menu. Let the screen fill up with colorful points. If you have a volume control, adjust it to the desired level—or turn off the sounds, if you wish. When you've seen and heard enough, interrupt the program with CTRL-BREAK. Save it as GRAFIXO1.BAS from the File menu.

SCREEN 1 is a graphics mode with 320 columns, numbered from 0 through 319 from left to right across the screen, and 200 rows, numbered from 0 through 199 from the top to the bottom of the screen, as shown in Figure 2-9.

When used in SCREEN 1, the COLOR statement specifies the background color (0-7) and one of two color palettes to be used for the foreground color.

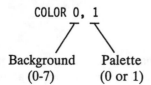

COLOR 0, 1

Background   Palette
(0-7)   (0 or 1)

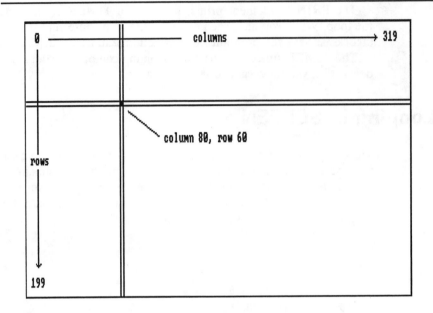

FIGURE 2-9. SCREEN 1 numbering

The colors for each palette are shown in Table 2-4. A foreground color is chosen for the point from the specified palette (1) and used in the PSET statement. The PSET statement also specifies the graphics column and row where the point is to be displayed, as shown here:

```
PSET (319 * RND, 199 * RND), 4 * RND
       |              |        |
       |              |        |
     Column         Row      Color
```

The SOUND statement in Program GRAFIX01 produces random frequencies in the range 40 to 3039 with a duration of 5 clock ticks.

LOOKING AT FILES

You now have several files on the disk that you are using to save programs. You can look at all the files that have a .BAS extension by accessing the Open... option of the File menu.

Color Number	Palette 0	Palette 1
0	Background	Background
1	Green	Cyan
2	Red	Magenta
3	Brown	White

Note The background color for each palette is the color selected in a previous COLOR statement (numbers 0-7 in Table 2-3).

═══ **TABLE 2-4.** SCREEN 1 Foreground Colors

Press: ALT, F, O

to access the Open dialog box, as shown by the screen in Figure 2-10. (The list for your disk may be different.)

ERASING A FILE

To erase any of the listed files, return to the QBasic Control Center, move to the Immediate window, and use the QBasic KILL statement.

If you have no further use for your first program, ALBERT01, erase it from the disk. First, press the ESC key to remove the Open dialog box and return to the Control Center. Then,

Press: F6   (to move the cursor to the Immediate window)
Type: **KILL "A:ALBERT01.BAS"**

Be sure that you have included the double quotation marks and the .BAS extension. Then

Press: ENTER

No indication is given that the file was deleted, so access the Open dialog box again to see that the file has been eliminated.

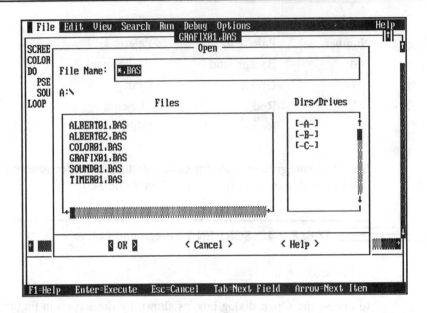

FIGURE 2-10. Files on drive A

Press: ALT, F, O

The active disk should now list the files shown in Figure 2-11. You can also erase any file by leaving QBasic, going to DOS, and using the ERASE or DEL command from DOS.

CLOSING DOWN QBASIC

This concludes the session on tiny programs. You will use everything that you learned in this chapter as you proceed through the book.

You can leave QBasic and return to DOS from the File menu. Access the File menu, and use ↓ to move the highlight to the last option, Exit. Then press ENTER. You can also leave QBasic and return to DOS by using this shortcut:

Press: ALT, F, X

SUMMARY

In this chapter, you learned what a QBasic program is. You entered several programs in the View window and ran them. You used the F4 key to move back and forth between the Output screen and the View window. You learned to save programs with the Save As... option and to copy programs to your printer with the Print option of the File menu. After adding lines to a program, you saved the modified program under a new name. You learned to load a program by using the Open... option of the File menu. You entered, ran, and saved programs that executed nonending loops. You erased a file from the disk.

Your QBasic vocabulary was enlarged to include the following keywords:

BEEP	DATE$	LOOP	SCREEN 1
CLS	DO	PRINT	SOUND
COLOR (in SCREEN 0)	KILL	PSET	TIME$
COLOR (in SCREEN 1)	LOCATE	RND	TIMER

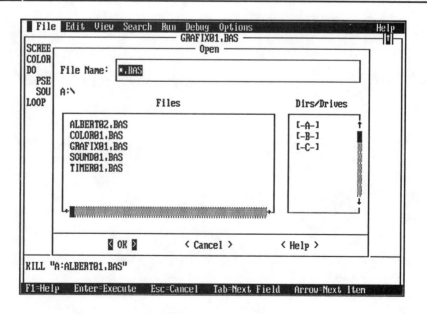

FIGURE 2-11.   One file deleted

NUMBER CRUNCHING

In this chapter, you will learn how to use the computer to do calculations. You will write short programs in the View window. You will use the arithmetic operators (+, −, *, /) and the exponentiation operator (^) with numbers and variables that represent numbers. You will also learn about QBasic *variables* and a number of ways to assign or acquire values of variables in programs.

ARITHMETIC OPERATIONS

You will now use the arithmetic operators +, −, *, and / to specify the operations of addition, subtraction, multiplication, and division in some very small programs.

To tell the computer to do arithmetic, you can use a PRINT statement consisting of the keyword PRINT followed by a numerical expression (such as 3 + 4 or 3 − 4). The computer evaluates the numerical expression (does the arithmetic) and then prints the result in the Output screen. For example, you could write a short program that clears the Output screen, adds the numbers 3 and 4, and prints the result.

First, clear the computer's memory by selecting the New option on the File menu. You can press ALT, press F, and press ENTER — or you can use the following shortcut, pressing each key in order (no need to press ENTER):

Press: ALT, F, N   (File menu, New option)

Now enter the following short program in the View window. Type each line and press ENTER.

```
CLS
PRINT 3 + 4
```

To run the program, press these keys in succession:

Press: ALT, R, S   (Run menu, Start option)

You can also use the shortcut: SHIFT-F5.

The Output screen appears and the computer prints the following:

```
7
```

Examine the result displayed on the Output screen. Then press any key to return to the QBasic Control Center.

Now try another program:

```
CLS
PRINT 15 - 3
```

You can modify the previous program quickly by moving the cursor to the beginning of the arithmetic expression, as shown here:

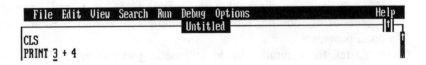

To erase the character at the cursor:

Press: DEL

The cursor stays where it was, but the 3 is erased. All other characters in the expression move to the left one place. Hold down the DEL key until all characters in the expression are deleted. If you hold the DEL key down after all characters have been erased, you will hear a series of short sounds informing you that there are no more characters to be deleted. You now see

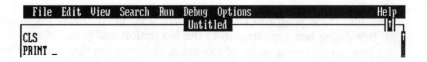

The cursor remains where it was. Now you can type a new expression:

Type: **15 − 3**
and press ENTER

You now have a program that subtracts the value 3 from the value 15. Run the program:

Press: ALT, R, S
or
Press: SHIFT-F5

The computer displays the Output screen with a new value:

12

Examples

You know how to enter programs, run them, and return to the View window of the Control Center. A series of short program examples follows. Enter and run each program.

After running a program, you can delete the expression in the PRINT statement by using the DEL key as in the previous addition example. Then enter the expression for the new program. Alternatively, you can use the New option in the File menu to clear the View window for a new program.

If you decide to select the New option to enter a program rather than just change the arithmetic expression, you will see this dialog box when the New option is selected:

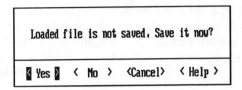

Because these programs are short, there is no need to save them. Therefore, if this dialog box appears, tab to the No option and press ENTER.

For the following series of examples, the program that you type and run is shown under the heading "Enter." The results of a run of the program are shown under the heading "Output Screen."

1. Albert Outlander is 74 inches tall. Convert his height to centimeters. One inch equals 2.54 centimeters.

Enter	Output Screen
CLS	
PRINT 74 * 2.54	187.96

2. An ancient ruler named Zalabar measured 100 centimeters from the tip of his nose to the end of his outstretched arm. How long is that in inches?

Enter	Output Screen
CLS	
PRINT 100 / 2.54	39.37008

Does that number look familiar? Perhaps you recall that 100 centimeters equals 1 meter. One meter equals 39.37008 inches, a little more than 1 yard.

3. People usually give their height in feet and inches. If you ask Albert how tall he is, he will probably tell you that he is 6 feet, 2 inches tall. It is easy to write a PRINT statement to convert feet and inches to inches.

Enter	Output Screen
CLS	
PRINT 6 * 12 + 2	74

The computer first does the multiplication (6 times 12) and then the addition (plus 2). In evaluating an expression, the computer does multiplications and divisions first and then additions and subtractions.

4. Almost everyone gets a monthly bill from a utility company. Gas is measured in therms and electricity in kilowatt-hours. Gas is charged at the rate of $0.44826 per therm for the first 84 therms and $0.84849 per therm for additional therms. Compute the amount paid for 97 therms of gas (84 therms at the lower rate plus 13 therms at the higher rate).

Enter	Output Screen
CLS	
PRINT 84 * .44826 + 13 * .84849	48.68421

In evaluating this expression, the computer first does both multiplications; then it adds the two multiplication results to get the final result. Rounded to the nearest penny, the result is $48.68.

5. Before he reached his full stature, King Kong was once 37 feet, 8 inches tall. How tall was he in meters?

Enter	Output Screen
CLS	
PRINT (37 * 12 + 8) * 2.54 / 100	11.4808

Note the use of parentheses. The computer does the arithmetic inside the parentheses first; then it multiplies that result by 2.54 and then divides by 100.

6. At the beginning of an auto trip, the odometer showed 31,832 miles. At the end of the trip it read 32,219 miles. The car used 9.3 gallons of gas. How many miles per gallon did the car get on the trip?

Enter	Output Screen
CLS	
PRINT (32219 - 31832) / 9.3	41.6129

7. Suppose that your favorite team has won 38 games and lost 24. You can compute its win percentage like this:

Enter	Output Screen
CLS	
PRINT 38 / (38 + 24)	.6129032

The computer first does the arithmetic inside the parentheses, adding 38 and 24 to obtain 62. It then divides 38 by this result. Newspapers usually round the percentage to three places after the decimal point. This result would be reported as .613. Your team is doing very well!

INTEGER QUOTIENT AND REMAINDER

Some applications require the use of *integer division,* which computes an integer quotient and an integer remainder. For example, suppose that you want to convert 73 ounces to pounds and ounces. With paper and pencil, you could do it like this:

```
        4  ◄─── Integer quotient
   16 ⌐73
       64
       ──
        9  ◄─── Remainder of integer division
```

QBasic provides two operations that you can use for this type of calculation. Use the backslash (\) to obtain the integer quotient and the MOD operation to obtain the integer remainder. QBasic uses a slash (/) for regular division and a backslash (\) for integer division. The MOD operation is also known as *modulus arithmetic.*

Integer quotient: 73 \ 16
Integer remainder: 73 MOD 16

Enter the following program to compute and display the integer quotient and remainder on dividing 73 by 16:

```
CLS
PRINT 73 \ 16, 73 MOD 16
```

When you run the program, the Output screen shows:

4   9

If one of the two numbers entered for the operation (called *operands*) is a noninteger, it is rounded to the nearest integer prior to the computation. For example:

72.9 \ 16 = 4 and 72.9 MOD 16 = 9
72.4 \ 16 = 4 and 72.4 MOD 16 = 8

In the preceding operations, 72.9 is first rounded to 73, and 72.4 is rounded to 72. Note that the remainder is 9 for 72.9 MOD 16 and 8 for 72.4 MOD 16. Following are some additional examples in short programs.

Examples

1. Suppose you pack 200 eggs in cartons, each containing 1 dozen eggs, and perhaps have some eggs left over. How many cartons do you need and how many eggs will be left over?

Enter   **Output Screen**

```
CLS
PRINT 200 \ 12, 200 MOD 12          16       8
```

It looks like you will need 17 cartons, with 16 of them full and one carton two-thirds full.

2. Convert 12,345 seconds to hours, minutes, and seconds in this order: First, convert 12,345 seconds to hours and minutes:

hours = 12345 \ 3600
minutes = (12345 MOD 3600) \ 60

Then convert the left-over minutes to seconds:

seconds = (12345 MOD 3600) MOD 60

Enter   **Output Screen**

```
CLS
PRINT 12345 \ 3600                      3
PRINT (12345 MOD 3600) \ 60            25
PRINT (12345 MOD 3600) MOD 60         45
```

You can see that 12,345 seconds equals 3 hours, 25 minutes, 45 seconds.

3. Perhaps you would like to identify the results, as follows:

Enter

```
CLS
PRINT 73 \ 16; "pounds,"; 73 MOD 16; "ounces"
```

The Output screen shows

```
4 pounds, 9 ounces
```

The computer prints the value of 73 \ 16, then prints the string "pounds," then prints the value of 73 MOD 16, and then prints the string "ounces" at the end of the line. The semicolons that separate the items in the PRINT statement cause each item to be printed immediately following the previous item.

EXPONENTS AND THE EXPONENTIATION OPERATION

In this section, you use the exponentiation operator (^) to compute the *power* of a number. .

A room has a floor that is 12 feet square. That is, the floor is square, and each side of the square is 12 feet long. What is the area of the room in square feet? Here are two ways to compute the area.

The first program uses multiplication.

Enter	Output Screen
`CLS` `PRINT 12 * 12`	144

The next program uses the exponentiation operator (^) to compute the square of 12, also called the second power of 12. To type the exponentiation symbol (^), hold down a SHIFT key and press the key that has both the number 6 and the exponentiation symbol.

Enter	Output Screen
CLS	
PRINT 12 ^ 2	144

Now suppose that the room has a lofty ceiling, exactly 12 feet high. A fortuitous coincidence! The room is 12 by 12 by 12. Therefore, the volume of the room is 12 times 12 times 12, or 12 cubed. Another way to say "12 cubed" is "12 to the third power," or "the third power of 12." You can compute the volume in cubic feet in two ways.

Multiplication (*):	PRINT 12 * 12 * 12
Exponentiation (^):	PRINT 12 ^ 3

The following program does it both ways.

Enter	Output Screen
CLS	
PRINT 12 * 12 * 12	1728
PRINT 12 ^ 3	1728

In math books, squares and cubes of numbers are indicated by means of superscript numbers. The numbers 12 squared and 12 cubed are shown here in both standard math notation and QBasic notation.

Math Notation	QBasic Notation	Meaning
12^2	12 ^ 2	12 squared, or 12 to the second power
12^3	12 ^ 3	12 cubed, or 12 to the third power

In an expression such as 12 ^ 3, the number 12 is the *base,* and 3 is the *exponent.* The exponent tells how many times the base is to be used as a factor. Here are some examples:

Expression	Base	Exponent	Equivalent Using Multiplication
12 ^ 2	12	2	12 * 12
12 ^ 3	12	3	12 * 12 * 12
2 ^ 7	2	7	2 * 2 * 2 * 2 * 2 * 2 * 2

Exponents can be very useful. It is much easier to write

    2 ^ 7

than to write

    2 * 2 * 2 * 2 * 2 * 2 * 2

A computer has 256K, 512K, 640K, or more bytes of memory. *K* is an abbreviation of the metric term "kilo," which means 1000. A kilogram is 1000 grams; a kilometer is 1000 meters. However, 1K bytes actually means 2 ^ 10 bytes. The following program uses the exponentiation operator (^) to compute the number of bytes in 1K and 640K:

```
CLS
PRINT 2 ^ 10          '1K bytes
PRINT 640 * 2 ^ 10    '640k bytes
```

 The information following the apostrophe in the second and third lines is not executed. These lines contain comments describing the value to be printed.

In evaluating the numerical expression, 640 * 2 ^ 10, the computer first computes the value of 2 ^ 10 and then multiplies that result (1024) by 640.

When you run the program, the Output screen displays

```
1024
655360
```

FLOATING-POINT NUMBERS

Computer memories are getting bigger. Memories of 1, 2, or more megabytes are increasingly common. The term "mega" is also borrowed from the metric system. In metric, it means 1 million. However, in referring to the size of computer memories or hard disk storage capacity, it means 2 ˆ 20 (2 to the twentieth power, or the twentieth power of 2).

How many bytes are in a megabyte? Write a QBasic program to find out. Print the value of 1 megabyte (2 ˆ 20); then print the value of the number of bytes on a 40-megabyte (40 * 2 ˆ 20) hard disk.

```
CLS
PRINT 2 ^ 20              '1 megabyte
PRINT 40 * 2 ^ 20         '40 megabytes
```

When you run this program, the Output screen shows

```
1048576
4.194304E+07
```

One megabyte equals 1,048,576 bytes, not 1,000,000 bytes. Forty megabytes equals 40 times 1 megabyte, so 40 megabytes equals 40 times 1,048,576.

QBasic prints this large number as a *floating-point number*. Read it like this: 4.194304E+07 is 4.194304 times 10 ˆ 7 (10 to the seventh power). Floating-point notation is very similar to scientific notation used in math, science, and engineering books, as shown here:

Floating-point notation: 4.194304E+07

Scientific notation: 4.194304×10^7

Floating-point notation is simply a shorthand way of expressing large numbers. A floating-point number has two parts: a *mantissa* and an *exponent*. The mantissa and exponent are separated by the letter E (for exponent), as shown here:

Floating-point number: 4.194304E+07

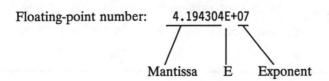

         Mantissa   E   Exponent

In a floating-point number, the exponent is always a power of 10. Table 3-1 gives more examples of large numbers shown in ordinary notation, floating-point notation, and scientific notation.

The national debt of the United States is about 3 trillion dollars and the population is about 250 million. You can use floating-point numbers to write a program that computes the debt for each person. Enter the following program:

```
CLS
PRINT 3E12 / 250E6
```

When you press the ENTER key after typing the PRINT statement, QBasic reformats the line so that the program looks like this:

```
CLS
PRINT 3E+12 / 2.5E+08
```

Don't worry about the format; 3E+12 is the same value as 3E12 and 2.5E+08 is the same value as 250E6. QBasic likes to display things in a standard manner; that way, programs have a consistent look and are easier to read and understand.

When you run the program, the Output screen shows

```
12000
```

The debt for each person in this country is $12,000! Three trillion equals 3 times $10 \wedge 12$ (3E+12 in floating-point notation). Two hundred fifty million equals 250 times $10 \wedge 6$. In floating-point notation, this is 250E+06. Note that you can write 3 trillion as 3E12 instead of 3E+12. Also, you can write 250 million as 250E+06, 250E6, or 2.5E+08.

Number	Ordinary Notation	Floating-Point Notation	Scientific Notation
Population of the earth	5000000000	5E+09	5×10^9
Three trillion	3000000000000	3E+12	3×10^{12}
Miles in one light year	5865696000000	5.865696E+12	5.865696×10^{12}

TABLE 3-1. Examples of Large Number Notations

Very Small Numbers

As you have seen, QBasic does a good job of representing large numbers by means of floating-point notation. QBasic is equally adept at representing very small numbers.

A recent experiment determined that a frightened snail moves at the speed of 1 inch every 4 seconds. How fast is that in feet per second and miles per second? Let's see; the snail moves at 0.25 inches per second. Divide that number by 12 to get its speed in feet per second. Because there are 5280 feet in a mile, divide the snail's speed in feet per second by 5280 to get its speed in miles per second.

```
CLS
PRINT .25 / 12              'feet per second
PRINT .25 / 12 / 5280       'miles per second
```

In the second calculation, 0.25 is divided by 12; then the result is divided by 5280. If you enter the snail's speed as 0.25, QBasic will reformat it as .25. Run the program.

The Output screen shows

```
2.083333E-02
3.945707E-06
```

QBasic prints these very small numbers as floating-point numbers with a mantissa and a negative exponent. The mantissa and exponent are separated by the letter E. Read the miles-per-second speed this way: three point nine four five seven zero seven times ten to the minus six. In math, science, and other high-tech books, you might see this number written in scientific notation as 3.945707×10^{-6}.

Floating-point notation:	3.945707E−06
Scientific notation:	3.945707×10^{-6}

Hydrogen is universal stuff. It began with the big bang that created the universe and is everywhere. The hydrogen atom is very small and light. The mass of the hydrogen atom is about 1.67×10^{-27} kilograms.

Floating-point notation:	1.67E−27
Scientific notation:	1.67×10^{-27}
Ordinary notation:	.00000000000000000000000000167

As you can see, you can type this number much more quickly in floating-point than in ordinary notation, and with less chance of a typing mistake.

TYPES OF NUMBERS

QBasic has several types of numbers: integers, long integers, single-precision numbers, double-precision numbers, and floating-point numbers. So far, you have seen three types—integers, single-precision numbers, and floating-point numbers—examples of which are shown here:

Integers:	3 4 −1 12
Single-precision numbers:	2.54 11.4808 655360
Floating-point numbers:	4.194304E+07 250E6 3.945707E−06

An *integer* is a whole number (that is, a number with no fractional part) in the range −32,768 to 32,767. An integer is stored in 2 bytes of memory.

A *single-precision number* can be an integer or noninteger with up to seven digits. A single-precision number is stored in 4 bytes of memory. This type of number is actually stored as a floating-point number.

A *floating-point number* is a number with a mantissa and an exponent. The mantissa can have up to seven digits. The exponent is in the range −39 to +38. A floating-point number is stored in 4 bytes of memory.

Exploring Number Patterns

Now explore a number pattern. Write a program to clear the screen and execute three PRINT statements, as follows:

```
CLS
PRINT 11 * 11
PRINT 111 * 111
PRINT 1111 * 1111
```

When you run the program, you may see a brief flash of the Output screen. Then the Overflow dialog box appears, as shown in Figure 3-1. Notice that the third PRINT statement is highlighted. QBasic is telling you that this program line resulted in a number that is too large to be represented as a seven-digit integer. It would "overflow" the space (2 bytes) allowed for integers.

Press: ENTER

to remove the dialog box. Then,

Press: F4

to see the Output screen, which should look like the one shown here:

121
12321

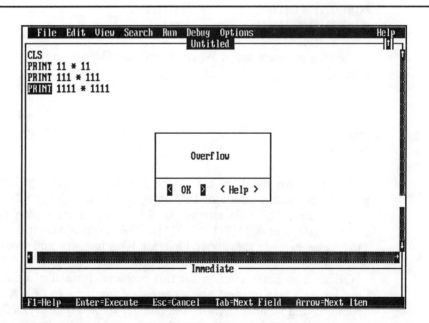

FIGURE 3-1. Overflow dialog box

The first two numbers are in the range of integers and were printed. However, the third expression (1111 * 1111) caused an overflow. Press F4 to return to the View window. When you return to the View window, the offending line is highlighted, another clue that it caused the overflow.

This problem has a simple solution. QBasic has a number type called a *long integer*. A long integer may be in the range -2,147,483,648 to +2,147,483,647. If one of the numbers being multiplied is a long integer, the result will also be a long integer. You specify a number as a long integer by appending an ampersand (&) to the end of the number; for example, 1111&.

Change the line to

```
PRINT 1111 * 1111&
```

To do this, move the cursor to the right end of the line, type an ampersand, and press ENTER. In addition to this change, add one more line to the program, typing an ampersand at the end of each statement, so that the program looks like this:

```
CLS
PRINT 11 * 11
PRINT 111 * 111
PRINT 1111 * 1111&          'modified
PRINT 11111 * 11111&        'added
```

Run the program again. When you do, the Output screen should look like this:

```
121
12321
1234321
123454321
```

The first two numbers are in the range of integers, and the last two numbers are in the range of long integers. Press any key to return to the View window. The next number in this series of increasing digits in the PRINT statement is 111111 * 111111&, the result of which is 12345654321. That value exceeds the upper limit for long integers and would cause an overflow.

QBasic also has a solution for this problem. Instead of using an ampersand (as for a long integer), use a pound, or number sign (#). A number sign appended to a number declares the number to be a *double-precision number*.

A double-precision number can have up to 16 digits. You can use double-precision numbers to compute the correct result of multiplying 111111 by 111111#. Add another PRINT statement so that the program looks like this:

```
CLS
PRINT 11 * 11
PRINT 111 * 111
PRINT 1111 * 1111&
PRINT 11111 * 11111&
PRINT 111111 * 111111#            'added line
```

Run the program with this addition. Since the number 111111# is a double-precision number, the expression 111111 * 111111# is evaluated as a double-precision result and the answer (12345654321) is printed correctly, as shown here:

```
121
12321
1234321
123454321
12345654321
```

You can also append the # sign to the first value of the expression:

```
PRINT 111111# * 111111
```

If any operand in an expression is double-precision, the computer treats the entire expression as double-precision.

If you continue the pattern of increasing the number of digits in the PRINT statement, you will eventually see a double-precision floating-point number, which will be the result of the following PRINT statement:

```
PRINT 111111111 * 111111111#       'nine digits each
```

This print statement will result in a value of

1.234567898765432D + 16

A double-precision floating-point number consists of a mantissa and an exponent separated by the letter D. The mantissa can have up to 16 digits. The exponent has the same range as single-precision numbers, −39 to +38. A double-precision number is stored in 8 bytes of memory.

Integers are whole numbers (no decimal point) in the range −32768 to 32767. An integer is stored in 2 bytes of memory. Long integers are whole numbers in the range −2,147,483,648 to +2,147,483,647. A long integer is stored in 4 bytes of memory. Single-precision numbers are real numbers (integer or noninteger) with up to seven digits and, possibly, a decimal point. A single-precision number can appear as a floating-point number consisting of a mantissa, the letter E, and an exponent. A double-precision number is a real number (integer or noninteger) with up to 16 digits and a decimal point. A double-precision number can appear as a double-precision floating-point number consisting of a mantissa, the letter D, and an exponent.

The result of a calculation might be outside QBasic's range of numbers. Here are some examples that use immediate PRINT statements in the Immediate window.

Examples

1. If a result is too large, QBasic displays an Overflow dialog box.
   In the Immediate window, enter

```
PRINT 1E40
```

The number 1E40 (1 times 10 to the 40th power) is too big for QBasic to handle. It displays the Overflow dialog box shown previously in Figure 3-1.

2. Division by zero is not allowed. If you try to divide by zero, you will see a Division by zero dialog box.
   In the Immediate window, enter

```
PRINT 1 / 0
```

Press ENTER, and the Division by zero dialog box appears.

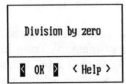

3. QBasic has a smallest positive number. If a result is smaller than this number, the result is replaced by 0. To search for this smallest positive number, enter and run the following short program. As you enter the PRINT statements, notice how QBasic changes your entries.

Enter	QBasic Changes
CLS	CLS
PRINT 1E-45	PRINT 0!
PRINT 2E-45	PRINT 1.401298E-45
PRINT 3E-45	PRINT 2.802597E-45
PRINT 4E-45	PRINT 4.203895E-45

All these numbers are very small but are non-zero. The way QBasic changes the values in the program indicates that the numbers that QBasic will use are not very precise. Run the program. The Output screen shows

```
0
1.401298E-45
2.802597E-45
4.203895E-45
```

You can see that 1E−45 is too small for QBasic to handle. Therefore, this too-small number is replaced by 0. QBasic's smallest positive number is approximately 1.4E−45. As expected, the other small numbers (which are close to 1.4E−45) are not very precise.

NUMERIC VARIABLES

Imagine that in the computer's memory, there are many "number boxes." Each number box can hold one number at any one time. A number box can hold, or store, different numbers at different times. Each number box has a name. The next illustration shows number boxes with the names *a, diameter,* and *Price.* Each number box contains a number.

a [7   ]   diameter [24   ]   Price [19.95   ]

The number 7 is in the number box named *a;* 24 is in the number box called *diameter;* the number box labeled *Price* contains the number 19.95.

In QBasic, a number box is called a *numeric variable.* The number in a number box is the *value* of the variable that identifies the box. Therefore,

- The value of the variable *a* is 7.

- The value of the variable *diameter* is 24.

- The value of the variable *Price* is 19.95.

You can create variable names subject to these limitations:

- A variable name can be a single letter or any combination of letters and digits up to 40 characters long.

- The first character must be a letter.

- You cannot use a QBasic keyword (such as BEEP, CLS, or PRINT) as a variable, but a keyword can be part of a variable. For example, "beeper" is all right even though it contains "beep."

Here are seven sample variable names:

a   diameter   price   pi   Qty   R2D2   GasRate

Note that letters may be uppercase (A, B, C . . .) or lowercase (a, b, c . . .).

QBasic lets you type variable names in lowercase, uppercase, or a mixture of uppercase and lowercase.

 If you use a variable more than once when entering a program, you should be aware that QBasic reformats all uses of the variable name to the case used in the latest entry. Therefore, if you first enter a variable as GasRate and later enter it as Gasrate, the first variable will be reformatted as Gasrate.

This feature makes it easy to reformat all occurrences of a variable name if you decide to change it while developing the program.

In this book, variable names appear in lowercase or a mixture of lowercase and uppercase letters. This makes it easy to distinguish variables from keywords (BEEP, CLS, PRINT, and so on), which always appear in uppercase letters.

Since QBasic has four types of numbers, it also has four types of numeric variables: *integer variables, long integer variables, single-precision variables,* and *double-precision variables.* An integer variable or long integer variable can have only integer values. A single-precision variable can have single-precision numbers as values. A double-precision variable can have double-precision numbers as values.

An integer variable consists of a variable name followed by a percent sign (%). The percent sign designates the variable as an integer variable.

Integer variables: n%   Qty%   Year%

A long integer variable consists of a variable name followed by an ampersand (&).

Long integer variables: m&   Count&   USdebt&

A single-precision variable consists of a variable name followed by no designator or by an exclamation point (!).

single-precision variables: x   Price   Price!   pi   pi!

A double-precision variable consists of a variable name followed by a number symbol (#).

double-precision variables: BigNumber#   LotsaBucks#   pi#

A variable name without a designator (%, &, !, or #) is automatically a single-precision variable. Single-precision variables suffice for most programming. You can use other variables when necessary. For example, you need double-precision variables for problems involving large amounts of money or in scientific work requiring extreme precision.

Assigning Values to Variables

You can assign a value to a variable and then print the value of that variable. Enter and run this three-line program:

```
CLS
a = 7
PRINT a
```

QBasic reserves a small part of memory (4 bytes) as a single-precision variable named *a,* and assigns the number 7 as the value of *a.* When you type

a = 7, you tell the computer to assign the value 7 to the variable named *a*. The PRINT statement tells the computer to print the value of *a*. Run the program to see the value of *a*, as shown here:

```
7               (the value of a)
```

The value of a variable remains the same until you change it. Move the cursor to the Immediate window. Then,

Type: **PRINT a**
and press ENTER

Again the computer prints 7, the value of *a*. Now, change the assignment statement in the program (a = 7) to

```
a = 1.47
```

Run the program with this new value. Your new number (1.47) will replace the old value of *a*. The Output screen displays the new value:

```
1.47
```

Add a line that assigns the value 3.14 to a new variable, *pi*, and prints the value of *pi*. The program should read

```
CLS
a = 1.47
PRINT a
pi = 3.14
PRINT pi
```

When you have entered the new lines, run the program. The Output screen shows

```
1.47
3.14
```

Both *pi* and *a* will maintain their values until changed.
Confirm this by printing both variables in the Immediate window. You can do this with a single PRINT statement, using a comma (,) between the two variables, as shown here:

```
PRINT a, pi        (in the Immediate window)
```

When you press the ENTER key, the following values are shown on the Output screen:

```
1.47                          (from program run)
3.14                          (from program run)
1.47          3.14            (from Immediate statement)
```

You can use variables in arithmetic expressions. Assign values to the variables *a* and *b;* then add, subtract, multiply, and divide the values of *a* and *b,* as in this program:

```
CLS
a = 7
b = 5
PRINT a + b, a - b, a * b, a / b
```

Enter the program and run it. You should see these results on the screen:

```
12            2            35            1.4
```

Examples

1. Two bicycles have wheels with diameters of 21 and 24 inches. How far does each bike travel in one turn of the wheels? The distance is the diameter multiplied by *pi* (π), where *pi* is approximately equal to 3.14. First, assign the value 3.14 to *pi,* and then compute and print the two distances:

```
CLS
pi = 3.14
PRINT pi * 21, pi * 24
```

Run the program and see the results:

```
65.94         75.36
```

The distances (65.94 and 75.36) are in inches. If you want the results in feet, change the PRINT statement to

```
PRINT pi * 21 / 12, pi * 24 / 12
```

When the program is run with this change, you will see the result as

```
5.495        6.28
```

2. The local sales tax rate is 6% (.06 as a decimal). You buy a computer game that costs $39.95. Write a program to calculate and print the sales tax on your purchase.

```
CLS
TaxRate = .06
PRINT 39.95 * TaxRate
```

Enter and run the program. The Output screen shows

```
2.397
```

Rounded to the nearest cent, the tax on the $39.95 computer game is $2.40.

You can use QBasic's PRINT USING statement to print results that are rounded to the nearest cent. Change the PRINT statement in the previous program to

```
PRINT USING "$$##.##"; 39.95 * TaxRate
```

Run the program with this modification. The result is now

```
$2.40
```

PRINT USING is a variation of the PRINT statement. It is a formatting command that allows you to provide a dollar sign automatically before numbers, decimal-point placement, and commas (if necessary). The PRINT USING format statement has many variations. The PRINT USING statement used in this program automatically provides a dollar sign; it also provides spacing for two digits before the decimal point and two after the decimal point, as shown here:

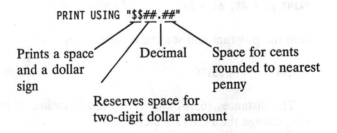

You will use more complex PRINT USING statements in future chapters.

ENTERING VARIABLE VALUES FROM THE KEYBOARD

The computer becomes a much more powerful and useful tool if you create programs that allow you to enter the values of variables as needed from the keyboard. The program can then do most of the work automatically.

The INPUT statement provides the means for entering values of variables as needed by a program. A simple INPUT statement consists of the keyword INPUT followed by a variable.

The next program illustrates the use of the INPUT statement to acquire a value of the variable *kwh*. Clear the View window and any program in memory with shortcut keys:

Press: ALT, F, N

Then, type each line and press ENTER. Here is the program:

```
CLS
LoRate = .08882
INPUT kwh
PRINT kwh * LoRate
```

To run the program,

Press: ALT, R, S
or
Press: SHIFT-F5

The program clears the screen, sets the value of *LoRate* to .08882, and then executes the INPUT statement. The INPUT statement prints a question mark on the screen, displays the blinking cursor, and waits at the top of the screen:

? _

The computer is waiting for you to enter a value of *kwh* and to press ENTER.

Type: **846**
and press ENTER

The computer accepts 846 as the value of *kwh* and computes and prints the cost of electricity on the Output screen below your entry, as shown here:

```
? 846
 75.14172
```

Run the program again and enter the number of your choice. Also try entering numbers such as 1, 10, or 100 so you can verify easily that the program is running correctly and producing the right answers.

If the cost per kilowatt-hour of electricity in your neighborhood is different from $.08882, change the value assigned to *LoRate*. For example, if the rate is $0.0765, change it as follows:

```
LoRate = .0765
```

Select the Save As. . . option in the File menu (ALT, F, A) and save the program with the file name KWH01.

Examples

1. The program for this example computes the amount of sales tax on the value of the variable *SalesAmount* entered in response to an INPUT statement. The sales tax rate of 6% is assigned to the variable *TaxRate*.

```
CLS
TaxRate = 6 / 100
INPUT SalesAmount
PRINT SalesAmount * TaxRate
```

Enter this program. Save it as SALETX01, and then run it. Three runs are shown, side by side.

```
? 1              ? 39.95          ? 1000000000
 .06              2.397            6E+07
```

Oops! The sales amount of 1000000000 causes the result to be printed in exponential notation. For large numbers, it is better to use double-precision, as in the next example.

2. The program in this example uses double-precision numbers and variables to compute the sales tax and total amount of sale (including tax) for large values of *SalesAmount#*. The sales tax is assigned to the variable *SalesTax#*. The total amount of the sale is computed and assigned to the variable *TotalAmount#*. Then the sales tax and the total amount are printed.

```
CLS
TaxRate# = 6 / 100#
INPUT SalesAmount#
SalesTax# = SalesAmount# * TaxRate#
TotalAmount# = SalesAmount# + SalesTax#
PRINT SalesTax#, Total Amount#
```

Enter and run this program. It handles a sale of $1 billion quite nicely, as shown on the Output screen:

```
? 1000000000
 60000000        1060000000
```

Save this program as SALETX02. Note that the double-precision variables are *TaxRate#, SalesAmount#, SalesTax#,* and *TotalAmount#*. The second line of the program uses a double-precision number (100#) to ensure that the value of *TaxRate#* will be as precise as possible. Numbers in QBasic are stored as binary (base 2) numbers. The decimal number .06 cannot be stored exactly as a binary number; a small round-off error occurs. This error is much less if you use a double-precision number for the computation.

3. A cube has six faces; each face is a square. The program in this example computes the area of a face and the cube's volume, given the value of *side,* the length of a side of the cube.

```
CLS
INPUT side
area = side ^ 2
volume = side ^ 3
PRINT area, volume
```

Run the program several times, entering different values for the variable *side.* Then save the program as CUBE01.

SUMMARY

You use the arithmetic operators (+, −, *, /), the integer quotient (\) and integer remainder (MOD), and the exponent operator (^) to make calculations. You can use the Immediate window to print immediate calculations or use the View window to write programs that calculate and print your results. Depending on the value of the numbers you are manipulating, you may use one of the following four number types:

- An *integer,* denoted by a percent sign (%) following the number or variable, is a whole number in the range −32,768 to +32767.

- A *long integer,* denoted by an ampersand (&) appended to the number or variable, is a whole number in the range −2,147,483,648 to +2,147,483,647.

- A *single-precision number,* denoted by an exclamation mark (!) added to the number or variable, is a real number of up to seven digits, plus a decimal point. If a single-precision number is too large to be represented in seven digits, the number is expressed in floating-point notation, rounded to seven digits with an exponent.

- A *double-precision number,* denoted by a number sign (#) added to the number or variable, is a real number of up to 16 digits, plus a decimal point. If a number cannot be expressed simply in 16 digits, then it is converted to floating-point notation.

A numeric variable represents number values. You use a variable to represent values that vary. It may be any combination of upper- and lower-case letters and numbers. The first character of a variable name must be a letter.

To make a program more general, use the INPUT keyword to ask for user input of values during program execution.

QBasic may reformat statements that you enter in the View window (such as altering spacing and capitalizing all keywords).

You use the PRINT USING statement to control the format of numbers when they are displayed. The PRINT USING formatting options include the ability to display leading dollar signs. You use the Save As. . . option in the File menu to save a program in the View window to a disk file.

Practice loading and running the programs that you saved to disk in this chapter:

KWH01.BAS	(Cost of Electricity with INPUT Statement)
SALETX01.BAS	(Calculate Sales Tax)
SALETX02.BAS	(Sales Tax and Total Amount)
CUBE01.BAS	(Area of a Side and Volume of a Cube)

chapter **4**

STRING
MANIPULATIONS

In this chapter you will learn

- How to make your programs more useful and your output more meaningful by using strings

- How to use the "enhanced" INPUT statement to identify information to be entered by someone who uses your program

- How to identify and format the information printed by your program

You will also learn how to make your programs more readable by including comments within a program that provide information about the program. This is part of good programming style. Programs that are written in good programming style can be read and understood by others—and by yourself a year later.

USING REMARKS IN YOUR PROGRAMS

It is good practice to put information at the beginning of a program to tell people something about the program. The *REM (REMark) statement* allows you to do this. When you run the program, it ignores any text that follows the REM keyword in a program line. You can use an apostrophe (') as an abbreviation for the REM keyword.

Now you will add three REM lines to Program KWH01 from the previous chapter. If you saved the program to the disk, load the program as follows:

1. Access the File menu, move the highlight to Open, and press ENTER.

2. Press TAB to move the cursor to the Dirs/Drives box of the Open dialog box and press the ↓ key until the highlight moves to the drive that has the programs from Chapter 3. Then,

    Press: ENTER

    This demonstration uses a data disk in drive A for saving and loading programs. The programs that were saved are listed in alphabetic order, like those shown in the Open dialog box of Figure 4-1.

3. Press TAB to move the cursor to the Files box. Then use the arrow keys to highlight the KWH01.BAS file. Press ENTER to load the file.

This loads the program, which should look like this:

```
CLS
LoRate = .08882
INPUT kwh
PRINT kwh * LoRate
```

When you load the program from the Open dialog box, the cursor appears under the C of CLS in the first line. Press ENTER if the cursor is there. If you have inadvertently moved the cursor, move it back to the C of CLS and press ENTER.

A blank line opens at the beginning of the program. Use the ↑ key to move the cursor to the beginning of the blank line and add the first three program lines that follow. Just type each line and press ENTER.

```
REM ** Cost of Electricity with INPUT **
' QBasic Made Easy, Chapter 4.  Filename: KWH02.BAS
' Written on a balmy day in May

CLS
LoRate = .08882
INPUT kwh
PRINT kwh * LoRate
```

The REM statement in the first line gives the title of the program. The second line uses an apostrophe (') instead of the word REM. It tells where the program originated (*QBasic Made Easy,* Chapter 4) and gives the file name (KWH02.BAS) under which the file will be saved on a disk. The third line is optional. You can include whatever comments you want in these first few lines. You might want to include the date the program was written or the date of the last time you modified the program.

Include the blank line after the three remark statements to serve as a blank line spacer that separates this block of descriptive information from

FIGURE 4-1. Programs on disk

the rest of the program, which does the actual work. Since QBasic does not remove blank lines from a program, the programs in this book usually include blank lines to enhance readability.

The information in REM statements is for people; the computer ignores it. From now on, most programs will have REM statements that will help you identify and understand them.

Save this program to disk by using the file name shown in the second remark: KWH02.BAS. The program produces the same results as program KWH01. The only difference is the remarks that you added.

Examples

Congratulations! You are the big winner on a TV game show. Your prize is selected as follows:

A number from 1 to 1000 is chosen at random. Call it *n*. You then select one, but only one, of the following prizes. You have 30 seconds to make your selection.

Prize Number 1: You receive n dollars.
Prize Number 2: You receive 1.01^n dollars.

For some values of *n*, prize 1 is larger; for other values of *n*, prize 2 is larger. Program TVSHOW01 (TV Game Show Winner with PRINT), which follows, displays the values of both prizes. It uses REM statements and prints strings to identify the prizes.

```
REM ** Big Winner on TV Game Show with PRINT Strings **
' QBasic Made Easy, Chapter 4.  File: TVSHOW01.BAS

CLS
INPUT n
PRINT "Prize #1:"; n
PRINT "Prize #2:"; 1.01 ^ n
```

Here are two sample runs of TVSHOW01.

```
? 100                 ? 700
Prize #1: 100         Prize #1: 700
Prize #2: 2.704811    Prize #2: 1059.153
```

WRITING MORE USEFUL PROGRAMS

The INPUT statement tells the computer to put a question mark on the screen and wait for a number to be entered. This is useful, but it would be more useful if the computer identified what sort of input it wanted. There is an easy way to do this.

Program 4-1, SALETX03 (Sales Tax with Enhanced INPUT Statement), is an improved sales tax program. It is similar to Program SALETX02 from Chapter 3, but it features an "enhanced" INPUT statement. Two sample runs are shown side by side here:

```
Amount of sale? 39.95        Amount of sale? 269
 2.397          42.347        16.14          285.14
```

The program line

```
INPUT "Amount of sale"; SalesAmount#
```

tells the computer to do the following:

1. Print the string "Amount of sale".

2. Print a question mark.

3. Wait for a number to be entered and assign it as the value of *SalesAmount#*.

```
REM ** Sales Tax with Enhanced INPUT Statement **
' QBasic Made Easy, Chapter 4. Filename: SALETX03.BAS

CLS
TaxRate# = 6 / 100#

INPUT "Amount of sale"; SalesAmount#

SalesTax# = SalesAmount# * TaxRate#
TotalAmount# = SalesAmount# + SalesTax#
PRINT SalesTax#, TotalAmount#
```

PROGRAM 4-1.   Sales Tax with Enhanced INPUT Statement

Note that the message to be displayed (Amount of sale) is enclosed in quotation marks and followed by a semicolon. The semicolon causes a question mark to be displayed following the INPUT message.

You can make the program even easier to use by changing the program so that it identifies the results as the amount of sales tax and the total amount of the sale, as shown in Program 4-2, SALETX04 (Sales Tax with Enhanced INPUT & PRINT Statements). Be sure to type all punctuation, including quotation marks ("). A sample run is shown here:

```
Amount of sale? 39.95
Amount of sales tax is 2.397
Total amount is 42.347
```

The program now identifies the required data to be entered (amount of sale) and the two results (amount of sales tax and total amount). A PRINT statement prints each result and also identifies the printed result.

The program line

```
PRINT "Amount of sales tax is"; SalesTax#
```

tells the computer to first print the string "Amount of sales tax is" and then print the value of *SalesTax#*. Note that the string and the variable are separated by a semicolon. Thus, the value of *SalesTax#* is printed as close as possible to the string. The string "Total amount is" is printed in a similar way along with the value of *TotalAmount#*.

```
REM ** Sales Tax with Enhanced INPUT & PRINT Statements **
' QBasic Made Easy, Chapter 4. Filename: SALETX04.BAS

CLS
TaxRate# = 6 / 100#

INPUT "Amount of sale"; SalesAmount#

SalesTax# = SalesAmount# * TaxRate#
TotalAmount# = SalesAmount# + SalesTax#
PRINT "Amount of sales tax is"; SalesTax#
PRINT "Total amount is"; TotalAmount#
```

PROGRAM 4-2. Sales Tax with Enhanced INPUT & PRINT Statements

Examples

1. You can use Program 4-3, KWH03 (Cost of Electricity with Enhanced INPUT & PRINT), to compute the cost of electricity for values of kwh charged at the low rate of $0.08882. A sample run is shown here:

```
Kilowatt-hours at low rate? 789
The cost of electricity is 70.07898
```

2. In 1990, the population of the Earth was about 5.3 billion people and increasing at the rate of 1.8% per year. Program 4-4, POPUL01 (Projected World Population), uses these values to estimate the population *n* years from 1990. A sample run follows:

```
Number of years after 1990? 20
Projected population: 7.572363E+09
```

The projected world population in 2010 (20 years after 1990) is about 7.6 billion people. Note that Program POPUL01 does not use double-precision variables or numbers, even though large numbers are involved. The current world population and growth rate are only estimates. Single-precision arithmetic is adequate for this calculation.

```
REM ** Cost of Electricity with Enhanced INPUT & PRINT **
' QBasic Made Easy, Chapter 4. Filename: KWH03.BAS

CLS
LoRate = .08882

INPUT "Kilowatt-hours at low rate"; kwh

PRINT "The cost of electricity is"; kwh * LoRate
```

PROGRAM 4-3. Cost of Electricity with Enhanced INPUT & PRINT

```
REM ** Projected World Population **
' QBasic Made Easy, Chapter 4. Filename: POPUL01.BAS

CLS
Pop1990 = 5.3E+09
GrowthRate = 1.8 / 100

INPUT "Number of years after 1990"; n

PRINT "Projected population:"; Pop1990 * (1 + GrowthRate) ^ n
```

PROGRAM 4-4. Projected World Population

3. For a given value of *n*, which is greater, *n* dollars or $1.01 \char`\^ n$ dollars? Use Program 4-5, TVSHOW02 (Big Winner on a TV Game Show With INPUT String), to find out. Two sample runs are shown here:

```
Enter an integer from 1 to 1000: 100
Prize #1: 100
Prize #2: 2.704811

Enter an integer from 1 to 1000: 700
Prize #1: 700
Prize #2: 1059.153
```

```
REM ** Big Winner on a TV Game Show with INPUT string **
' QBasic Made Easy, Chapter 4. Filename: TVSHOW02.BAS

CLS

INPUT "Enter an integer from 1 to 1000: ", n

PRINT "Prize #1:"; n
PRINT "Prize #2:"; 1.01 ^ n
```

PROGRAM 4-5. Big Winner on a TV Game Show with INPUT
String

In the program line

```
INPUT "Enter an integer from 1 to 1000: ", n
```

a comma (,) separates the string "Enter an integer from 1 to 1000: " and the variable *n*. This comma suppresses printing of the question mark normally supplied by the INPUT statement. If you want a question mark, use a semicolon; if you don't want a question mark, use a comma.

FORMATTING THE PRINTED RESULTS

Program 4-6, SALETX05 (Sales Tax with TAB Function) prints the amount of the sale entered from the keyboard, the amount of the sales tax, and the total amount of the sale, including sales tax. Note two new things in this program:

- The first PRINT statement is an "empty" PRINT statement. It causes a blank line to be printed. You can control and improve the appearance of printed results by using PRINT statements to insert appropriate blank lines.

```
REM ** Sales Tax with TAB Function **
' QBasic Made Easy, Chapter 4. Filename: SALETX05.BAS

CLS
TaxRate# = 6 / 100#

INPUT "Amount of sale"; SalesAmount#

SalesTax# = SalesAmount# * TaxRate#
TotalAmount# = SalesAmount# + SalesTax#

PRINT
PRINT "Amount of sale is"; TAB(30); SalesAmount#
PRINT "Amount of sales tax is"; TAB(30); SalesTax#
PRINT "Total amount is"; TAB(30); TotalAmount#
```

PROGRAM 4-6. Sales Tax with TAB Function

- The TAB function in the last three PRINT statements tells the computer to move the cursor to the column specified in parentheses. TAB(30) moves the cursor to column 30.

A sample run of Program SALETX05 is shown here:

```
Amount of sale? 1

Amount of sale is        1
Amount of sales tax is   .06
Total amount is          1.06
```

Although the values of *SalesAmount#*, *SalesTax#*, and *TotalAmount#* are all printed beginning in column 30, the decimal points do not line up correctly. To solve this problem, use a variation of the PRINT statement called PRINT USING. The PRINT USING statement lets you specify the appearance and positioning of numbers. It also provides the means for rounding numbers to a given number of decimal places.

The following statement tells the computer to print the value of *SalesAmount#* with up to nine digits before the decimal point and two digits following the decimal point, rounded, if necessary:

```
PRINT USING "########.##"; SalesAmount#
```

Program 4-7, SALETX06 (Sales Tax with PRINT USING), uses three PRINT USING statements. Since all three numbers are printed with the same PRINT USING format string ("#########.##"), they line up vertically along the decimal point, as shown in the following run:

```
Amount of sale? 39.95

Amount of sale is        39.95
Amount of sales tax is    2.40
Total amount is          42.35
```

The following pair of statements prints one line on the screen:

```
PRINT "Amount of sale is"; TAB(30);
PRINT USING "########.##"; SalesAmount#
```

```
REM ** Sales Tax with PRINT USING **
' QBasic Made Easy, Chapter 4. Filename: SALETX06.BAS

CLS
TaxRate# = 6 / 100#

INPUT "Amount of sale"; SalesAmount#

SalesTax# = SalesAmount# * TaxRate#
TotalAmount# = SalesAmount# + SalesTax#

PRINT
PRINT "Amount of sale is"; TAB(30);
PRINT USING "########.##"; SalesAmount#

PRINT "Amount of sales tax is"; TAB(30);
PRINT USING "########.##"; SalesTax#

PRINT "Total amount is"; TAB(30);
PRINT USING "########.##"; TotalAmount#
```

═══════════ **PROGRAM 4-7.** Sales Tax with PRINT USING

The PRINT statement prints the string "Amount of sale is" and then tabs over to column 30. The semicolon following TAB(30) holds the cursor at column 30 so that the information printed by the PRINT USING statement will begin there. The PRINT USING statement prints the value of *SalesAmount#* as specified by the format string: *"#########.##"*, as illustrated here:

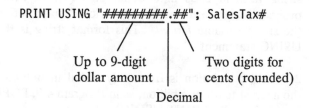

Each pair of PRINT and PRINT USING statements following the first pair also work together to produce one line of print. Note that all numbers are shown with two decimal places, as specified by the format string in the

PRINT USING statements. The format string in Program SALETX05 limits the printed number to, at most, nine digits before the decimal point. If a printed number is more than 999999999.99, the program prints a percent sign (%) in front of the number, as shown here:

```
Amount of sale? 1000000000

Amount of sale is        %1000000000.00
Amount of sales tax is    60000000.00
Total amount is          %1060000000.00
```

This problem has an easy solution: use a format string that allows more digits before the decimal point. The following PRINT statement allows up to 12 digits before the decimal point:

```
70 PRINT USING "###########.##"; SalesAmount#
```

Examples

1. Program 4-8, TVSHOW03 (Big Winner on a TV Game Show with PRINT USING), assigns a format string ("#####.##") to the string variable *format$* and then uses *format$* in two PRINT USING statements. A sample run follows:

```
Enter an integer from 1 to 1000: 700

Prize #1:        700.00
Prize #2:       1059.16
```

You can invent your own string variables, such as *format$*. Note that a string variable ends in a dollar sign ($). In Program TVSHOW03, the program assigns a format string enclosed in quotation marks as the value of the string variable *format$*. This format string is then used in the PRINT USING statements.

2. World population is frequently stated in billions of people, rounded to the nearest tenth of a billion, as in Program 4-9, POPUL02 (Projected World Population with PRINT USING).
Here is a run of POPUL02.

```
Number of years after 1990? 20
Projected population:  7.6 billion people
```

```
REM ** Big Winner on a TV Game Show with PRINT USING **
' QBasic Made Easy, Chapter 4. Filename: TVSHOW03.BAS

CLS

INPUT "Enter an integer from 1 to 1000: ", n

format$ = "#####.##"

PRINT

PRINT "Prize #1:"; TAB(20);
PRINT USING format$; n

PRINT "Prize #2:"; TAB(20);
PRINT USING format$; 1.01 ^ n
```

═══ **PROGRAM 4-8.**   Big Winner on a TV Game Show with PRINT
USING

```
REM ** Projected World Population with PRINT USING **
' QBasic Made Easy, Chapter 4. Filename: POPULO2.BAS

CLS
Pop1990 = 5.3
GrowthRate = 1.8 / 100
format$ = "##.#"

INPUT "Number of years after 1990"; n

People = Pop1990 * (1 + GrowthRate) ^ n

PRINT "Projected population: ";
PRINT USING format$; People;
PRINT " billion people"
```

═══ **PROGRAM 4-9.**   Projected World Population with PRINT USING

A value of 5.3 is assigned to the variable *Pop1990*. This is the number of billions of people. The format string allows up to 99.9 billion people to be printed by the PRINT USING statement. The PRINT and PRINT USING statements work together to print one line, as follows:

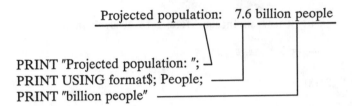

LEARNING MORE ABOUT THE PRINT USING STATEMENT

The PRINT USING statement has many variations. Among the most useful of these are printing dollar signs ($) before numbers and automatically putting commas in very large numbers. These features are shown in Program 4-10, SALETX07 (Sales Tax with Dollars & Commas in Printout). In the following sample run, note the dollar sign ($) before each number and the commas embedded in the number:

```
Amount of sale? 1000000000

Amount of sale is         $1,000,000,000.00
Amount of sales tax is       $60,000,000.00
Total amount is           $1,060,000,000.00
```

The format string "$$###,###,###,###.##" is assigned to the string variable *format$*. This format string, used in the PRINT USING statements, tells the computer to print a number as follows:

- The double dollar sign ($$) causes a space and a dollar sign to be printed to the left of the number.

- The 12 number signs (#) separated by commas allow up to 12 digits of the number to be printed, with commas inserted every three digits. If fewer than 12 digits are printed, spaces are printed instead, in this case to the left of the dollar sign.

- The decimal point causes a decimal point to be printed in the number.

```
REM ** Sales Tax with Dollars & Commas in Printout **
' QBasic Made Easy, Chapter 4. Filename: SALETX07.BAS

CLS
TaxRate# = 6 / 100#

INPUT "Amount of sale"; SalesAmount#

SalesTax# = SalesAmount# * TaxRate#
TotalAmount# = SalesAmount# + SalesTax#

format$ = "$$###,###,###,###.##"

PRINT
PRINT "Amount of sale is"; TAB(30);
PRINT USING format$; SalesAmount#

PRINT "Amount of sales tax is"; TAB(30);
PRINT USING format$; SalesTax#

PRINT "Total amount is"; TAB(30);
PRINT USING format$; TotalAmount#
```

≡≡≡ **PROGRAM 4-10.**   Sales Tax with Dollars & Commas in Printout

- The two number signs to the right of the decimal point cause two digits to be printed to the right of the decimal point. If necessary, the number being printed is rounded to two places.

    If you own stocks, you might find Program 4-11, STOCKS01 (Value of Stocks With REM Statements), useful. It computes and prints the value of a block of stock shares, given the number of shares and the price per share. A sample run is shown here:

```
Number of shares? 1200
Price per share ? 37.50

The value is        $45,000.00
```

The format string "$$############,.##" is equivalent to the format string "$$###,###,###,###.##" used previously in Program SALETX07. In either case, the program prints commas every three digits in the part of the number to the left of the decimal point.

```
REM ** Value of Stocks with REM Statements **
' QBasic Made Easy, Chapter 4. Filename: STOCKS01.BAS

REM ** Set up **
CLS

REM ** Get number of shares and price per share **
INPUT "Number of shares"; NumberOfShares#
INPUT "Price per share "; PricePerShare#

REM ** Compute value of this block of stock **
Value# = NumberOfShares# * PricePerShare#

REM ** Print the value of this block of stock **
PRINT
PRINT "The value is ";
PRINT USING "$$###########,.##"; Value#
```

PROGRAM 4-11. Value of Stocks with REM Statements

USING REM STATEMENTS TO OUTLINE YOUR PROGRAM

Suppose that you keep your money in a bank account that pays regular interest, compounded periodically. Program 4-12, INTRST01 (Future Value of Money -- Compound Interest) computes the value of money (principal) invested at a particular interest rate per period, compounded for a given number of periods.

Before looking at the program, examine the following sample runs and think about how you would write the program. The first sample is for $1 invested at 1% interest, compounded for one period. This is used to test the program. The answer should be $1.01.

```
Principal amount invested ($)? 1
Interest rate per period (%) ? 1
Number of interest periods    ? 1

At maturity, the value will be              $1.01
```

Now suppose that you have a balance of $500 on a credit card that charges 1.5% interest per month, and you put off paying it for 12 months:

```
Principal amount invested ($)? -500
Interest rate per period (%) ? 1.5
Number of interest periods   ? 12

At maturity, the value will be                  -$597.81
```

The "investment" is entered as −500 as a reminder that you owe $500 and are paying interest. The result is −$597.81, the amount that you owe if you procrastinate for 12 months.

You might find it helpful to write an outline of the program in REM statements first. A possible outline is shown here:

```
REM ** Future Value of Money -- Compound Interest **
' QBasic Made Easy, Chapter 4.  Filename: INTRST01.BAS

REM ** Set up **

REM ** Get principal, interest rate, number of periods **

REM ** Compute future value **

REM ** Print the future value **
```

```
REM ** Future Value of Money -- Compound Interest **
' QBasic Made Easy, Chapter 4. Filename: INTRST01.BAS

REM ** Set up **
CLS
format$ = "$$###,###,###,###.##"

REM ** Get principal, interest rate, number of periods **
INPUT "Principal amount invested ($)"; Principal#
INPUT "Interest rate per period (%) "; Rate#
INPUT "Number of interest periods   "; Periods#

REM ** Compute future value **
Rate# = Rate# / 100
FutureValue# = Principal# * (1 + Rate#) ^ Periods#

REM ** Print the future value **
PRINT
PRINT "At maturity, the value will be ";
PRINT USING format$; FutureValue#
```

PROGRAM 4-12. Future Value of Money − Compound Interest

Once you have an outline for your program, you can expand it as shown in Program INTRST01.

The program has five blocks. Each block begins with a REM statement that tells what the block does. The first block gives the name of the program, where it was first published, and the file name of the program as stored on a disk.

The second block clears the screen and assigns a format string to a string variable. If there were any other program set-up to be done, this block would include those instructions also.

The third block uses INPUT statements to get values for the three variables used to compute the amount of interest and future value. All variables are double precision—useful for handling values that require a high degree of precision.

- *Principal#* is the amount invested, in dollars and cents.

- *Rate#* is the interest rate per interest period. Enter 1 for 1%, 1.5 for 1.5%, and so on.

- *Periods#* is the number of periods over which the interest is compounded. For example, if the interest is compounded monthly for one year, enter 12 as the value of *Periods#*.

The fourth block calculates the future value. The interest rate is first converted to a decimal fraction (*Rate#* = *Rate#* / 100#), which is used in the formula to compute the future value. Note the use of the exponentiation operator (^) in the computation of *FutureValue#*.

The fifth and final block prints the value of the future value, preceded by the string "At maturity, the value will be". The format string assigned to *format$* causes the printed number to have a leading dollar sign and commas every three digits.

Examples

1. Program 4-13, INTRST02 (Future Value of Money -- Print to Printer) prints the values that you enter and the final result on the printer. Here is a sample run, as printed on the printer:

```
Principal amount invested:        $1,000.00
Interest rate per period:              1.00
Number of interest periods:           12.00

At maturity, the value will be:   $1,126.83
```

```
REM ** Future Value of Money -- Print to Printer **
' QBasic Made Easy, Chapter 4. Filename: INTRST02.BAS

REM ** Set up **
CLS
format1$ = "$$###,###,###,###.##"
format2$ = "###,###,###,###.##"

REM ** Get principal, interest rate, number of periods **
INPUT "Principal amount invested ($)"; Principal#
INPUT "Interest rate per period (%) "; RatePerPeriod#
INPUT "Number of interest periods   "; Periods#

REM ** Compute future value **
Rate# = RatePerPeriod# / 100
FutureValue# = Principal# * (1 + Rate#) ^ Periods#

REM ** Print all values to the printer **
LPRINT "Principal amount invested:"; TAB(32);
LPRINT USING format1$; Principal#
LPRINT "Interest rate per period:"; TAB(34);
LPRINT USING format2$; RatePerPeriod#
LPRINT "Number of interest periods:"; TAB(34);
LPRINT USING format2$; Periods#
LPRINT
LPRINT "At maturity, the value will be:"; TAB(32);
LPRINT USING format1$; FutureValue#
```

═══ **PROGRAM 4-13.**　Future Value of Money — Print to Printer

The values of *Principal#* and *FutureValue#* are printed with dollar signs, and the values of *RatePerPeriod#* and *Periods#* are printed without dollar signs. The format string assigned to *format1$* causes a space and a dollar sign to be printed when used to print *Principal#* and *FutureValue#*. The format string assigned to *format2$* does not do this. Note that the values in the TAB function are chosen to make sure that the decimal points line up vertically.

 To print information to the printer, use LPRINT or LPRINT USING instead of PRINT and PRINT USING.

2. Program 4-14, POPUL03 (Projected World Population with REM Statements), is a revision of Program POPUL02. A REM outline of Program POPUL03 is shown here:

```
REM ** Projected World Population with REM Statements **
' QBasic Made Easy, Chapter 4.  Filename: POPUL03.BAS

REM ** Set up **

REM ** Get the number of years after 1990 **

REM ** Compute projected population in billions of people **

REM ** Print projected population in billions of people **
```

If you run Program POPUL03 and enter the same value you did for Program POPUL02, the result will be the same.

```
REM ** Projected World Population with REM Statements **
' QBasic Made Easy, Chapter 4. Filename: POPUL03.BAS

REM ** Set up **
CLS
Pop1990 = 5.3
GrowthRate = 1.8 / 100
format$ = "##.#"

REM ** Get the number of years after 1990 **
INPUT "Number of years after 1990"; n

REM ** Compute projected population in billions of people **
People = Pop1990 * (1 + GrowthRate) ^ n

REM ** Print projected population in billions of people **
PRINT "Projected population: ";
PRINT USING format$; People;
PRINT " billion people"
```

PROGRAM 4-14.   Projected World Population with REM Statements

LEARNING MORE ABOUT STRINGS AND STRING VARIABLES

A string is a group of characters, one after another in, of course, a string. A string can be

A name	Christopher
A telephone number	707-555-1212
A message	Trust your psychic tailwind
A date	1-1-91
A time	8:30:57
A format string	$$###,###,###.##
Gibberish	123Bz#m%@

You have seen strings enclosed in quotation marks:

```
DATE$ = "1-1-91"

TIME$ = "8:30:57"

PRINT USING "$$###,###,###.##"; TotalAmount#
```

The quotation marks enclose the string but are not part of the string. They tell the computer where the string begins and ends.

A string can be the value of a *string variable*. You can think of a string variable as a labeled box that can hold, or store, a string:

format$ | $$###,###,###,###.## |

You specify a string variable by using a name followed by a dollar sign ($). The name can be any combination of letters and numbers, but the first character must be a letter. Here are some examples of string variables:

DATE$	TIME$	format$	Strng$
Address$	City$	State$	Agent007$

Two of these, DATE$ and TIME$, are special string variables. They are QBasic keywords. The string variable *format$* was created for use in previous programs.

 Most keywords may not be used as variables. For example, you may not use *String$* as a string variable because STRING$ is a QBasic keyword. However, note the use of *Strng$* in the previous examples, as a string variable that sounds and looks like *String$*.

You can assign a value to a string variable in the same way that you assign a value to a numeric variable. For example, clear the Output screen from the Immediate window. Then assign a value to the string variable *Naym$* in the Immediate window, as follows:

Type: **Naym$ = "Albert Outlander"**
and press ENTER

Verify that Albert's name is now the value of *Naym$* (also in the Immediate window):

Type: **PRINT Naym$**
and press ENTER

After pressing ENTER, you should see Albert's name on the Output screen:

```
Albert Outlander
```

Program 4-15, STRNGS01 (Print Two Strings in Various Ways), demonstrates several ways to print two strings with a single PRINT statement. All the PRINT statements use an apostrophe (') to include a remark at the end of a program line. This remark is ignored by the computer but provides information about the line for you to read.

Study the program and the printed results to learn more about strings, commas, and semicolons in PRINT statements and the use of a plus sign (+) to *catenate* (join) strings. Table 4-1 shows each PRINT statement together with the result printed by the statement. The program prints the values of *FirstName$* and *LastName$* in seven ways, as follows:

```
Albert       Outlander
AlbertOutlander
Albert Outlander
```

```
AlbertOutlander
Albert Outlander
Outlander, Albert
Outlander, Albert
```

The program line

```
PRINT FirstName$, LastName$            'Note comma
```

contains a remark ('Note comma). You can annotate your programs in this way in order to make them more readable. The computer ignores the apostrophe and everything to its right.

Examples

1. You can assign the value of a variable to another variable. After doing so, both variables have the same value. For example, assign the value of

---

```
REM ** Print Two Strings in Various Ways **
' QBasic Made Easy, Chapter 4. Filename: STRNGS01.BAS

REM ** Set up **
CLS

REM ** Assign values to string variables **
FirstName$ = "Albert"
LastName$ = "Outlander"

REM ** Print values of 2 string variables in various ways **
PRINT FirstName$, LastName$            'Note comma
PRINT FirstName$; LastName$            'Note semicolon
PRINT FirstName$; " "; LastName$       'Put in a space
PRINT FirstName$ + LastName$           'Use + to join 2 strings
PRINT FirstName$ + " " + LastName$     'Use + to join 3 strings
PRINT LastName$; ", "; FirstName$      'Reverse order
PRINT LastName$ + ", " + FirstName$    'Another way to do it
```

═══ **PROGRAM 4-15.**   Print Two Strings in Various Ways

Statement	Result
PRINT FirstName$, LastName$	AlbertOutlander
PRINT FirstName$; LastName$	AlbertOutlander
PRINT FirstName$; " "; LastName$	Albert Outlander
PRINT FirstName$ + LastName$	AlbertOutlander
PRINT FirstName$ + " " + LastName$	Albert Outlander
PRINT LastName$; ", "; FirstName$	Outlander, Albert
PRINT LastName$ + ", " + FirstName$	Outlander, Albert

TABLE 4-1. PRINT Statements and Results from Program STRNGS01

DATE$ to the string variable *Today$,* and then print the values of both DATE$ and Today$. The Enter column is to be entered in the Immediate window.

Enter   **Output Screen**

```
CLS
Today$ = DATE$
PRINT Today$, DATE$          01-24-1991      01-24-1991
```

You can assign the value of TIME$ to a variable called, say, *StartTime$.* Momentarily, these two variables will have the same value. However, as you know, TIME$ marches on, while *StartTime$* remains the same.

Enter   **Output Screen**

```
CLS
StartTime$ = TIME$
PRINT StartTime$, TIME$      07:59:53        08:01:06
```

2. You can use a plus sign (+) to catenate (join) strings and assign the result to a variable. The example that follows catenates the value of DATE$, two spaces, and the value of TIME$ and then assigns the result to the variable *DateTime$.*

Enter   **Output Screen**

```
CLS
DateTime$ = DATE$ + "  " + TIME$
PRINT DateTime$              01-24-1991  08:06:35
```

In a PRINT statement, you can use the plus sign (+) or a semicolon (;) to catenate strings:

```
PRINT DATE$ + "   " + TIME$
PRINT DATE$; "   "; TIME$
```

USING INPUT WITH STRING VARIABLES

You can use INPUT to acquire a value for a string variable. Program 4-16, STRNGS02 (Enter Strings with INPUT and PRINT) uses an INPUT statement to acquire a value for the string variable *Strng$*. This variable is used in lieu of String$, which is a QBasic keyword (STRING$). The program uses an endless DO...LOOP to allow you to try many strings without having to restart the program each time. Enter and run the program. It clears the screen, prints a question mark, displays the cursor, and waits for you to enter a value for the string variable *Strng$,* as shown here:

```
? _
```

```
REM ** Enter strings with INPUT and PRINT **
' QBasic Made Easy, Chapter 4. Filename: STRNGS02.BAS
' Press CTRL-BREAK to stop

REM ** Set up **
CLS

REM ** Get a string and print it; then loop **
DO
  INPUT Strng$
  PRINT Strng$
  PRINT
LOOP
```

PROGRAM 4-16.   Enter Strings with INPUT and PRINT

Enter Albert Outlander's name:

Type: **Albert Outlander**
and press ENTER

The computer accepts Albert's name as the value of *Strng$*, prints the value of *Strng$*, and then loops back to the INPUT statement and waits for a new value of *Strng$*. The screen looks like this:

```
? Albert Outlander
Albert Outlander

? _
```

Now enter Albert's name in reverse order—last name, a comma, first name:

Type: **Outlander, Albert**
and press ENTER

Oops! This causes a problem. You will see the following on the screen:

```
? Outlander, Albert

Redo from start
? _
```

The "Redo from start" message denotes that something is wrong with your entry. If you are using INPUT to enter a string that contains a comma, you must enclose the entire string in quotation marks. To correct the entry, enter Albert's name in reverse order, enclosed in quotation marks:

Type: **"Outlander, Albert"**
and press ENTER

This time the computer should accept the string containing a comma. The screen will look like this:

```
? "Outlander, Albert"
Outlander, Albert

? _
```

Here is another example showing entry of a string containing a comma, with and without quotation marks:

```
? January 1, 1991

Redo from start
? "January 1, 1991"
January 1, 1991

? _
```

Enter some more values of *Strng$*. When you are finished, use CTRL-BREAK to stop the program.

USING LINE INPUT WITH STRING VARIABLES

When you are entering strings that contain punctuation, you can also use QBasic's LINE INPUT statement in place of INPUT. Program 4-17,

```
REM ** Enter strings with LINE INPUT and PRINT **
' QBasic Made Easy, Chapter 4. Filename: STRNGS03.BAS
' Press CTRL-BREAK to stop

REM ** Set up **
CLS

REM ** Get a string and print it; then loop **
DO
  LINE INPUT "? "; Strng$
  PRINT Strng$
  PRINT
LOOP
```

PROGRAM 4-17.   Enter Strings with LINE INPUT and PRINT

STRNGS03 (Enter Strings with LINE INPUT and PRINT), uses LINE INPUT. Here is a sample run showing three string entries, two with punctuation:

```
? Albert Outlander
Albert Outlander

? Outlander, Albert
Outlander, Albert

? 3005 Maryana Dr., #5
3005 Maryana Dr., #5

? _
```

Notice that you do not have to enclose your entry with quotation marks when using LINE INPUT. Also notice that in the program, the LINE INPUT statement includes a string containing a question mark and space ("? "):

```
LINE INPUT "? "; Strng$
```

LINE INPUT does not automatically print a question mark for a prompt. If you want a question mark, include it in a string prompt.

Using WRITE to Display Information

You can use a WRITE statement to display information on the screen in place of PRINT. Program 4-18, STRNGS04 (Enter Strings with LINE INPUT and WRITE) uses a WRITE statement in place of the PRINT statements used in Program STRNGS03. Enter and run the program. Here is a sample run:

```
? Albert Outlander
"Albert Outlander"

? Outlander, Albert
"Outlander, Albert"

? 3005 Maryana Dr., #5
"3005 Maryana Dr., #5"

? _
```

```
REM ** Enter strings with LINE INPUT and WRITE **
' QBasic Made Easy, Chapter 4. Filename: STRNGS04.BAS
' Press CTRL-BREAK to stop

REM ** Set up **
CLS

REM ** Get a string and print it; then loop **
DO
   LINE INPUT "? "; Strng$
   WRITE Strng$
   WRITE
LOOP
```

═══ **PROGRAM 4-18.**   Enter Strings with LINE INPUT and WRITE

The WRITE statement prints quotation marks at the start and end of each string that it prints. When no value or variable follows a WRITE statement, the program prints a blank line, just as in a PRINT statement.

Examples

1. Program 4-19, NAME01 (Name Everywhere with Color & Sound (IN-PUT)) begins by asking for your name. After you type your name, or any string, the program fills the screen with the name or string in many colors, accompanied by random "music." As usual, to find out what a program does, enter it into memory and run it. First, you see

```
Your name? _
```

Alice, having recently returned from Wonderland, tried it. She typed a quotation mark ("), her name, two spaces, and a quotation mark, as follows:

```
Your name? "Alice  "_
```

```
REM ** Name Everywhere with Color & Sound (INPUT) **
' QBasic Made Easy, Chapter 4. Filename: NAME01.BAS

REM ** Set up **
CLS

REM ** Use INPUT to get a value of Name$ **
INPUT "Your name"; Naym$

REM ** Use a GOTO loop to print name with color & sound **
DO                                      'Top of GOTO loop
   COLOR 31 * RND, 8 * RND
   PRINT Naym$;
   SOUND 3000 * RND + 1000, .25
LOOP                                    'Bottom of GOTO loop
```

PROGRAM 4-19. Name Everywhere with Color & Sound (INPUT)

Then she pressed ENTER. The screen filled quickly with her name in many foreground colors on assorted background colors, accompanied by strange music reminiscent of her recent adventure. Note that each copy of Alice's name is followed by two spaces.

Stop the program and then run it again. Type Alice's name with two trailing spaces, but not enclosed in quotation marks, like this:

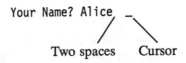

Two spaces   Cursor

After you press ENTER, again you will see Alice's name everywhere, but without the two spaces you typed. Without quotation marks, the computer ignores leading or trailing spaces in a string you enter.

Run the program again, enclosing Alice and two spaces in quotation marks, and the spaces will be printed. As an alternative, change the INPUT statement to

```
LINE INPUT "Your name? "; Naym$
```

Be sure to include the question mark, followed by a space, in the prompt string. If you run the program with this change and include two spaces after typing in the name, the spaces will be displayed on the screen.

EXITING FROM A LOOP

Program 4-20, GRAFIX02 (Stars Twinkling With Music in SCREEN 1) uses QBasic's PSET statement to put colored points at random places on the screen. The twinkling points are accompanied by an appropriate musical accompaniment. When you run the program, the message "Press space bar to quit" appears near the center of the screen.

Enter the program. Then run it. Watch, and listen a bit. Tiny points that seem to twinkle in a black sky appear on the screen. With a little (or maybe a lot) of imagination, the music seems to play, "Twinkle, Twinkle Little Star." When you want to stop the music (and the stars), press the SPACEBAR as the

```
REM ** Stars Twinkling with Music in SCREEN 1  **
' QBasic Made Easy, Chapter 4. Filename: GRAFIX02.BAS

REM ** Set up **
SCREEN 1: CLS

REM ** Print quit message then twinkle stars loop **
LOCATE 12, 8: PRINT "Press space bar to quit"
DO                              'Top of loop
  kolor = RND * 3
  row = RND * 199: column = RND * 319
  IF INKEY$ = " " THEN EXIT DO       'Escape from loop
  PSET (column, row), kolor
  SOUND 4000 * RND + 800, .75
LOOP                            'Bottom of loop
END
```

PROGRAM 4-20. Stars Twinkling with Music in SCREEN 1

message says. Figure 4-2 shows the screen after the SPACEBAR has been pressed. You can see how the screen looks when you interrupt the program. Another message, "Press any key to continue," is now displayed at the bottom of the screen, signifying that the program is over. Press any key to return to the View window, where you can study the program.

The Set up block selects the graphics screen mode (SCREEN 1) and clears it. Then the program prints the quit message near the center of the screen by using a LOCATE statement:

```
LOCATE 12,8: PRINT "Press space bar to quit"
```

You saw an endless DO...LOOP previously in Chapter 2, "Tiny Programs." You also used RND, SOUND, and PSET in Chapter 2. A technique to exit from the DO...LOOP is introduced in this program:

```
IF INKEY$ = " " THEN EXIT DO
```

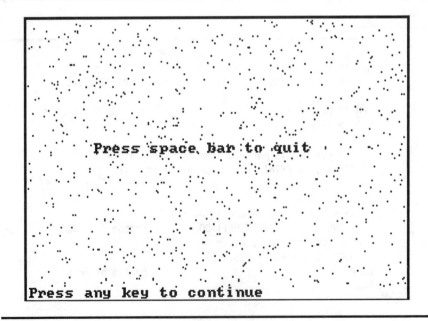

Press space bar to quit

Press any key to continue

FIGURE 4-2. Output of Program GRAFIX02

INKEY$ is a string function that reads a character from the keyboard. If no key has been pressed, the value of INKEY$ is the null (or empty) string. The null string is represented by a pair of quotation marks with nothing between them (""). If the SPACEBAR has been pressed, the value of INKEY$ will be a string consisting of one space (" ").

```
IF INKEY$ = " " THEN EXIT DO
        /                /
   If this is true    Then do this
```

If the SPACEBAR has not been pressed, INKEY$ = " " is false and the program keeps looping through the DO . . . LOOP, putting stars on the screen. When you press the SPACEBAR, the key press is detected by INKEY$ (INKEY$ = " " is true); the THEN clause of the IF . . . THEN statement is executed. An exit is made from the DO . . . LOOP and the program ends.

This program uses an END statement, which is optional. When you write longer and more complex programs, you may need an END statement at the end of your program.

SUMMARY

This chapter emphasized the use of remarks (REM and ') to annotate your programs. In addition, you learned to use several string and formatting techniques to make your programs more readable and easier to use.

You can enhance the INPUT statement by adding string prompts to tell the user what kind of entry is needed. Strings can also be used in PRINT statements to identify results of calculations.

You can align printed output by using the TAB function, commas, semicolons, and catenation. You can format output with PRINT USING statements. For example, the following PRINT USING statements are equivalent and format large money amounts with a leading space and dollar sign, a comma between each three digits in the dollar amount, and a decimal point followed by cents (rounded to the nearest penny):

```
PRINT USING "$$########,.##"; Amount#
PRINT USING "$$###,###,###.##"; Amount#
```

Programs should be broken into functional blocks with a line space between blocks and a leading REM statement in each block. You can use REM statements to make an outline of a program before writing other statements.

You use LPRINT in place of PRINT to send information to your printer instead of the display screen. You can use WRITE in place of PRINT to send information to the display screen. WRITE encloses the information in quotation marks.

A string can be a value assigned to a string variable. String variables have a dollar sign ($) appended to their names. You can use INPUT or LINE INPUT to enter values for string variables from the keyboard. If the values to be entered for string variables contain punctuation marks, you must enclose the values in quotation marks when using INPUT but not when using LINE INPUT.

Last of all, you learned to use INKEY$ to detect a keypress and used the detection to make an exit from a loop (EXIT DO).

chapter 5

CONTROL STRUCTURES

QBasic has several *control structures* that you can use to make your programs more useful. In this chapter, you will learn how to do the following:

- Use IF, Block IF, and SELECT CASE for making decisions
- Use the loop structures WHILE . . . WEND and FOR . . . NEXT
- Use the DO . . . LOOP with conditions.

Previous chapters introduced strings and string variables. You will learn more about strings in this chapter and use them in several programs.

USING THE IF STATEMENT FOR DECISION MAKING

The IF statement tells the computer to make a simple decision. It tells the computer to do a certain operation if a given condition is true. However, if the condition is false (not true), the operation is not done. Here is a simple IF statement:

```
IF number = 0 THEN EXIT DO
```

This IF statement tells the computer:

- If the value of the numeric variable *number* is equal to 0, then exit the DO...LOOP.
- If the value of the numeric variable *number* is not equal to 0, then don't exit.

Here is another way to think about it:

- If the value of *number* is equal to 0, execute the statement following the keyword THEN.
- If the value of *number* is not equal to 0, don't execute the statement following the keyword THEN.

The preceding IF statement has the form

IF *condition* THEN *statement*

In this form, the *statement* can be any QBasic statement. The *condition* is usually a comparison between a variable and a value, between two variables, or between two expressions.

Examples

1. Program 5-1, NORP01 (Negative or Positive with IF statements), tests a number entered from the keyboard to determine whether the number is negative or positive. In the first block, the program is named; then the book and chapter are listed along with the file name under which the program is saved.

```
REM ** Negative or Positive with IF statements **
' QBasic Made Easy, Chapter 5.  File: NORP01.BAS
```

```
REM ** Negative or Positive with IF Statements **
' QBasic Made Easy, Chapter 5.  Filename: NORPO1.BAS

REM ** Set up **
n$ = "negative"
p$ = "positive"

REM ** Tell what to do **
CLS
PRINT "Enter a number and I will tell you whether"
PRINT "your number is negative or positive"
PRINT "Enter 0 to quit"

REM ** Ask for a number **
DO                               'Top of loop
  PRINT
  INPUT "Enter a number: ", number

  ' Tell about the number
  IF number < 0 THEN PRINT n$
  IF number > 0 THEN PRINT p$
  IF number = 0 THEN EXIT DO
LOOP                             'Bottom of loop
END
```

═══ **PROGRAM 5-1.**   Negative or Positive with IF Statements

In the second block, messages are assigned to string variables, as shown here:

```
REM ** Set up **
n$ = "negative"
p$ = "positive"
```

The "Tell what to do" section follows:

```
REM ** Tell what to do **
CLS
PRINT "Enter a number and I will tell you whether"
PRINT "your number is negative or positive."
PRINT "Enter 0 to quit"
```

The rest of the program is a DO...LOOP that acquires a number entered from the keyboard and then tells whether the number is negative or positive. If you enter a 0, the loop is exited and the program ends. The loop is shown here:

```
REM ** Ask for a number **
DO                                      'Top of loop
  PRINT
  INPUT "Enter a number: ", number
  'Tell about the number
  IF number < 0 THEN PRINT n$
  IF number > 0 THEN PRINT p$
  IF number = 0 THEN EXIT DO
LOOP                                    'Bottom of loop
```

If you enter a negative number, the first IF statement causes the value of *n$* ("negative") to be printed. If your number is positive, the second IF statement prints the value of *p$* ("positive"). If you enter 0, the program activates the third IF statement and exits the loop. The LOOP statement marks the bottom of the loop; it sends control back to the top of the loop. When the loop is exited, the END statement stops the program. A sample run is shown in Figure 5-1.

2. Program 5-2, KWH04 (Cost of Electricity with IF Statement), compares the value of *kwh* that you enter with the baseline value of 846. The program then computes the cost of electricity in one of two ways.

If the value of *kwh* is less than or equal to 846:

```
KwhCost = kwh * LoRate
```

If the value of *kwh* is greater than 846:

```
KwhCost = 846 * LoRate + (kwh - 846) * HiRate
```

These cost decisions are made by IF statements in the program. A sample run is shown here for a value of *kwh* less than 846. The cost is computed by the first IF statement:

```
Enter number of kilowatt-hours: 789

Total cost of electricity is       $70.08
```

```
Enter a number and I will tell you whether
your number is negative or positive.
Enter 0 to quit

Enter a number: -32
negative

Enter a number: 64
positive

Enter a number: .000007
positive

Enter a number: -123456
negative

Enter a number: 0




Press any key to continue
```

FIGURE 5-1.   Output of Program NORP01.BAS

The next sample run is for a value of *kwh* greater than the baseline value of 846. The cost is computed by the second IF statement:

```
Enter number of kilowatt-hours: 1435

Total cost of electricity is     $154.80
```

For a third run to test the program, try a value of 846. The cost should be computed as $75.14.

Adding ELSE to the IF Statement

You can add ELSE clauses to IF . . . THEN statements when more than one decision must be made. However, ELSE clauses lead to long statements that extend beyond the right edge of the screen. As you are entering a long statement that extends beyond the right edge of the View window, the text window scrolls to the right so that you can see what you are entering.

```
REM ** Cost of Electricity with IF Statement **
' QBasic Made Easy, Chapter 5.  Filename: KWH04.BAS

REM ** Set up **
CLS
LoRate = .08882
HiRate = .13524
format$ = "$$###,###.##"

REM ** Get number of kilowatt-hours (kwh) **
INPUT "Enter number of kilowatt-hours: ", kwh

REM ** Compute cost of electricity **
IF kwh <= 846 THEN KwhCost = kwh * LoRate
IF kwh > 846 THEN KwhCost = 846 * LoRate + (kwh - 846) * HiRate

REM ** Print cost of electricity **
PRINT
PRINT "Total cost of electricity is";
PRINT USING format$; KwhCost
END
```

PROGRAM 5-2.   Cost of Electricity with IF Statement

However, once this happens, you cannot see the complete line. For example, you could write the IF statements in Program KWH04 as one long statement by using an ELSE clause like this:

```
IF kwh <= 846 THEN KwhCost = kwh * LoRate ELSE IF kwh > 846
THEN KwhCost = 846 * LoRate + (kwh - 846) * HiRate
```

This long statement will not fit on one line in this book. It will fit on one line in QBasic, but you will not be able to see all of it at one time. When you use QBasic, the View window scrolls to the right when you reach the right side of the screen. You can enter up to 256 characters on a program line. As the View window scrolls to the right, the characters at the extreme left cannot be seen.

Here is what you see when the window is scrolled to the left:

```
REM ** Compute cost of electricity **
IF kwh <= 846 THEN KwhCost = kwh * LoRate ELSE KwhCost = 846 * LoRate + (kwh -
```

Here is what you can see when the line is scrolled to show the right end of the statement:

```
cost of electricity **
HEN KwhCost = kwh * LoRate ELSE KwhCost = 846 * LoRate + (kwh - 846) * HiRate
```

You can see the inconvenience of this situation. QBasic has a Block IF . . . THEN structure that can handle multiple IF . . . THEN decisions with ease, as you will see in the next section. It is a good idea to use the Block IF structure for multiple decisions. Use the simple IF . . . THEN statement for single decisions.

BLOCK IF . . . THEN STRUCTURES

The Block IF structure greatly expands the usefulness and readability of the single-line IF . . . THEN . . . ELSE statement. Here is an example that is used in Program 5-3, NORP02 (Negative or Positive with Block IF):

```
IF number < 0 THEN          'If this condition is true,
   PRINT n$                 'do this
ELSEIF number > 0 THEN      'If this condition is true,
   PRINT p$                 'do this
ELSE                        'If conditions 1 and 2 are false,
   EXIT DO                  'do this
END IF
```

Enter and run Program NORP02. If you use the same entries as you did for Program NORP01, the results should be the same.

In writing a Block IF structure, note that

- The first line of a Block IF structure is an IF clause, and the last line is END IF.

- A line beginning with IF or ELSEIF must end with THEN.

- Each conditional clause (IF, ELSEIF, and ELSE) may be followed by any number of statements.

- END IF includes a blank space; ELSEIF does not.

```
REM ** Negative or Positive with Block IF **
' QBasic Made Easy, Chapter 5.   Filename: NORPO2.BAS

REM ** Set up **
n$ = "negative"
p$ = "positive"

REM ** Tell what to do **
CLS
PRINT "Enter a number and I will tell you whether"
PRINT "your number is negative or positive."
PRINT "Enter 0 to quit"

REM ** Ask for a number **
DO                                      'Top of loop
  PRINT
  INPUT "Enter a number: ", number

  ' Tell about the number
  IF number < 0 THEN
    PRINT n$
  ELSEIF number > 0 THEN
    PRINT p$
  ELSE
    EXIT DO
  END IF
LOOP                                    'Bottom of loop
END
```

━━━━ **PROGRAM 5-3.** Negative or Positive with Block IF

Examples

1. Program 5-4, KWH05 (Cost of Electricity with Block IF), uses Block IF instead of the two IF statements of Program KWH04:

```
REM ** Compute cost of electricity in Block IF **
IF kwh <= 846 THEN
  KwhCost = kwh * LoRate
ELSE
  KwhCost = 846 * LoRate + ( kwh - 846) * HiRate
END IF
```

Enter and run Program KWH05. If you enter the same values as you did in Program KWH04, the results should be the same.

```
REM ** Cost of Electricity with Block IF **
' QBasic Made Easy, Chapter 5.  Filename: KWH05.BAS

REM ** Set up **
CLS
LoRate = .08882
HiRate = .13524
format$ = "$$###,###.##"

REM ** Get number of kilowatt-hours (kwh) **
INPUT "Enter number of kilowatt-hours: ", kwh

REM ** Compute cost of electricity in Block IF **
IF kwh <= 846 THEN
  KwhCost = kwh * LoRate
ELSE
  KwhCost = 846 * LoRate + (kwh - 846) * HiRate
END IF

REM ** Print cost of electricity **
PRINT
PRINT "Total cost of electricity is";
PRINT USING format$; KwhCost
END
```

PROGRAM 5-4.   Cost of Electricity with Block IF

2. Program 5-5, GRAFIX03 (Circles and Sounds with Block IF), draws colorfully filled circles at random places on the screen. The frequency and duration of the accompanying sounds depend on the size of the circle being drawn. The radius of the circle is randomly chosen and assigned to the variable *radius.*

The CIRCLE statement is used here in a simple form: specifying the *column* and *row* for the circle's center, the circle's *radius,* and the color number used to draw the circle (3):

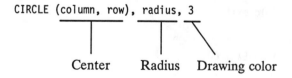

```
CIRCLE (column, row), radius, 3
```

    Center   Radius   Drawing color

Within the Block IF structure, the appropriate sounds are made, and the interior of each circle is painted (filled with color). The sound made and the color used for PAINT depend on the random value selected for *radius:*

```
IF radius < 4 THEN
  SOUND 4000, .25
  PAINT (column, row), 3, 3
ELSEIF radius >= 4 AND radius < 7 THEN
  SOUND 1000, .5
  PAINT (column, row), 1, 3
ELSE
  SOUND 400, .875
  PAINT (column, row), 2, 3
END IF
```

```
REM ** Circles and Sounds with Block IF **
' QBasic Made Easy, Chapter 5.  Filename: GRAFIX03.BAS

REM ** Set up **
SCREEN 1: CLS
LOCATE 2, 2: PRINT "Press spacebar to quit"

REM ** Select random size and color for circle **
DO
  radius = RND * 8 + 2
  column = RND * 319: row = RND * 199

  'Draw circle and make sounds
  CIRCLE (column, row), radius, 3
  IF radius < 4 THEN
    SOUND 4000, .25
    PAINT (column, row), 3, 3
  ELSEIF radius >= 4 AND radius < 7 THEN
    SOUND 1000, .5
    PAINT (column, row), 1, 3
  ELSE
    SOUND 400, .875
    PAINT (column, row), 2, 3
  END IF

  ' Delay and possible exit
  start! = TIMER
  DO WHILE TIMER < start! + .2: LOOP
  IF INKEY$ = " " THEN EXIT DO
LOOP
END
```

PROGRAM 5-5. Circles and Sounds with Block IF

Be sure that you enter the keyword ELSEIF with no spaces. If you enter the
ELSEIF clause with a space (as ELSE IF), you will see the following dialog
box:

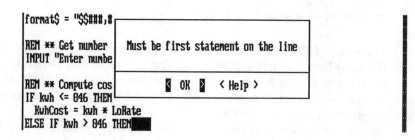

This message may not mean much to you, but it signifies that something is
wrong in the line where the highlight shows. If this message appears, press
ENTER to erase the dialog box and return to the View window. Move the
cursor to the blank space between ELSE and IF and press the DEL key to
erase the blank space.

Notice that the ELSEIF condition is composed of two parts, both of which
must be true for the statements in the ELSEIF statement block to be
executed:

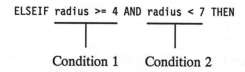

The SOUND statement produces sounds of the specified frequency and
duration. The PAINT statement is introduced here. It colors the inside of
the circle and specifies the circle boundary by setting these values:

• The screen location to begin painting (*column, row*)

• The color to be used for painting

• The border (of the circle) color at which the painting stops

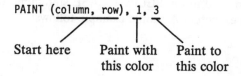

The program uses a short time delay to coordinate the timing of the sounds with the circle drawing:

```
start! = TIMER
DO WHILE TIMER < start! + .2: LOOP
```

The value of TIMER is assigned to *start!,* a single-precision variable, before the delay loop is entered. Single precision is used so that the delay can be in fractions of a second. The DO . . . LOOP has a condition, WHILE TIMER < *start!* + .2, that causes the time delay. As long as the condition is true, program execution remains in the DO . . . LOOP. When the TIMER value is equal to (or greater than) *start!* + .2, the time delay ends. The loop is exited. (The DO . . . LOOP is discussed in more detail later in this chapter.)

If you wish, you may consolidate the delay on one line, as follows:

```
start! = TIMER: DO WHILE TIMER < start! + .2: LOOP
```

You should note that the time delay loop, the IF . . . THEN block, and the random radius and column selections are all contained in another (outer) DO . . . LOOP. You can make an exit from the outer DO . . . LOOP by pressing the SPACEBAR because of the following statement, located near the end of the outer loop:

```
IF INKEY$ = " " THEN EXIT DO
```

Enter and run Program GRAFIX03. Figure 5-2 shows a sample run after the SPACEBAR has been pressed.

USING THE SELECT CASE STRUCTURE FOR MULTIPLE DECISIONS

SELECT CASE is a multiple-decision structure. Depending on the value of the variable or expression used in the SELECT CASE statement, one of the blocks in the structure is executed. A simple example follows:

```
SELECT CASE number
  CASE 1
    PRINT "one"
  CASE 2
    PRINT "two"
  CASE ELSE
    PRINT "not one or two"
END SELECT
```

There are three blocks that might be executed based on the value of *number:* CASE 1, CASE 2, or CASE ELSE. For any value of *number,* only one CASE block is executed. If the value of *number* is 1, the CASE 1 block is executed and the computer prints "one." If the value of *number* is 2, the CASE 2 block is executed and the computer prints "two." For any value of *number* other than 1 or 2, the CASE ELSE block is executed and the computer prints "not one or two."

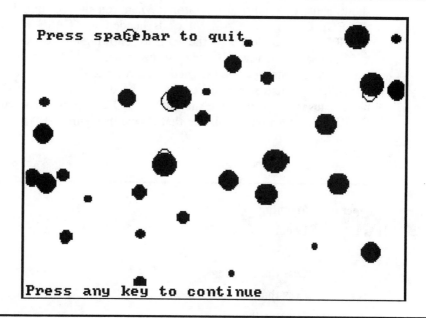

FIGURE 5-2.   Output of Program GRAFIX03.BAS

Examples

1. Program 5-6, NORP03 (Negative or Positive with SELECT CASE), uses the SELECT CASE structure in place of the Block IF ... THEN structure used in Program NORP02:

```
SELECT CASE number
  CASE IS < 0
    PRINT n$
  CASE IS > 0
    PRINT p$
  CASE ELSE
    EXIT DO
END SELECT
```

Program NORP03 uses relational expressions for the value of *number* in the first and second CASE blocks. You have already used relational expressions with the relational operator (=) to assign values to variables. Table 5-1 shows a list of relational operators. When you use relational operators in SELECT CASE, the CASE block is headed by "CASE IS". If you type "CASE" only, QBasic inserts the word IS following the keyword CASE.

If *number* is negative, the string value assigned to n$ is printed. If *number* is positive, the string value assigned to p$ is printed. If the number you enter is neither negative nor positive, it must be 0. Therefore, the CASE ELSE block causes an exit from the DO ... LOOP. Enter and run Program NORP03. A run would look like that shown in Figure 5-1.

Operator	Meaning
=	Equal
< >	Not equal
<	Less than
< =	Less than or equal to
>	Greater than
> =	Greater than or equal to

TABLE 5-1. Relational Operators

```
REM ** Negative or Positive with SELECT CASE **
' QBasic Made Easy, Chapter 5.  Filename: NORPO3.BAS

REM ** Set up **
n$ = "negative"
p$ = "positive"

REM ** Tell what to do **
CLS
PRINT "Enter a number and I will tell you whether"
PRINT "your number is negative or positive."
PRINT "Enter 0 to quit"

REM ** Ask for a number **
DO                                      'Top of loop
  PRINT
  INPUT "Enter a number: ", number

  ' Tell about the number
  SELECT CASE number
    CASE IS < 0
      PRINT n$
    CASE IS > 0
      PRINT p$
    CASE ELSE
      EXIT DO
  END SELECT
LOOP                                    'Bottom of loop
END
```

PROGRAM 5-6. Negative or Positive with SELECT CASE

2. Program 5-7, GRAFIX04 (Rectangles and Sounds with SELECT CASE), draws randomly sized and placed rectangles on the screen with a musical accompaniment. The program uses SELECT CASE to select colors and sounds.

The method for drawing rectangles is a variation of the LINE statement, shown here:

```
LINE (column, row)-(column + size, row + size), 3, B
```

One corner   Opposite corner   Color   Make a box

```
REM ** Rectangles and Sounds with SELECT CASE **
' QBasic Made Easy, Chapter 5.  Filename: GRAFIX04.BAS

REM ** Set up **
SCREEN 1: CLS
LOCATE 2, 2: PRINT "Press spacebar to quit"

REM ** Select random size and color for circle **
DO
  size = RND * 16 + 2
  column = RND * 319: row = RND * 199
  inc = size / 2: kolor = RND * 3

  ' Draw rectangle and make sounds
  LINE (column, row)-(column + size, row + size), 3, B
  SELECT CASE size
    CASE 2 TO 6
      SOUND 4000, .25
      PAINT (column + inc, row + inc), kolor, 3
    CASE 6 TO 12
      SOUND 1000, .5
      PAINT (column + inc, row + inc), kolor, 3
    CASE ELSE
      SOUND 400, .875
      PAINT (column + inc, row + inc), kolor, 3
  END SELECT

  ' Delay and possible exit
  start! = TIMER
  DO WHILE TIMER < start! + .2: LOOP
  IF INKEY$ = " " THEN EXIT DO
LOOP
END
```

PROGRAM 5-7. Rectangles and Sounds with SELECT CASE

When you use the LINE statement to draw one line, the column and row values for each end point of the line are given. The coordinates (*column, row*) of each end point are enclosed in parentheses. A hyphen (-) separates the two coordinate pairs. However, when you use the B (Box option), as in this program, the computer interprets the column and row values (given in parentheses) as opposite corners of a box. It then draws all four sides of the box. The color value used, 3, is optional. If you omit the color value when using the B option, you must include its comma to prevent the letter B from being interpreted as a color number variable. You would write the statement this way:

```
LINE (column, row)-(column + size, row + size), , B
```

The space between the commas that precede the B in this form of the LINE statement is optional.

The size of the rectangle's sides, the column and row to start drawing the rectangle, and the color used for painting are randomly chosen at the beginning of the DO ... LOOP. The increment to the column and row for starting to paint is computed from the random size of the rectangle's sides:

```
DO
  size = RND * 16 + 2
  column = RND * 319: row = RND * 199
  inc = size / 2: kolor = RND * 3
```

The rectangles are drawn by the LINE statement; then the program uses SELECT CASE to produce the sounds and color the rectangles:

```
SELECT CASE size
  CASE 2 TO 6
    SOUND 4000, .25
    PAINT (column + inc, row + inc), kolor, 3
  CASE 6 TO 12
    SOUND 1000, .5
    PAINT (column + inc, row + inc), kolor, 3
  CASE ELSE
    SOUND 400, .875
    PAINT (column + inc, row + inc), kolor, 3
END SELECT
```

The form of the CASE heading for the first two CASE blocks in this program specifies a range of values: 2 TO 6 and 6 TO 12. You use the keyword TO between the starting and ending values when a range of values is used in this CASE form. The randomly selected values of size range from 2 to 18. For any value over 12, the CASE ELSE block is used.

Objects that you paint must be closed (no gaps between points), and painting must start within the closed object. Otherwise, paint will spill out and go everywhere. An increment (*inc*) is added to the *column* and *row* variables in the PAINT statement to specify the point for starting to paint. This value is one-half the magnitude of the variable *size* so that the starting paint point will be inside the rectangle.

Figure 5-3 shows a sample run of GRAFIX04. Run the program, listen to the music, and watch the rectangles fill up the screen.

USING FOR . . . NEXT LOOPS FOR EASY COUNTING

Counting loops occur frequently in programs. QBasic has a loop structure designed to make counting easy. It is called the FOR . . . NEXT loop. Here is a short program using a FOR . . . NEXT loop:

```
CLS

FOR number = 1 TO 10
  PRINT number,
NEXT number
```

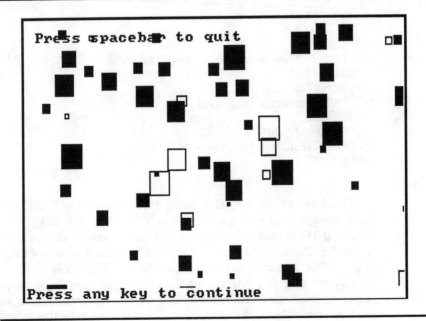

FIGURE 5-3. Output of Program GRAFIX04.BAS

Enter the program in the View window and run it. The FOR ... NEXT loop generates and prints the integers from 1 to 10. Here is the output of a run:

1	2	3	4	5
6	7	8	9	10

The FOR ... NEXT loop tells the computer to count from 1 to 10, as illustrated here:

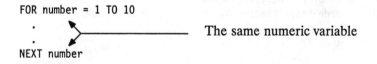

```
FOR number = 1 TO 10
```
      First number   Last number

As the computer counts from 1 to 10, each value is assigned to the variable *number.* This value is printed by the PRINT statement, which is inside the FOR ... NEXT loop.

A FOR ... NEXT loop begins with a FOR statement, ends with a NEXT statement, and can have any number of statements in between. A numeric variable must follow the keyword FOR. The same numeric variable follows the keyword NEXT:

```
FOR number = 1 TO 10
    .
    .
NEXT number
```
    The same numeric variable

This numeric variable can be used in statements between the FOR and NEXT statements, as in the following:

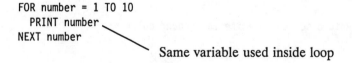

```
FOR number = 1 TO 10
   PRINT number
NEXT number
```
    Same variable used inside loop

A FOR statement defines a sequence of values for the variable that follows the keyword FOR.

Examples

1. The default screen colors are white letters on a black screen. You can use the COLOR statement to tell the computer to print in any of 16 colors, including black (COLOR 0) and the standard white (COLOR 7). Of course, if you print in black on a black screen, you won't see it. Program 5-8, COLORS02 (A Colorful FOR ... NEXT Loop), prints one line in each of the 15 colors from 1 to 15 and tells you the color number in which it prints.

Run the program. If you have a color system, you will see 15 vivid colors. Figure 5-4 shows a black and white printout. Most of the work is done by the FOR ... NEXT loop shown here:

```
REM ** FOR...NEXT loop prints in 15 foreground colors **
FOR kolor = 1 TO 15
  COLOR kolor
  PRINT "This is color number"; kolor
NEXT kolor
```

Since COLOR is a keyword, the program uses a sound-alike word (*kolor*) as the numeric variable for the sequence of color numbers, 1 through 15.

```
REM ** A Colorful FOR...NEXT Loop **
' QBasic Made Easy, Chapter 5.  Filename: COLORS02.BAS

REM ** Set up **
CLS

REM ** FOR...NEXT loop prints in 15 foreground colors **
FOR kolor = 1 TO 15
  COLOR kolor
  PRINT "This is color number"; kolor
NEXT kolor

REM ** Return screen to white foreground color **
COLOR 7
PRINT
PRINT "This is in the default screen color"
END
```

PROGRAM 5-8. A Colorful FOR ... NEXT Loop

```
This is color number 1
This is color number 2
This is color number 3
This is color number 4
This is color number 5
This is color number 6
This is color number 7
This is color number 8
This is color number 9
This is color number 10
This is color number 11
This is color number 12
This is color number 13
This is color number 14
This is color number 15

This is in the default screen color




Press any key to continue
```

FIGURE 5-4. Output of Program COLORS02.BAS

This variable appears in all four lines of the FOR ... NEXT loop. The statement

```
COLOR kolor
```

tells the computer to set the foreground color to the color specified by the value of the numeric variable *kolor*. The PRINT statement prints the information in this color. On exiting from the FOR ... NEXT loop, the program sets the foreground color to the default color, as follows:

```
REM ** Return screen to white foreground color **
COLOR 7
PRINT
PRINT "This is in the default screen color"
```

Color numbers from 0 to 15 designate nonblinking colors. Color number 0 is black and was not included in the color sequence. (Black characters on a black screen are invisible.) Color numbers from 16 to 31 designate blinking colors. If you would like to see blinking colors, change the FOR statement to the following:

```
FOR kolor = 17 TO 31
```

After making this change, run the program again to see the blinking colors.

2. The FOR . . . NEXT loops that you have seen so far count up, from a lower to a higher number. You can also count down, from a higher number to a lower number. To do so, include a STEP clause, as shown in the following short program:

```
CLS

FOR number = 10 TO 0 STEP -1
  PRINT number,
NEXT number
```

Here is a sample run:

10	9	8	7	6
5	4	3	2	1
0				

3. You can put any number in a STEP clause. The number following STEP defines the amount by which the variable following FOR changes each time. For example, in the following FOR . . . NEXT loop, the variable k has this sequence of values: 1, 3, 5, 7, 9.

```
FOR k = 1 TO 9 STEP 2
  PRINT k,
NEXT k
```

Enter and run the program.

The following FOR . . . NEXT loop uses a noninteger STEP size. The values of x are 0, .25, .50, .75, and 1.

```
FOR x = 0 TO 1 STEP .25
  PRINT x,
NEXT x
```

Enter and run it.

LEARNING MORE ABOUT THE DO . . . LOOP

A DO . . . LOOP is more versatile than WHILE . . . WEND (discussed later in this chapter) and FOR . . . NEXT loops because it can test for a condition at the beginning, the end, or even inside the loop. Most of the DO . . . LOOP structures that you have used previously have been endless loops. In some programs, you could exit the loop by pressing the SPACEBAR (detected by INKEY$). In the programs GRAFIX03 and GRAFIX04, a timing loop contained a condition that was true or false. When the condition became false, the program automatically executed an exit. This loop, which is written on one line, is shown again here:

```
start! = TIMER: DO WHILE TIMER < start! + .2: LOOP
```

Even though the TIMER is checked, there are no statements inside the loop. It does nothing but loop and check the TIMER to see if it is time to leave. Such a loop is useful for time delays.

Sound Effects Using DO UNTIL

Have you ever wondered how arcade games make all those strange sounds? Enter the following program in the View window:

```
CLS

DO UNTIL INKEY$ = CHR$(27)
  FOR frequency = 100 TO 300
    SOUND frequency, .25
  NEXT frequency
LOOP
```

In this program, the FOR . . . NEXT loop makes a sequence of very short sounds, starting at 100 Hz and ending at 300 Hz. Thus you hear a rapidly rising pitch. Run the program.

Press: ESC

to quit. There may be a slight delay before the sound stops and the bottom of the FOR . . . NEXT loop is reached. The program will then end.

Each keyboard character is assigned an ASCII code. The code 27 is assigned to the ESC key. When you press the ESC key, its ASCII code (27) is assigned to INKEY$. The UNTIL condition in the DO statement then becomes true, and the program exits the loop.

Now change the beginning and ending values of the FOR statement to 300 and 100 Hz with a STEP value of −1, as shown here:

```
CLS

DO UNTIL INKEY$ = CHR$(27)
  FOR frequency = 300 TO 100 STEP -1
    SOUND frequency, .25
  NEXT frequency
LOOP
```

Enter and run this program to hear a familiar arcade game sound—a sound with a rapidly falling pitch. The frequency lowers quickly from 300 Hz to 100 Hz in steps of −1 Hz. The sequence of values is

300, 299, 298 . . . 100

Sound Effects Using LOOP WHILE

Now put both ideas together into Program 5-9, SOUND02 (Siren Song). As the name suggests, it makes a sound like a siren. The sound goes up, down, up, down, and so on. Press ESC to quit. When the end of the current FOR . . . NEXT loop is reached, the program ends. Program SOUND02 uses another variation of the DO . . . LOOP. The program displays a message telling how to exit from the loop near the end of the loop and places the condition after the LOOP keyword.

```
DO
  .

  .
  LOCATE 2, 2: PRINT "Press ESC to quit"
LOOP WHILE INKEY$ <> CHR$(27)
```

As long as you have not pressed the ESC key, the condition INKEY$ < > CHR$(27) is true—another pass is made through the loop. When you press ESC, an exit is made after the completion of the current sequence of FOR . . . NEXT loops.

```
REM ** Siren Song **
' QBasic Made Easy, Chapter 5.  Filename: SOUND02.BAS

REM ** Set up **
CLS
duration = .125

REM ** Make a rising, then falling sound **
DO
  FOR frequency = 523 TO 1046              'Rising pitch
    SOUND frequency, duration
  NEXT frequency

  FOR frequency = 1046 TO 523 STEP -1     'Falling pitch
    SOUND frequency, duration
  NEXT frequency

  LOCATE 2, 2: PRINT "Press ESC to quit";
LOOP WHILE INKEY$ <> CHR$(27)
END
```

PROGRAM 5-9. Siren Song

You can make the pitch rise and fall at different rates by changing the frequencies in the FOR statements. For example, to make the pitch rise and fall more quickly, change the frequencies as shown here:

```
FOR frequency = 523 TO 1046 STEP 2        'Rising pitch

FOR frequency = 1046 TO 523 STEP -2       'Falling pitch
```

Sound Effects Using LOOP UNTIL

Use Program 5-10, SOUND03 (Sound Effects Experimenter), to experiment with FOR ... NEXT loops and find effects to your liking. It contains yet another variation of the DO ... LOOP.

Enter and run the program. To get a rising pitch, enter a smaller number for the beginning frequency, a larger number for the ending frequency, and a positive step size, as shown in this sample run:

Beginning frequency? 500

Ending frequency   ? 1000

Frequency step size? 10

Duration each sound? .125

Number of times   ? 5

The last item entered, "Number of times," is the number of times that you want the entire sound repeated. When you run the program using the preceding numbers, you will hear the sound whoop, whoop, whoop, whoop, whoop.

```
REM ** Sound Effects Experimenter **
' QBasic Made Easy, Chapter 5.  Filename: SOUND03.BAS

REM ** Set up **
CLS

DO
  REM ** Get parameters for experiment **
  LOCATE 1, 1: INPUT "Beginning frequency"; BeginFreq
  LOCATE 3, 1: INPUT "Ending frequency   "; FinalFreq
  LOCATE 5, 1: INPUT "Frequency step size"; StepSize
  LOCATE 7, 1: INPUT "Duration each sound"; duration
  LOCATE 9, 1: INPUT "Number of times    "; NmbrTimes

  REM ** Make the sound **
  FOR k = 1 TO NmbrTimes
    FOR frequency = BeginFreq TO FinalFreq STEP StepSize
      SOUND frequency, duration
    NEXT frequency
  NEXT k

  REM ** Go back for a new set of data **
  PRINT : PRINT "Press a key to go again, ESC to quit";
  kbd$ = INPUT$(1): CLS
LOOP UNTIL kbd$ = CHR$(27)
END
```

PROGRAM 5-10. Sound Effects Experimenter

The program uses a condition using the keyword UNTIL with the LOOP keyword at the end of the DO . . . LOOP in Program SOUND03. After each sequence of sounds, the "GO back for a new set of data" block contains instructions for continuing or quitting. The computer waits for a keypress. Press ESC to quit; press any other key to try a new experiment with a new set of values:

```
 PRINT : PRINT "Press a key to go again, ESC to quit";
 kbd$ = INPUT$(1): CLS
LOOP UNTIL kbd$ = CHR$(27)
```

The INPUT$(1) statement interrupts the program. The number 1 in parentheses tells the computer to wait until one keystroke has been made. When you press a key, the ASCII code for that key is assigned to the string variable *kbd$*. The LOOP condition specifies that the loop is to be continued *until* the value of *kbd$* is equal to CHR$(27). Remember, 27 is the ASCII code for the ESC key. When you press ESC, the condition "UNTIL kbd$ = CHR$(27)" becomes true; the program exits from the loop.

To obtain a sound with a falling pitch, enter a larger number for the beginning frequency, a smaller number for the ending frequency, and a negative step size, as shown here:

```
Beginning frequency? 3000

Ending frequency   ? 1000

Frequency step size? -100

Duration each sound? .25

Number of times    ? 10
```

The INPUT statements that acquire the preceding information are in the "Get parameters for experiment" block of the program. Each INPUT statement is preceded by a LOCATE statement that positions the cursor. For example, the statement

```
LOCATE 7, 1
```

puts the cursor at line 7, column 1 of the screen. The string in the INPUT statement, "Duration each sound", is printed at the cursor position. You can use a LOCATE statement to put the cursor anywhere on the screen. For example, you could use LOCATE 12, 40 to put the cursor at line 12, column 40.

Block "Make the sound", shown next, features *nested* FOR...NEXT loops: a loop within a loop. The sounds are made in the *inner loop*. This loop is nested inside the *outer loop,* which counts the number of times (*NmbrTimes*) that the inner loop is executed.

```
REM ** Make the sound **
FOR k = 1 TO NmbrTimes
   FOR frequency = BeginFreq TO FinalFreq STEP StepSize
     SOUND frequency, duration
   NEXT frequency
NEXT k
```

The inner loop makes the rising or falling sound. The outer loop controls the number of times the rising or falling sound is made. Note that the entire inner loop is indented within the outer loop. This is an element of programming style intended to help you read and understand the program more easily.

A BIT ABOUT WHILE . . . WEND LOOPS

If you have used GW-BASIC or BASICA, you are probably familiar with the WHILE...WEND loop structure. QBasic also has WHILE...WEND loops. Since the DO...LOOP is more versatile, its use has replaced that of WHILE...WEND. Although this is probably the last time you will see a WHILE...WEND loop in this book, here is some brief information about this structure.

The WHILE...WEND loop is similar to the DO...LOOP but not as flexible. The WHILE...WEND loop repeats a set of statements while a condition is true. The loop begins with a WHILE statement, ends with a WEND statement, and can have any number of statements in between. The WHILE statement must contain an expression that serves as a condition, which can be true or false. If the condition is true, the loop continues; if the condition is false, the loop ends, and the program continues with the line following the WEND statement (if there is a line).

In the following WHILE...WEND timer loop, the condition in the WHILE statement is "TIMER < start! + 20". If the TIMER is read and assigned to the variable *start!* before the program enters the loop, the condition will be true until 20 seconds after the value was assigned to *start!*. Therefore, the loop continues for approximately 20 seconds.

```
CLS
start! = TIMER
WHILE TIMER < start! + 20
  LOCATE 2, 2: PRINT "Start time  "; start!
  LOCATE 3, 2: PRINT "Timer reads "; TIMER
WEND
```

Enter and run this program. The value of the starting time is printed in the upper-left corner of the Output screen, and the value of TIMER is printed just below it.

The statements inside the WHILE ... WEND loop are repeated until the condition in the WHILE statement is true (approximately 20 seconds after the start time). The TIMER values are printed in hundredths of seconds. You can see the values increase until the value is at least 20 seconds past the value of *start!*. Notice that the value of *start!* does not change, but the value of TIMER does. Here is a sample run of the program after the exit from the loop:

```
Start time   37727.11
TIMER reads  37747.11
```

The loop was exited when the TIMER read 20.00 seconds from the start time.

SUMMARY

You learned about QBasic's control structures in this chapter. These control structures allow you to group decision-making, counting, and repeated statements logically.

You use simple IF ... THEN statements to make single decisions. A simple IF ... THEN statement has the following form:

IF *condition* THEN *statement*

You use Block IF statements in choosing among multiple decisions; they are composed of blocks of statements, as follows:

```
IF condition 1 THEN
  statement block 1
ELSEIF condition 2 THEN (Optional block)
```

```
  statement block 2
ELSE
  statement block 3
END IF
```

SELECT CASE offers a wider variety for making multiple decisions. It has the following form:

```
SELECT CASE variable
  CASE 1
statement block 1
  CASE 2
statement block 2
      .
      .
      .    (additional cases if needed)
CASE ELSE
  statement block n (last case)
END SELECT
```

The CASE formats of SELECT CASE may also use relational operators, as follows:

```
CASE IS < 0
```

You may also state a range of values in a CASE format, as follows:

```
CASE 2 TO 6
```

You also learned to use FOR ... NEXT loops for counting and performing operations in fixed increments. A FOR ... NEXT loop has this form:

```
FOR variable = StartValue TO EndValue STEP increment
  block of statements
NEXT variable
```

You learned that the versatile DO ... LOOP comes in many varieties:

Never ending loops

```
DO
  block of statements
LOOP
```

Conditional loops

```
DO WHILE condition
  block of statements
LOOP
```

```
DO UNTIL condition
  block of statements
LOOP
```

```
DO
  block of statements
LOOP WHILE condition
```

```
DO
  block of statements
LOOP UNTIL condition
```

You also learned a bit about WHILE . . .WEND:

```
WHILE condition
  block of statements
WEND
```

chapter 6

EDITING AND DYNAMIC DEBUGGING

In this chapter you will learn to use some of QBasic's editing and debugging tools. You will learn

- How to use the Edit menu to access the editing tools
- How to use the Debug menu to access the debugging tools
- How to use keystrokes to control the cursor, scroll the View window, and select text for editing

From the Edit menu, you can remove sections of a program, copy sections of a program from one place to another, and cut sections of a program and paste them elsewhere in the program.

From the Debug menu, you can execute a program one statement at a time, set breakpoints to interrupt a program so that you can examine the current values of variables, and remove breakpoints when you are through using them.

EDITING

When you write programs, especially long or complex programs, you often need to edit them. Editing ranges from simple one-letter changes to removing or copying a portion of a program. QBasic provides several useful and powerful editing tools to simplify and enhance your programming.

In previous chapters, you used some editing keys: BACKSPACE, DEL, CTRL-Y, ←, →, ↑, ↓, and ENTER. Now you will learn to use other helpful editing keys as well as options on the Edit menu.

Editing Keys

In addition to the editing keys just mentioned, there are other simple yet powerful keys that you can use to make changes quickly in a program. Table 6-1 lists some of the editing keys that you will find useful when writing programs.

Many of the keys included in Table 6-1 are self explanatory. For example, pressing HOME moves the cursor to the beginning of the line, and pressing END moves the cursor to the end of the line. Others, however, are more complex and require some discussion.

When a program is too large to be displayed in the View window, as much of it as possible is displayed. To see the next windowful, press PGUP. To see the previous windowful, press PGDN. PGUP and PGDN allow you to scroll your program within the View window, one windowful at a time.

You may also want to scroll up or down one line at a time in order to display lines that are out of sight above or below the window. To scroll down one line, press CTRL-↓. To scroll up one line, press CTRL-↑.

A program may not only be too long to be displayed in a single window, it may also be too wide. If a program line has more than 78 characters, the line cannot be displayed completely in the View window. For example, here is a line that was shown in Chapter 5, "Control Structures," that extends beyond the right edge of the View window because it has more than 78 characters:

```
REM ** Compute cost of electricity **
IF kwh <= 846 THEN KwhCost = kwh * LoRate ELSE KwhCost = 846 * LoRate + (kwh -
```

You moved the window to the right to see the "hidden" part of the line. You pressed the following key combination:

```
CTRL-PGDN
```

When you pressed this key combination, you saw the end of the line, as shown here:

```
cost of electricity **
HEN KwhCost = kwh * LoRate ELSE KwhCost = 846 * LoRate + (kwh - 846) * HiRate
```

Cursor Controls	Keys
Left one character	←
Right one character	→
Left one word	CTRL-←
Right one word	CTRL-→
Up one line	↑
Down one line	↓
Beginning of current line	HOME
End of current line	END
Beginning of next line	CTRL-ENTER
Beginning of program	CTRL-HOME
End of program	CTRL-END

Scrolling Controls	Keys
Up one line*	CTRL-↑
Down one line**	CTRL-↓
Up one page (window)	PGUP
Down one page (window)	PGDN
Left one window	CTRL-PGUP
Right one window	CTRL-PGDN

* Window moves up, text scrolls down

** Window moves down, text scrolls up

TABLE 6-1.   Cursor and Scrolling Control Keys

To see the beginning of the line, you moved the window back to the left by pressing

CTRL-PGUP

To avoid this situation, most program lines in this book are short so that they can be seen in their entirety in the View window.

As you write more and larger programs, the editing features of QBasic will become increasingly useful. Experiment with various editing keys as you write and modify the programs in the rest of this chapter.

Using the Editing Keys

To practice using the editing keys, enter the program shown in Figure 6-1. Include any errors that you see in the program. You might even make mistakes additional to the ones included in this program.

```
REM ** QBasic Made Easy Program File Names **
' QBasic Made Easy, Chapster 6.  File: 1REMFILE.BAS
' REM program - contains programm file names, descriptions

REM ** Chapster 2. Tiny Programs **
' ALBERTO1.BAS   Date, Time, and Nome
' ALBERTO2.BAS   Date, Time, Name and String
' COLORSO1.BAS   Name in many colors
' GRAFIXO1.BAS   PSET, SOUND
' TIMERO1.BAS    Changing TIMER

REM ** Chapter 3. Number Crunching **
' CUBEO1.BAS     INPUT side, Print Area and Volume
' KWHO1.BAS      INPUT kwh, Print Cost
' SALETXO1.BAS   INPUT Amount, Print Tax
' SALETXO2.BAS   INPUT Amount, Print Tax and Total

REM ** Chapter 4. String Manipulations **
' INTRSTO1.BAS   INPUT Info, PRINT USING Future Value

REM ** Chapter 5. Control Structures **

REM ** Chapter 6. Editing and Dynmaic Debugging **
```

FIGURE 6-1. A program for editing practice

Notice that this program consists only of REM statements and therefore has no executable statements. As you write more programs, this REM program will become increasingly useful. When you want to review or use a particular program, you can use 1REMFILE to determine the correct program to load. The program is named 1REMFILE so that, when saved, it will always appear at the beginning of the list of programs displayed in the Open dialog box from the File menu. Because the program is at the beginning of the list, you can load and scan it quickly to find the desired program.

Now, using some of the editing keys listed in Table 6-1, correct the errors in this program. Press CTRL-HOME to move the cursor to the beginning of the program if it is not already there. The first mistake occurs in the third line of the program, so press ↓ until the cursor is at the first character of this line:

```
' REM program - contains programm file names, descriptions
```

The word "programm" in this line needs to be changed to "program". Press CTRL-→ until the cursor is on the "p" of "programm", and then press → until the cursor is under the second "m" in "Programm":

```
' REM program - contains programm file names, descriptions
```

When the cursor is on the extra "m", press DEL to delete that letter.

≡≡*note*≡≡ You could also press CTRL-→ until the cursor is on "file" and then press ← until the cursor is on the second "m" of "programm".

Press HOME to move the cursor to the beginning of the line, and then press ↓ until the cursor is at the line that contains the next error:

```
REM ** Chapster 2. Tiny Programs **
```

Use any combination of editing keys you wish to correct the spelling of "Chapster" to "Chapter". You could put the cursor under the "s" in "Chapster" and press DEL. You could also put the cursor under the "t" in "Chapster" and press BACKSPACE. When this line has been corrected, move the cursor to the line that contains the next error:

```
' ALBERTO1.BAS   Date, Time, and Nome
```

Press: END

The cursor will move to the end of the line. Press ← to move the cursor to the "o" of "Nome", delete that letter, and type an "a" to spell the correct word, "Name".

You could also move the cursor to the "m" of "Nome", use BACKSPACE to delete the "o", and type an "a" to replace the deleted letter "o".

Yet another way to correct the error is to move the cursor to the "o" of "Nome", press the INS key to change to the overtype edit mode (the cursor is now a character block: ■), and then type the letter "a" to overwrite the "o". Then press the INS key a second time to change back to the insert edit mode (the cursor once again looks like the underline character, _).

When you type a character while in the insert edit mode, the character typed is displayed at the cursor position. The character that was at the cursor, and all characters to its right, are shifted one position to the right. When you type a character in the overtype edit mode, the character at the cursor position is replaced by the character you type. You can toggle back and forth between the insert edit mode and the overtype edit mode by pressing the INS key.

The last error occurs in the last line of the program, but it does not show in the current View window. To see it, press PGDN and move the cursor to this line, which contains the error:

```
REM ** Chapter 6. Editing and Dynmaic Debugging **
```

Change "Dynmaic" to "Dynamic", correct any additional errors you find, and then save this temporary program under the file name 1REMFILE.BAS so that you can load it later in its present form.

Experiment with the cursor and scrolling keys for a while. Next you will add some lines and learn how to use other editing keys to delete one line or an entire block from a program.

INSERTING LINES   Add a few "throwaway" lines to 1REMFILE. Later you will delete these lines. To insert new lines, first create space in your program for those lines. Move the cursor until it is just below the line that lists the program INTRST01.BAS, like this:

```
REM ** Chapter 4. String Manipulations **
' INTRST01.BAS   INPUT Info, PRINT USING Future Value

REM ** Chapter 5. Control Structures **
```

Then type the following three lines, pressing ENTER after each line:

>   Type: **' Throw away line #1**
>
>   **' Throw away line #2**
>
>   **' Throw away line #3**

DELETING A SINGLE LINE   To delete a single line from your program, you move the cursor to the line that is to be deleted and press CTRL-Y. Suppose that you want to delete the line that you just inserted:

```
' Throw away line #3
```

Place the cursor anywhere on this line and press CTRL-Y. The line disappears. Even though CTRL-Y removes the complete line from the program, it doesn't just throw it away. It removes it from the program and copies it to a special area of memory called a *buffer* (also referred to as the *clipboard*). You will learn more about the clipboard in the Edit Menu section of this chapter.

SELECTING BLOCKS OF TEXT   You can delete an entire block of text without having to press CTRL-Y several times. Deleting a block involves a technique known as *selecting*. To select a block for deletion or other manipulation, you move the cursor to the beginning of the first line of the block that you want to delete. Then you press SHIFT and hold it down while pressing ↓ until all of the lines to be deleted have been highlighted. The highlighted text is the selected text. Many of the editing operations that follow use this method.

DELETING A BLOCK OF TEXT   Now use the selecting technique to delete the two remaining throwaway lines. First, move the cursor to the beginning of throwaway line #1:

```
' Throw away line #1
' Throw away line #2
```

Press and hold SHIFT and then press ↓ twice to highlight the two lines. Those lines have now been selected. The screen in Figure 6-2 shows the selected text in the View window. To delete the two lines that are highlighted, press DEL. The selected text disappears from the View window.

Text may be selected in several other ways. Table 6-2 shows keypress combinations for selecting text.

The Edit Menu

Press ALT-E to see the Edit menu shown in Figure 6-3. The first option, Cut, is highlighted. Notice the status bar at the bottom of the screen. The status bar

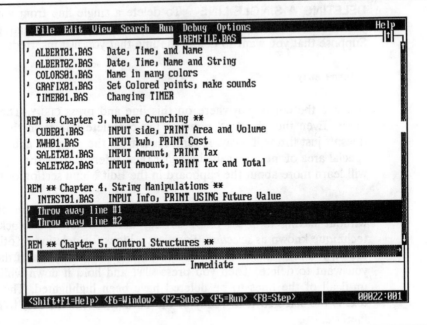

```
  File  Edit  View  Search  Run  Debug  Options                    Help
                          1REMFILE.BAS                              ↕
' ALBERT01.BAS   Date, Time, and Name
' ALBERT02.BAS   Date, Time, Name and String
' COLORS01.BAS   Name in many colors
' GRAFIX01.BAS   Set Colored points, make sounds
' TIMER01.BAS    Changing TIMER

REM ** Chapter 3. Number Crunching **
' CUBE01.BAS     INPUT side, PRINT Area and Volume
' KWH01.BAS      INPUT kwh, PRINT Cost
' SALETX01.BAS   INPUT Amount, PRINT Tax
' SALETX02.BAS   INPUT Amount, PRINT Tax and Total

REM ** Chapter 4. String Manipulations **
' INTRST01.BAS   INPUT Info, PRINT USING Future Value
▌ Throw away line #1
' Throw away line #2

REM ** Chapter 5. Control Structures **
▐
─────────────────────────── Immediate ───────────────────────────

<Shift+F1=Help> <F6=Window> <F2=Subs> <F5=Run> <F8=Step>    00022:001
```

FIGURE 6-2. Two lines selected

Text Selected	Key Combination
Character to left	SHIFT- ←
Character to right	SHIFT- →
Word to left	SHIFT-CTRL- ←
Word to right	SHIFT-CTRL- →
Current line	SHIFT-↓
Line above	SHIFT-↑
Screen up	SHIFT-PGUP
Screen down	SHIFT-PGDN
To beginning of file	SHIFT-CTRL-HOME
To end of file	SHIFT-CTRL-END

TABLE 6-2. Text Selection Key Combinations

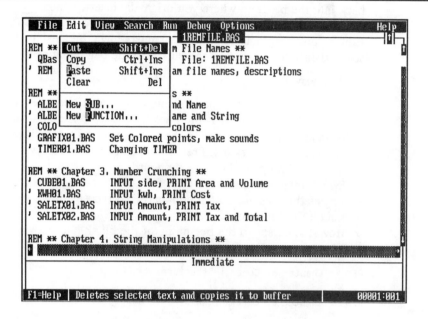

FIGURE 6-3. The Edit menu

tells you that the Cut option "Deletes selected text and copies it to buffer." (The *buffer* and the *clipboard* are two terms for the same feature.)

Press the ↓ key to highlight the Copy option. Again, notice the status bar at the bottom of the screen. The information in the status bar has changed to reflect that the Copy option "Copies selected text to buffer."

Press ↓ to highlight the Paste option. The status bar now informs you that the Paste option "Inserts buffer contents at current location."

Press ↓ to highlight the Clear option. The status bar now says that the Clear option "Deletes selected text without copying it to buffer."

You will use these four options in this chapter. The last two options, New SUB and New FUNCTION, will not be used until Chapter 8, "FUNCTION and SUB Procedures."

CUT TEXT TO CLIPBOARD AND PASTE IT BACK   Insert the three throwaway lines

```
' INTRST01.BAS    INPUT Info, PRINT USING Future Value
' Throw away line #1
' Throw away line #2
' Throw away line #3
```

back into the program where you originally inserted them.

To delete the three lines that you inserted, you use the Cut option on the Edit menu. Before using Cut, you must select the text to be deleted. To select the three lines, move the cursor to the beginning of the first line:

```
' Throw away line #1
```

Press SHIFT and hold it while pressing ↓ until all three lines are highlighted. The highlighting means that the lines have been selected.

To delete these lines, access the Cut option on the Edit menu, as shown by the screen in Figure 6-4. Press ENTER, and the three lines are deleted from the program and placed on the clipboard.

Even though you cut three lines from the program, you can recover them as long as they remain on the clipboard. To recover them, you use the Paste option on the Edit menu.

Move the cursor to the beginning of the blank line between the following REM statements:

```
REM ** Chapter 5. Control Structures **

REM ** Chapter 6. Editing and Dynamic Debugging **
```

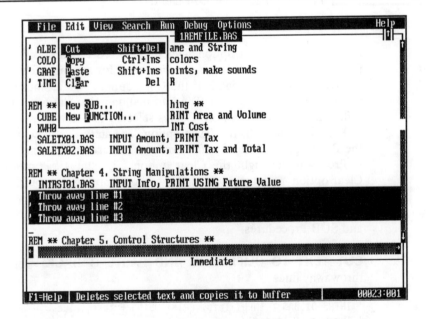

FIGURE 6-4. Cutting three selected lines

Access the Paste option on the File menu, as shown here:

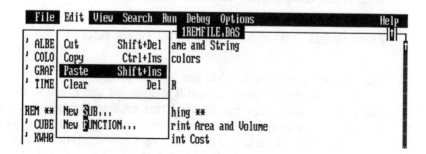

When you have highlighted the Paste option, press ENTER to paste the three lines from the clipboard into the program. The lines should appear like this:

```
REM ** Chapter 5. Control Structures **
' Throw away line #1
' Throw away line #2
' Throw away line #3

REM ** Chapter 6. Editing and Dynamic Debugging **
```

You have now cut a block of text from one place in the program (automatically placing it on the clipboard) and pasted it (from the clipboard) into another place in the program. This sequence is called "cut and paste."

 The previous contents of the clipboard are erased when a cut or CTRL-Y operation is made. Therefore, if you want to retain a block of text that has been cut, you must use the Paste operation before using Cut again.

Experiment with cutting and pasting. For example, cut a block from the middle of the program and paste it at the bottom. Then cut the same block from the bottom and paste it back where it was originally.

COPYING AND PASTING   Because you have just been experimenting with deleting and pasting, the program in memory may not be in its corrected form. Load 1REMFILE.BAS from disk to put it back into memory. You will see the "Loaded file is not saved. Save it now?" dialog box. Since you don't need to save the program that you have been practicing with, access the No response and press ENTER.

You will use the Copy and Paste options in the Edit menu with this program. When you use the Copy option, you must first select the line or block of text being copied. Select the following line:

```
' INTRST01.BAS   INPUT Info, PRINT USING Future Value
```

Now choose Copy from the Edit menu; then press ENTER.

Notice that the selected text is still highlighted and is still in the program. The Copy option copies the selected text to the clipboard but leaves the program otherwise untouched. Remember, the clipboard contains only the text from the most recent CTRL-Y, Cut, or Copy operation. Therefore, the clipboard now contains only the one line that you just copied. To make use of the text on the clipboard, you must paste it into the program.

The Paste option in the Edit menu inserts the contents of the clipboard at the current cursor position. First remove the highlight by moving the cursor up or down one line. Then move the cursor back down to the first position below the line that you just copied, as you see here:

```
REM ** Chapter 4.  String Manipulations
' INTRST01.BAS   INPUT Info, PRINT USING Future Value
_

REM ** Chapter 5. Control Structures
```

Select the Paste option in the Edit menu and press ENTER. The line is now in the program twice:

```
REM ** Chapter 4.  String Manipulations
' INTRST01.BAS   INPUT Info, PRINT USING Future Value
' INTRST01.BAS   INPUT Info, PRINT USING Future Value
_

REM ** Chapter 5. Control Structures
```

Modify the line that you just pasted into the program so that it looks like this:

```
' INTRST02.BAS   INPUT Info, LPRINT USING Future Value
```

The block of programs for Chapter 4 should now have the following two programs:

```
REM ** Chapter 4.  String Manipulations
' INTRST01.BAS   INPUT Info, PRINT USING Future Value
' INTRST02.BAS   INPUT Info, LPRINT USING Future Value
```

Use as many of the editing keys and editing tools as you wish to complete this program so that it contains all the programs in each of the chapters. It should also contain a REM statement for each chapter in the book. Because there are many file names and blocks of text that are similar, use Copy and Paste. When you have finished, your new program should be similar to Program 6-1, 1REMFILE (QBasic Made Easy Program File Names). Save the file under the same name, 1REMFILE.BAS, replacing the previous file with that name.

```
REM ** QBasic Made Easy Program File Names **
' QBasic Made Easy, Chapter 6.  File: 1REMFILE.BAS
' REM program - contains program file names, descriptions

REM ** Chapter 2. Tiny Programs **
' ALBERT01.BAS   Date, Time, and Name
' ALBERT02.BAS   Date, Time, Name and String
' COLORS01.BAS   Name in many colors
' GRAFIX01.BAS   Set Colored points, make sounds
' TIMER01.BAS    Changing TIMER

REM ** Chapter 3. Number Crunching **
' CUBE01.BAS     INPUT side, PRINT Area and Volume
' KWH01.BAS      INPUT kwh, PRINT Cost
' SALETX01.BAS   INPUT Amount, PRINT Tax
' SALETX02.BAS   INPUT Amount, PRINT Tax and Total

REM ** Chapter 4. String Manipulations **
' GRAFIX02.BAS   Set points to music
' INTRST01.BAS   INPUT Info, PRINT USING Future Value
' INTRST02.BAS   INPUT Info, LPRINT USING Future Value
' KWH02.BAS      INPUT Info, PRINT Cost
' KWH03.BAS      Enhanced INPUT and PRINT, kwh
' NAME01.BAS     PRINT name in color and make sound
' POPUL01.BAS    Projected population
' POPUL02.BAS    Projected population
' POPUL03.BAS    Projected population with many REMs
```

PROGRAM 6-1. QBasic Made Easy Program File Names

```
' SALETX03.BAS    Enhanced INPUT Amount, PRINT Tax and Total
' SALETX04.BAS    Enhanced INPUT and PRINT
' SALETX05.BAS    Enhanced INPUT and PRINT with TABs
' SALETX06.BAS    Enhanced INPUT and PRINT USING
' SALETX07.BAS    Enhanced INPUT, Commas and $ in PRINT USING
' STOCKS01.BAS    Value of Stocks
' STRNGS01.BAS    Strings in various PRINT formats
' STRNGS02.BAS    INPUT and PRINT Strings
' STRNGS03.BAS    LINE INPUT and PRINT Strings
' STRNGS04.BAS    Enter Strings and write them
' TVSHOW01.BAS    INPUT number, PRINT number, 1.01 ^ number
' TVSHOW02.BAS    Enhanced INPUT, PRINT, exponent
' TVSHOW03.BAS    Enhanced INPUT, PRINT USING, exponent

REM ** Chapter 5. Control Structures **
' COLORS02.BAS    PRINT colored text
' GRAFIX03.BAS    Colored circles and sound
' GRAFIX04.BAS    Colored rectangles and sound
' KWH04.BAS       Cost of Electricity, IF/THEN
' KWH05.BAS       Electricity, Block IF/THEN
' NORP01.BAS      Negative or Positive
' NORP02.BAS      Negative or Positive
' NORP03.BAS      Negative or Positive
' SOUND02.BAS     Siren Song
' SOUND03.BAS     Sound Effects Experimenter

REM ** Chapter 6. Editing and Dynamic Debugging **
' 1REMFILE.BAS    QBasic Made Easy Program File Names

REM ** Chapter 7. Function Junction **

REM ** Chapter 8. FUNCTION and SUB Procedures **

REM ** Chapter 9. Data Structures **

REM ** Chapter 10. Arrays **

REM ** Chapter 11. Sequential Files **

REM ** Chapter 12. Random-access Files **

REM ** Chapter 13. Your QBasic Backpack **
```

PROGRAM 6-1. QBasic Made Easy Program File Names
(continued)

CLEARING TEXT   The Clear option in the Edit menu deletes lines from text but does not copy them to the clipboard. The deleted text is gone, just as if you had used the DEL key. To use the Clear option, first put the three throwaway lines that you used before back into the program, following the REM statement of Chapter 6 in Program 1REMFILE:

```
REM ** Chapter 6. Editing and Dynamic Debugging **
' 1REMFILE.BAS   QBasic Made Easy Program File Names, REM
' Throw away line #1
' Throw away line #2
' Throw away line #3

REM ** Chapter 7. Function Junction **
```

Select the three throwaway lines with SHIFT-↓; then access the Clear option in the Edit menu. Press ENTER, and the lines are gone. Remember, use the Clear option only when you want to delete text. It does not put anything on the clipboard. Use Cut or Copy to copy selected text to the clipboard. The shortcut for Clear is the DEL key.

More Editing

If Program 1REMFILE is not in the View window, load it now. You will edit it to make a new, more complete REM file program. The new program will contain the programs created in each chapter in the book as well as the QBasic keywords used in each program. This program can help when you need an example of how to use a particular keyword or how to write a particular block of a program.

Use as many editing keys and editing tools as you wish to create the new program. Many programs include the same, or nearly the same, keywords; you may find it easier to use Copy and Paste to enter them than to retype them. When you are finished, save Program 6-2, 2REMFILE (QBasic Made Easy Program File Names, Keywords) as 2REMFILE.BAS.

As you progress through this book, add the names of the programs that you write to both 1REMFILE and 2REMFILE to keep them up to date. These programs will be a helpful tool if you continue to update them.

```
REM ** QBasic Made Easy Program File Names, Keywords **
' QBasic Made Easy, Chapter 6.  File: 2REMFILE.BAS
' REM program - contains program file names, descriptions

REM ** Chapter 2. Tiny Programs **
' ALBERT01.BAS    Date, Time, and Name
'                 BEEP, CLS, DATE$, PRINT, TIME$
' ALBERT02.BAS    Date, Time, Name and String
'                 BEEP, CLS, DATE$, PRINT, TIME$
' COLORS01.BAS    Name in many colors
'                 CLS, COLOR, DO...LOOP, PRINT, RND
' GRAFIX01.BAS    Set Colored points, make sounds
'                 CLS, COLOR, DO...LOOP, PSET, RND, SCREEN 1,
'                 SOUND
' TIMER01.BAS     Changing TIMER
'                 CLS, DO...LOOP, LOCATE, PRINT, TIMER

REM ** Chapter 3. Number Crunching **
' CUBE01.BAS      INPUT side, PRINT Area and Volume
'                 CLS, INPUT, PRINT
' KWH01.BAS       INPUT kwh, PRINT Cost
'                 CLS, INPUT, PRINT
' SALETX01.BAS    INPUT Amount, PRINT Tax
'                 CLS, INPUT, PRINT
' SALETX02.BAS    INPUT Amount, PRINT Tax and Total
'                 CLS, INPUT, PRINT

REM ** Chapter 4. String Manipulations **
' GRAFIX02.BAS    Set points to music
'                 CLS, DO...LOOP, END, EXIT DO, IF...THEN,
'                 INKEY$, LOCATE, PRINT, PSET, RND, SCREEN 1,
'                 SOUND
' INTRST01.BAS    INPUT Info, PRINT USING Future Value
'                 CLS, INPUT, PRINT, PRINT USING, REM
' INTRST02.BAS    INPUT Info, LPRINT USING Future Value
'                 CLS, INPUT, LPRINT, LPRINT USING, REM
' KWH02.BAS       INPUT Info, PRINT Cost
'                 CLS, INPUT, PRINT, REM
' KWH03.BAS       Enhanced INPUT and PRINT, kwh
'                 CLS, INPUT, PRINT, REM
```

PROGRAM 6-2.   QBasic Made Easy Program File Names, Keywords

```
' NAME01.BAS      PRINT name in color and make sound
'                 CLS, COLOR, DO...LOOP, INPUT, PRINT, REM,
'                 SOUND
' POPUL01.BAS     Projected population
'                 CLS, INPUT, PRINT, REM
' POPUL02.BAS     Projected population
'                 CLS, INPUT, PRINT, PRINT USING, REM
' POPUL03.BAS     Projected population with many REMs
'                 CLS, INPUT, PRINT, PRINT USING, REM
' SALETX03.BAS    Enhanced INPUT Amount, PRINT Tax and Total
'                 CLS, INPUT, PRINT, REM
' SALETX04.BAS    Enhanced INPUT and PRINT
'                 CLS, INPUT, PRINT, REM
' SALETX05.BAS    Enhanced INPUT and PRINT with TABs
'                 CLS, INPUT, PRINT, REM, TAB
' SALETX06.BAS    Enhanced INPUT and PRINT USING
'                 CLS, INPUT, PRINT, PRINT USING, REM, TAB
' SALETX07.BAS    Enhanced INPUT, Commas and $ in PRINT USING
'                 CLS, INPUT, PRINT, PRINT USING, REM, TAB
' STOCKS01.BAS    Value of Stocks
'                 CLS, INPUT, PRINT, PRINT USING, REM
' STRNGS01.BAS    Strings in various PRINT formats
'                 CLS, PRINT, REM
' STRNGS02.BAS    INPUT and PRINT Strings
'                 CLS, DO...LOOP, INPUT, PRINT, REM
' STRNGS03.BAS    LINE INPUT and PRINT Strings
'                 CLS, DO...LOOP, LINE INPUT, PRINT, REM
' STRNGS04.BAS    Enter Strings and write them
'                 CLS, DO...LOOP, LINE INPUT, REM, WRITE
' TVSHOW01.BAS    INPUT number, PRINT number, 1.01 ^ number
'                 CLS, INPUT, PRINT, REM
' TVSHOW02.BAS    Enhanced INPUT, PRINT, exponent
'                 CLS, INPUT, PRINT, REM
' TVSHOW03.BAS    Enhanced INPUT, PRINT USING, exponent
                  CLS, INPUT, PRINT, PRINT USING, REM

REM ** Chapter 5. Control Structures **
' COLORS02.BAS    PRINT colored text
'                 CLS, COLOR, FOR...NEXT, PRINT, REM
```

PROGRAM 6-2. QBasic Made Easy Program File Names,
Keywords (*continued*)

```
' GRAFIX03.BAS    Colored circles and sound
'                 CIRCLE, CLS, DO...LOOP, DO WHILE...LOOP,
'                 ELSE, ELSEIF, END, END IF, EXIT DO,
'                 IF...THEN block, INKEY$, REM, SCREEN 1,
'                 SOUND, TIMER
' GRAFIX04.BAS    Colored rectangles and sound
'                 CASE, CASE ELSE, CLS, DO...LOOP,
'                 DO WHILE...LOOP, END, END SELECT, INKEY$,
'                 LINE, REM, SCREEN 1, SOUND, TIMER
' KWH04.BAS       Cost of Electricity, IF...THEN
'                 CLS, IF...THEN, INPUT, PRINT, PRINT USING,
'                 REM
' KWH05.BAS       Electricity, Block IF...THEN
'                 CLS, ELSEIF, END IF, IF...THEN block, INPUT,
'                 PRINT, PRINT USING, REM
' NORP01.BAS      Negative or Positive
'                 CLS, DO...LOOP, END, EXIT DO, IF...THEN,
'                 INPUT, PRINT, REM
' NORP02.BAS      Negative or Positive
'                 CLS, DO...LOOP, ELSE, ELSEIF, END IF,
'                 EXIT DO, IF...THEN block, INPUT, PRINT, REM
' NORP03.BAS      Negative or Positive
'                 CASE ELSE, CASE IS,  CLS, DO...LOOP, END,
'                 END SELECT, EXIT DO, INPUT, PRINT, REM,
'                 SELECT CASE
' SOUND02.BAS     Siren Song
'                 CHR$(n), CLS, DO...LOOP WHILE, FOR...NEXT,
'                 INKEY$, REM, STEP
' SOUND03.BAS     Sound Effects Experimenter
'                 CHR$(n), CLS, DO...LOOP UNTIL, END,
'                 FOR...NEXT, FOR...NEXT nested, INPUT,
'                 INPUT$(n), LOCATE, REM, SOUND, STEP

REM ** Chapter 6. Editing and Dynamic Debugging **
' 1REMFILE.BAS    QBasic Made Easy Program File Names
'                 REM
' 2REMFILE.BAS    QBasic Made Easy Program File Names, Keywords
'                 REM

REM ** Chapter 7. Function Junction **
```

PROGRAM 6-2. QBasic Made Easy Program File Names, Keywords (*continued*)

```
REM ** Chapter 8. FUNCTION and SUB Procedures **

REM ** Chapter 9. Data Structures **

REM ** Chapter 10. Arrays **

REM ** Chapter 11. Sequential Files **

REM ** Chapter 12. Random-access Files **

REM ** Chapter 13. Your QBasic Backpack **
```

═══════ **PROGRAM 6-2.**   QBasic Made Easy Program File Names,
Keywords (*continued*)

Using the Search Menu

You can use the Search menu to find a character, a word, or a string within a program. The Search menu also has an option for finding the next occurrence of that character, word, or string. A third option allows you to find and change a character, word, or string.

You can use the Search menu to search Program 2REMFILE. Load that program now. Searches are made from the cursor location to the end of the file. Make sure the cursor is at the beginning of the file before starting a search. When the cursor is properly located,

Press: ALT, S

to access the Search menu, as shown by the screen in Figure 6-5. The highlight is on the Find... item. Notice that the status bar reads, "Finds specified text." The ellipses (...) indicate that you need to supply more information with this selection. Before accessing the Find dialog box, scan the other options on the menu:

Press: ↓

to highlight the second item, Repeat Last Find. Notice that the status bar now reads, "Find next occurrence of text specified in previous search."

Press: ↓

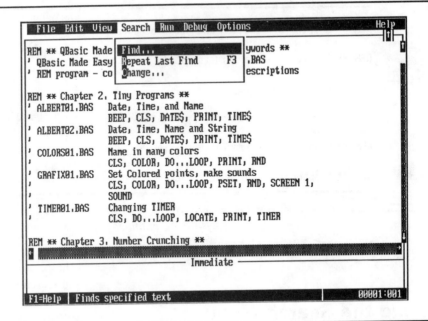

```
     File  Edit  View  Search  Run  Debug  Options                    Help
```

FIGURE 6-5.   The Search menu

to highlight Change. . ., the third item. The status bar changes again to read, "Finds and changes specified text."

Move the highlight back to Find. . ., the first item.

Press: ENTER

and you see the Find dialog box, as shown here:

Notice the small rectangle labeled "Find What:" located under the title of the dialog box. In the example, the box contains the keyword REM. Yours may show something different. This is where you enter the string that you want to find.

Search Program 2REMFILE for the word "Input" in the following way. First,

Type: **Input**

in the Find What: box. As you start typing, the word previously highlighted in the Find What: box disappears. It is replaced by the string you type. Do not press ENTER yet. Instead,

Press: TAB

The cursor moves to the empty brackets to the left of the Match Upper/ Lowercase option.

Press: SPACEBAR

This selects the option. The letter X appears in the brackets to indicate that the option has been selected. This means that the search will be for the word you entered in the exact way you entered it (uppercase letters to match uppercase letters and lowercase letters to match lowercase letters). Next,

Press: TAB

to move the cursor to the empty brackets to the left of the Whole Word option.

Press: SPACEBAR

to select this option. This option causes the program to overlook strings in which the selected search string, "Input", is embedded. The program will find only an occurrence in which the specified text is surrounded by spaces, punctuation marks, or other characters not considered parts of a word. Letters of the alphabet, digits 0-9, and !, #, %, and & are considered parts of a word.

The Find dialog box now looks like this:

```
┌──────────────────── Find ────────────────────┐
│                 ┌────────────────────────────┐│
│ Find What:      │Input                       ││
│                 └────────────────────────────┘│
│                                               │
│                                               │
│   [X] Match Upper/Lowercase      [X] Whole Word│
│                                               │
├───────────────────────────────────────────────┤
│    ▌ OK ▐        < Cancel >        < Help >    │
└───────────────────────────────────────────────┘
```

Now that both options have been selected,

Press: ENTER

to begin the search.

The dialog box disappears, and after a short period of time, the following dialog box appears:

```
┌─────────────────────────┐
│                         │
│ Match not found         │
│                         │
│                         │
│ ▌ OK ▐  < Help >        │
└─────────────────────────┘
```

The search has revealed that the word "Input" (in that exact form) does not appear in the file. Input is a QBasic keyword; it should appear in all uppercase letters. Remove the dialog box and access the Search menu again. With the Find. . . option highlighted,

Press: ENTER

to access the Find dialog box. Notice that both options still show an X enclosed in brackets, indicating that the options are still selected.

Make sure that the word "Input" is still in the Find What: box. If it is not, enter it again in the same way. Then

Press: TAB

to move the cursor below the X in the brackets to the left of the Match Upper/Lowercase option.

Press: SPACEBAR

The X disappears. The brackets are empty again. This means that the search will not match uppercase and lowercase letters. It will find INPUT, InPuT, or any other combination of uppercase and lowercase letters that spell the word as entered.

Press: ENTER

to start another search. After a short period of time, the text in the View window changes to display the first occurrence of the search word that is found. The word is highlighted, as shown by the screen in Figure 6-6. You

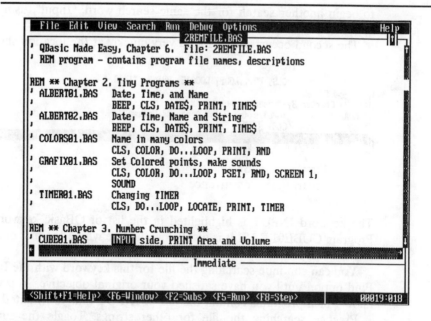

```
┌─ File  Edit  View  Search  Run  Debug  Options                         Help ─┐
│                          ═ 2REMFILE.BAS ═                                  ↕│
│ ' QBasic Made Easy, Chapter 6.  File: 2REMFILE.BAS                         ↑│
│ ' REM program - contains program file names, descriptions                   │
│                                                                             │
│ REM ** Chapter 2. Tiny Programs **                                          │
│ ' ALBERT01.BAS   Date, Time, and Name                                       │
│ '                BEEP, CLS, DATE$, PRINT, TIME$                             │
│ ' ALBERT02.BAS   Date, Time, Name and String                                │
│ '                BEEP, CLS, DATE$, PRINT, TIME$                             │
│ ' COLORS01.BAS   Name in many colors                                        │
│ '                CLS, COLOR, DO...LOOP, PRINT, RND                           │
│ ' GRAFIX01.BAS   Set Colored points, make sounds                            │
│ '                CLS, COLOR, DO...LOOP, PSET, RND, SCREEN 1,                │
│ '                SOUND                                                       │
│ ' TIMER01.BAS    Changing TIMER                                             │
│ '                CLS, DO...LOOP, LOCATE, PRINT, TIMER                        │
│                                                                             │
│ REM ** Chapter 3. Number Crunching **                                       │
│ ' CUBE01.BAS     INPUT side, PRINT Area and Volume                          │
│ ■                                                                          ↓│
│ ───────────────────────── Immediate ──────────────────────────────────────│
│                                                                             │
└─<Shift+F1=Help> <F6=Window> <F2=Subs> <F5=Run> <F8=Step> ──── 00019:018 ───┘
```

FIGURE 6-6. INPUT keyword found

now know that this keyword appears in the program CUBE01.BAS as part of the program's description.

This is the first occurrence of INPUT in the program. To find the next occurrence of INPUT, search the file from the current cursor location instead of from the beginning of the file. To do so, access the Search menu again.

Press: ↓

to select the second item, Repeat Last Find, as shown here:

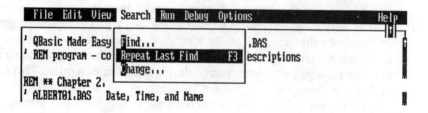

```
┌─ File  Edit  View  Search  Run  Debug  Options              Help ─┐
│                    ┌─────────────────────┐                        │
│ ' QBasic Made Easy │ Find...             │ .BAS                    │
│ ' REM program - co │ Repeat Last Find F3 │ escriptions             │
│                    │ Change...           │                         │
│ REM ** Chapter 2.  └─────────────────────┘                        │
│ ' ALBERT01.BAS   Date, Time, and Name                             │
```

Press: ENTER

to begin another search for the same search word, "Input", using the same options.

The second occurrence is found very quickly at the location shown here:

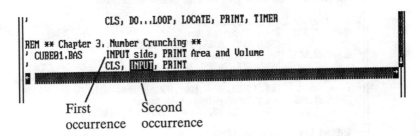

First   Second
occurrence   occurrence

The keyword INPUT is highlighted in the list of QBasic keywords used in Program CUBE01.BAS. It is just below the line where the first occurrence of INPUT was found.

You can continue searching the file for this keyword with the Repeat Last Find option until you have satisfied your original objective. You would then know which programs contain the use of INPUT that you wanted.

Practice searching the file for other strings. Toggle the Find options (Match Upper/Lowercase and Whole Word) on and off so that you know how they work. Search the file for parts of words, such as "pop". With Whole Word toggled off, you may find many such occurrences. Try many combinations of strings and options.

DYNAMIC DEBUGGING

Debugging is the term used to refer to the trial-and-error process of finding all the errors in long programs. Bugs occur in programs for a myriad of reasons. They are usually caused by simple oversights and typographical errors, but sometimes they occur because of the programmer's misunderstanding of how the program is to accomplish its task.

It is very easy, especially when writing large and complex programs, to make errors that are not easily identified. Often, you will not know what error has occurred until you check the order in which a program runs and how the values of variables change during program execution. This is known as *dynamic debugging*.

QBasic provides some powerful dynamic debugging tools: *tracing, stepping through a program,* and *using breakpoints*. In the sections that follow, you will learn to use all three techniques.

Using the Debug Menu

To see the tools that you have for debugging programs, access the Debug menu shown in Figure 6-7. When the menu appears, the first option, Step, is highlighted. Use the ↓ key to highlight each item on the Debug menu, and look at the status bar at the bottom of the screen to see the function of each option.

Step	Executes next program statement
Procedure Step	Executes next program statement, tracing over procedure calls
Trace On	Highlights statement currently executing
Toggle Breakpoint	Sets/clears breakpoint at cursor location
Clear All Breakpoints	Removes all breakpoints
Set Next Statement	Makes the statement at the cursor the next statement to execute

The Procedure Step option will not be used in this chapter. Procedures are discussed in Chapter 8, "FUNCTION and SUB Procedures."

TRACING A PROGRAM   You will use the Trace On option in the Debug menu first. When you use this option, each statement of the program is automatically highlighted as it is executed. The execution of the program is slowed down so that you can see the order in which the statements are executed. Trace On allows you to study the *logic* of the program to see if the statements are being executed in the order that you expected.

Leave the Debug menu and select the New option in the File menu. Then enter the following program in the View window:

```
CLS

FOR number = 1 TO 10
  PRINT number
NEXT number
```

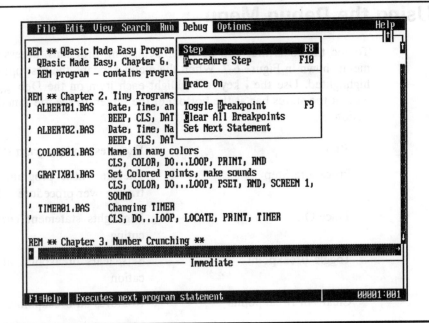

FIGURE 6-7.   The Debug menu

To trace the program execution, you must toggle the Trace On option in the Debug menu. When Trace On is not turned on, the option looks like this:

Notice the blank space to the left of the words "Trace On". The empty space is a clue that Trace On is not active. With the highlight at the Trace On selection, press ENTER. The Debug menu disappears, and your program appears in the View window. Access the Debug menu again to make sure that Trace On has been activated. The Trace On selection should now look like this:

Notice the marker that appears to the left of the words "Trace On". This marker signifies that Trace On is now active. Press ESC to go back to the View window.

To watch the program step through its statements, access the Run menu and select the Start option, just as if you were making a run of the program. When you select Start and press ENTER, the menu is erased. The Step operation begins. Each statement is highlighted as it is executed. You will see the statements highlighted in the following order:

```
CLS                      'first
FOR number = 1 TO 10     'second
   PRINT number          'third
NEXT number              'fourth
```

After "NEXT number" is executed the first time, the highlight alternates, as the loop is executed, between the following two statements:

```
   PRINT number
NEXT number
```

When the loop has been executed ten times, the program stops with the Output screen displaying the numbers 1 through 10, with the message "Press any key to continue" at the bottom of the screen. Press any key to return to the View window.

Add an END statement after the FOR ... NEXT loop and run the program again. The statements are executed in the same order. However, after the END statement is executed, the program stops in the View window. Remember, you can see what is in the Output screen by pressing F4. The output is the same but "Press any key to continue" is not displayed. Access the Debug menu and turn the Trace option off before going to the next section.

STEPPING THROUGH A PROGRAM You can completely control the execution of statements in a program by using the Step option on the Debug menu. When you use Step, the program halts before each instruction is executed and waits for you to press the F8 key.

Step through the previous program now. First, access the Run menu, shown here:

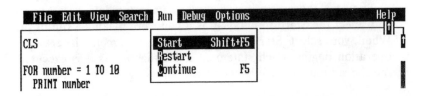

```
 File  Edit  View  Search  Run  Debug  Options                    Help
                                                                  ▐▌
CLS                        Start      Shift+F5                      ↑
                           Restart
FOR number = 1 TO 10       Continue        F5
  PRINT number                                                      ▐
```

The Start option is highlighted. Notice that the status bar reads, "Runs current program." You have used this option to run programs. (You will use the third option, Continue, in the next section in this chapter.)

Press: ↓

This moves the highlight from the Start option to the Restart option, as shown here:

```
 File  Edit  View  Search  Run  Debug · Options                   Help
                                                                  ▐▌
CLS                        Start      Shift+F5                      ↑
                           Restart       ·
FOR number = 1 TO 10       Continue        F5
  PRINT number                                                      ▐
```

Notice that the status bar now reads, "Clears variables in preparation for single stepping." Use this option for stepping through a program. While Restart is highlighted,

Press: ENTER

You will see that the first statement (CLS) is highlighted. Access the Debug menu. Notice that the Step option is highlighted. At the right of the highlight you will see that you can use F8 instead of the Step menu selection as a shortcut for executing the next statement. Use F8 in the future. If you forget what the shortcut is, you can always access the Debug menu. Since you are already in the Debug menu with Step highlighted,

Press: ENTER

This activates a single step. In between steps, the screen flashes briefly. The highlight skips over the blank line following the CLS statement and moves down to the next statement:

```
FOR number = 1 TO 10
```

Press: F8

to execute that statement. Then the highlight moves down to

```
PRINT number
```

Press: F8

again and the highlight moves down to

```
NEXT number
```

Each statement in the program has been executed. Now the execution of the loop is repeated. Pressing F8 moves the highlight alternately between these two statements:

```
PRINT number
NEXT number
```

You can press F4 at any time to see the display in the Output screen. If you press F4 after three passes through the FOR . . . NEXT loop, the Output screen shows

```
1
2
3
```

Continue pressing F8 until the loop has been completed ten times. Do not press the key too fast. Wait until the highlight moves to the next statement; otherwise, nothing will happen when you press F8.

When you press F8 again, the END statement is highlighted. One more press of the F8 key ends the program; the highlight is gone. Press F4 to see the Output screen, which shows all ten numbers.

USING BREAKPOINTS   You will use Program GRAFIX04 from Chapter 5 for the experiments in the rest of this chapter. Load GRAFIX04 now.

You can interrupt a program at any statement by setting a *breakpoint*. When you have interrupted the program, you can look at values of variables, the status of the Output screen, or other aspects of the program. You turn breakpoints on and off from the Debug menu.

Notice that the CASE blocks of Program GRAFIX04 have the form CASE *StartNumber* TO *EndNumber*:

```
SELECT CASE size
  CASE 2 TO 6
    SOUND 4000, .25
    PAINT (column + inc, row + inc), kolor, 3
  CASE 6 TO 12
    SOUND 1000, .5
    PAINT (column + inc, row + inc), kolor, 3
  CASE ELSE
    SOUND 400, .875
    PAINT (column + inc, row + inc), kolor, 3
END SELECT
```

The first CASE specifies a range of 2 to 6 for *size*. The second CASE specifies a range of 6 to 12. The value for *size* is determined by

```
size = RND * 16 + 2
```

The value of *size* will be greater than 2 and less than 18.

Set a breakpoint at each PAINT statement in the program by following these steps:

1. Move the cursor to the first PAINT statement.

2. Access the Debug menu.

3. Move the highlight down to Toggle Breakpoint.

4. Press ENTER.

The Debug menu disappears, and the first PAINT statement has a high-lighted background bar:

```
  SOUND 4000, .25
  PAINT (column + inc, row + inc), kolor, 3
  CASE 6 TO 12
```

Repeat the process for the other two PAINT statements so that all three have the highlighted background bar, as shown here:

```
    SOUND 4000, .25
      PAINT (column + inc, row + inc), kolor, 3
    CASE 6 TO 12
      SOUND 1000, .5
      PAINT (column + inc, row + inc), kolor, 3
    CASE ELSE
      SOUND 400, .875
      PAINT (column + inc, row + inc), kolor, 3
  END SELECT
```

The shortcut key for Toggle Breakpoints is F9. You may use F9 instead of accessing Toggle Breakpoints from the Debug menu.

You have now set a breakpoint at each of the PAINT statements. When you make a program run, the program will be interrupted at one of the three breakpoints if the SELECT CASE blocks have been set up correctly. When the program is interrupted, you can look at the Output screen to see its status and then continue to run the program by doing the following:

1. Access the Run menu.

2. Select the Continue option (shortcut F5).

3. Press ENTER.

Now it's time to put it all together and see how breakpoints work. You have already set up the breakpoints. All you have to do is access the Run menu and start the program.

The program begins, a sound is emitted from the speaker, and the program is then interrupted at one of the breakpoints. That breakpoint is highlighted in bright white letters. For example, if the value of *size* were greater than 12, the beep would be a low-frequency tone (400 cycles/sec.) and the third PAINT statement would be highlighted:

```
    SOUND 400, .875
    PAINT (column + inc, row + inc), kolor, 3
  END SELECT
```

Access the Output screen by pressing F4. You will see that one rectangle has been drawn on the screen but not painted. Since the breakpoint was set at the PAINT statement, that statement has not yet been executed. Press F4 to return to the View window. Then

Press: F5

Since F5 is the shortcut key for the Continue option in the Run menu, the program continues. The rectangle you just saw is painted, the program loops back to get the size of another rectangle, a sound is heard, and the program is interrupted at one of the three PAINT statements again, with that PAINT statement highlighted.

Press: F4

to see the Output screen. You will see that the first rectangle has been painted and a second rectangle has been drawn but not painted. (If the background color is selected for painting, the first rectangle's interior color will not change.) Press F4 to return to the View window. Then

Press: F5

to continue the program. Each time you continue the program by pressing F5, another value for *size* is selected, a sound is heard, a rectangle is drawn, and the program is interrupted at a breakpoint. Continue this cycle until you are satisfied that the range of values in the CASE blocks is correct and that all three breakpoints are working as planned.

Return to the View window. Then toggle the first breakpoint off. Do this by placing the cursor on the first PAINT statement. Then access the Debug menu, move the highlight to Toggle Breakpoint, and press ENTER. This turns off the breakpoint only where the cursor is located. The first breakpoint is no longer highlighted, but the other two breakpoints are still highlighted. You can also use the shortcut key F9 to toggle the breakpoint off.

If a breakpoint at the cursor is off, selecting Toggle Breakpoint (or pressing F9) turns it on. If the breakpoint is on, selecting Toggle Breakpoint (or pressing F9) turns it off.

If you want to turn all breakpoints off at once, use the Clear All Breakpoints option on the Debug menu. Do that now. Turn the remaining breakpoints off by following these steps:

1. Access the Debug menu.

2. Move the highlight down to Clear All Breakpoints.

3. Press ENTER.

The highlight bars of all the PAINT statements are now off. All breakpoints have been removed.

USING SET NEXT STATEMENT   The Set Next Statement option in the Debug menu changes the execution sequence of an interrupted program. You can interrupt your program with a breakpoint, move the cursor to the line where you want to continue, and use Set Next Statement to select that line as the next statement to be executed.

You may have noticed when running Program GRAFIX04 that some rectangles near the right edge and bottom edge of the screen were "clipped"; that is, only part of each rectangle was displayed. The rest was clipped off. You suspect that this condition is caused by the values of *column + inc* and *row + inc*. Since the maximum column value for the screen is 319, add three lines to the DO . . . LOOP, as shown here:

```
DO
   size = rnd * 16 + 2
   column = RND * 319: row = RND * 199
   inc = size / 2: kolor = RND * 3
   IF column + inc > 319 THEN        (Add this line)
     BEEP                            (Add this line)
   END IF                           (Add this line)
```

Now toggle a breakpoint at the BEEP statement. Put the cursor anywhere on the line containing BEEP; then press F9. The complete line is highlighted, as shown here:

```
IF column + inc > 319 THEN
   BEEP
END IF
```

If a rectangle will be clipped at the right edge of the screen, the breakpoint interrupts the program. This tells you that the value of *column + inc* is too great. You can continue the program with a new column value by using Set Next Statement and pressing F5 (Continue). The program continues where you selected Set Next Statement.

With the breakpoint set at BEEP, run the program. At some point the program will be interrupted, with the BEEP statement highlighted in bright white letters. The value of *column + inc* is too great. To get a new value for *column,* move the cursor to the statement where the value is assigned:

```
size = RND * 16 + 2
column = RND * 319: row = RND * 199
```

Access the Debug menu and move the highlight to Set Next Statement. Then

Press: ENTER

The column assignment statement is highlighted in bright white letters.

Press: F5

to continue the program from this statement. New values for *column* and *row* are selected, and the program continues. Eventually the condition will occur that causes the program to be interrupted again.

Now you know where the problem occurs. Since the variable *inc* is calculated by dividing *size* by 2, you can deduce that you must reduce the value of the random numbers selected for *column* and *row* by 9 (18 / 2). Therefore, change the *column* and *row* assignments to

```
column = RND * 310: row = RND * 190
```

Do not yet delete the IF . . . END IF block that you inserted. Run the program again with the *column* and *row* changes. Let it run until you are sure that the breakpoint does not cause an interruption.

When you are satisfied with the results,

Press: SPACEBAR

to end the program. Access the Debug menu and select Clear All Breakpoints. Remove the IF . . . END IF block and save the corrected program under the name it already has.

SUMMARY

Certain keys, called editing keys, allow you to edit a program quickly and more easily than by changing individual characters. The cursor and window scrolling keys are shown in Table 6-1. You used them to edit two REMFILE programs in this chapter.

You learned to select text with SHIFT-↓. Other methods of selecting text were shown in Table 6-2. Text to be deleted or moved must be selected before a Cut, Copy, or Clear option can be used from the Edit menu. Text from a Cut or Copy option is saved on the clipboard. Text from the Clear option is not saved. You can move text from the clipboard into a program with the Paste option in the Edit menu.

You used the Search menu to search and find strings contained in Program 2REMFILE. You can use the Search menu to find specified strings or to find and change specified strings.

The Debug menu contains tools for debugging programs that have errors. These tools include the following options:

Step	Executes next program statement
Trace On	Highlights statement being currently executed
Toggle Breakpoint	Sets/clears breakpoint at cursor location
Clear All Breakpoints	Removes all breakpoints
Set Next Statement	Makes the statement at the cursor the next statement to execute

You learned to use all the editing and debugging tools described here and are now prepared to create and develop longer and more complex programs.

chapter 7

FUNCTION JUNCTION

QBasic has a rich repertoire of built-in *functions.* A function is a keyword that, when used, returns a *value;* this value is the result computed by the function. QBasic has *numeric functions* and *string functions.* The value of a numeric function is a number; the value of a string function is a string. In other words, a numeric function returns a numeric value, and a string function returns a string value. String function names, like string variable names, end with a dollar sign ($).

Some functions require *arguments;* others do not. An argument is a number or string on which the function operates to produce the value of the function.

In this chapter, you will learn about some of the functions that are built into QBasic. You will also learn how to name and define your own *user-defined functions.* In particular, you will learn

- More about numeric functions used in previous chapters: RND, TIMER

- More about string functions used in previous chapters: CHR$, INKEY$, INPUT$(n)

- More about ASCII codes and characters

- Some new numeric functions: ABS, ASC, FIX, INSTR, INT, LEN, SGN, SQR, VAL

- Some new string functions: LCASE$, LEFT$, MID$, RIGHT$, SPACE$, STR$, STRING$, UCASE$

- Some new QBasic statements: DEF FN, DEF FN ... END DEF, RAN-DOMIZE

- How to name, define, and use your own user-defined functions

FUNCTIONS THAT DO NOT REQUIRE ARGUMENTS

The simplest type of function is one that does not require an argument. You have already used this type of function. For example, RND and TIMER are numeric functions that do not require an argument. INKEY$ is a string function that does not require an argument.

The INKEY$ String Function

INKEY$ scans the keyboard for a keypress. If a key or combination of keys has been pressed, the value of INKEY$ is a 1- or 2-byte string that corresponds to the key or key combination. If no key has been pressed, the value of INKEY$ is the null, or empty, string (""). INKEY$ does not wait for a keypress, as does the INPUT$ function, described later in this chapter.

Try the following program. It continues while the value of INKEY$ is the empty string (""). That is, it continues as long as you *don't* press a key.

```
DO
  PRINT "Press a key to stop me"
LOOP WHILE INKEY$ = ""
```

Enter and run the program. The screen then fills quickly with the message "Press a key to stop me." If you do not press a key, the condition INKEY$ = "" is true, and the DO ... LOOP continues. If you press a key, the condition becomes false, and the loop ends.

You can also write the program like this:

```
DO WHILE INKEY$ = ""
   PRINT "Press a key to stop me"
LOOP
```

Use the following program to learn more about INKEY$.

```
CLS
kbd$ = ""                                'Set kbd$ to empty string

DO WHILE kbd$ = ""                       'Loop while no key press
   PRINT "Press a key to stop me"
   kbd$ = INKEY$                         'kbd$ "remembers" key press
LOOP

PRINT : PRINT "You pressed "; kbd$       'Some keys are nonprinting
```

Run the program several times. Each time, use a different key or key combination to stop the program. You will frequently see the ESC key used as a means of "escaping" from a program. Run the program and press ESC. This key is printed as a small left-pointing arrow, as shown here:

```
Press a key to stop me
Press a key to stop me
Press a key to stop me

You pressed <-

Press any key to continue
```

You can write a DO ... LOOP that requires a preselected key as the interrupt key. To end the following DO ... LOOP, press the ESC key:

```
DO UNTIL INKEY$ = CHR$(27)
   PRINT "Press the ESC key to stop me"
LOOP
```

Run this program. Press several keys other than the ESC key; the program will continue to run. You must press the ESC key to stop the program.
    The statement:

```
DO UNTIL INKEY$ = CHR$(27)
```

tells the computer to continue the DO . . . LOOP until the value of INKEY$ is equal to the character whose ASCII code is 27. CHR$ is a string function. Its value is the character whose ASCII code number is enclosed in parentheses. For example, CHR$(32) is a space; CHR$(65) is the uppercase letter A; CHR$(27) is the ESC key. You will learn more about ASCII codes and the CHR$ function later in this chapter.

The TIMER Numeric Function

TIMER is a numeric function that does not require an argument. This function returns the number of elapsed seconds since midnight, according to the computer's clock. At midnight, the value of TIMER is 0. At high noon, the value of TIMER is 43200. At one minute before midnight, the value of TIMER is 86340. At one second before midnight, the value of TIMER is 86399. At midnight, the value of TIMER is reset to 0.

The following program uses both the TIMER numeric function and the INKEY$ string function:

```
CLS
TIME$ = "23:59:50"                '10 seconds before midnight

DO                                'Press a key to stop
  PRINT TIMER,
LOOP WHILE INKEY$ = ""            'Loop while no key press
```

This program sets the time to ten seconds before midnight and then starts printing the value of TIMER. Press a key (the SPACEBAR is a good choice) to stop the program. Use it to check your reaction time—how soon after midnight (TIMER = 0) can you stop the program? Part of a run is shown here, where the program was stopped a fraction of a second after the value of TIMER became 0:

86399.88	86399.94	86399.94	86399.94	86399.94
86399.94	86399.94	0	0	0
0	0	0	0	.05
.05	.05	.05	.05	.05
.1	.1	.1	.1	.1
.16	.16	.16	.16	.16
.16	.21	.21		

```
Press any key to continue
```

Note that the value of TIMER is usually printed with one or two decimal places to the right of the decimal point. The value of TIMER is precise to 1 clock tick. Since there are 18.2 clock ticks in 1 second, the value is precise to 1/18.2 second, or approximately 0.055 second. When the value of TIMER changes, it changes by either .05 or .06.

How long does it take your computer to multiply two numbers? Use the following program to find out:

```
CLS
start = TIMER
FOR k% = 1 TO 10000
  product = 1.23 * 4.56
NEXT k%
finish = TIMER
PRINT "Elapsed time:"; finish - start
```

This program was run on a computer that is rather slow by today's standards and produced the following result:

```
Elapsed time: 6.969727
```

The computer did 10,000 multiplications in about 7 seconds. The time for one multiplication is about 0.0007 second, or 0.7 thousandths of a second, or 0.7 *milliseconds*.

The RND Numeric Function

RND is a number function that does not require an argument. Its value is a *random number* between 0 and 1. The numbers generated by the RND function are not truly random, as are numbers obtained, for example, by rolling dice. Rather, RND generates *pseudorandom numbers*. To see the difference between truly random and pseudorandom numbers, run the following short program at least twice:

```
CLS
PRINT RND, RND, RND, RND
```

Two runs are shown here. Note that both runs produced the same set of numbers. First run:

```
.7055475        .533424        .5795186        .2895625
```

Second run:

.7055475　　　.533424　　　.5795186　　　.2895625

RND generates the same sequence of numbers each time you run the program. These numbers are pseudorandom; if RND generated truly random numbers, the numbers produced would be unpredictable.

You can avoid this replication of so-called random numbers by using the RANDOMIZE statement with the TIMER function, as shown in the next program:

```
RANDOMIZE TIMER
CLS
PRINT RND, RND, RND, RND
```

Two sample runs of this program produced different sequences of random numbers. First run:

.5486872　　　.3790051　　　.9177755　　　.649792

Second run:

.4725153　　　.6075207　　　.2322286　　　.7064326

Run the program several times. You will see a different sequence of numbers each time. Use a RANDOMIZE TIMER statement in your programs if you want your RND numbers to seem random.

The RND function generates a random number between 0 and 1, but never 0 or 1. That is, RND is a random number greater than 0 and less than 1. Thus,

0 < RND < 1

To obtain random numbers in another range of values, just multiply RND by an appropriate number. For example, 10 * RND is a random number between 0 and 10, but never 0 or 10. That is, 10 * RND is a random number greater than 0 and less than 10:

0 < 10 * RND < 10

You will see more examples that use the RND function as you continue through this chapter.

NUMERIC FUNCTIONS THAT REQUIRE ARGUMENTS

A QBasic function usually operates on an argument to compute the value of the function. The value of the function depends on the value of the argument. The argument is enclosed in parentheses and follows the name of the function.

The FIX and INT Numeric Functions

FIX is a numeric function of a numeric argument. It returns the integer part of its numeric argument. For example:

FIX(3.14) = 3   FIX(-3.14) = -3   FIX(.99) = 0

INT is a numeric function of a numeric argument. It returns the *greatest integer* value of the argument. INT(*number*) is the greatest integer that is less than or equal to the value of *number*. Some examples of the INT function are shown here:

Nonnegative numbers	Negative numbers
INT(0) = 0	INT(−1) = −1
INT(3.14) = 3	INT(−3.14) = −4
INT(.99) = 0	INT(−.99) = −1

Use the following program to learn more about the FIX and INT numeric functions:

```
CLS
DO
  INPUT "Argument, please"; argument
  PRINT "FIX(argument) is "; FIX(argument)
  PRINT "INT(argument) is "; INT(argument)
  PRINT
LOOP
```

Press CTRL-BREAK to end the program.

Figure 7-1 shows a sample run. For integer arguments, FIX and INT return the same result. The results are also the same for positive noninteger arguments. For negative noninteger arguments, however, the values differ by one, as you can see in Figure 7-1.

The ABS and SGN Numeric Functions

ABS is a numeric function of a numeric argument. It returns the *absolute value* of the argument. SGN is a numeric function of a numeric argument. Its value is −1, 0, or 1, as defined here:

If *number* is negative, then SGN(*number*) is −1.
If *number* is zero, then SGN(*number*) is 0.
If *number* is positive, then SGN(*number*) is 1.

Use the following program to learn more about ABS and SGN:

```
CLS
DO
  INPUT "Number, please"; number
  PRINT "ABS(number) is: "; ABS(number)
  PRINT "SGN(number) is: "; SGN(number)
LOOP
```

```
Argument, please? 1
FIX(argument) is 1
INT(argument) is 1

Argument, please? -1
FIX(argument) is -1
INT(argument) is -1

Argument, please? -.123
FIX(argument) is 0
INT(argument) is -1

Argument, please? _
```

FIGURE 7-1. Values of FIX and INT functions

Figure 7-2 shows a sample run of this program. Try it yourself; enter both negative and positive numbers as the values of *number*. Note that for negative numbers, the absolute value (ABS) is the corresponding positive number.

You can use the ABS and SGN functions with the FIX or INT function to round a number. The following program rounds a number to two decimal places:

```
CLS
DO
  INPUT "Number, please"; nmbr
  rounded = SGN(nmbr) * FIX(100 * ABS(nmbr) + .5) / 100
  PRINT "Rounded value: "; rounded
  PRINT
LOOP
```

Figure 7-3 shows a sample run. Table 7-1 shows how the rounded values are calculated.

This program may behave somewhat erratically for numbers that end with a 5 in the third decimal place (for example, try .385, .445, or .695). This happens because QBasic uses *binary numbers*. The decimal numbers that you enter are converted to binary numbers. That's okay for integers, but most decimal fractions cannot be represented exactly as a binary QBasic number. QBasic's binary numbers are close enough to the real thing for most purposes, but keep in mind that tiny errors are possible; they are called *binary roundoff errors*.

```
Number, please? 7
ABS(number) is:  7
SGN(number) is:  1

Number, please? 0
ABS(number) is:  0
SGN(number) is:  0

Number, please? -1.23
ABS(number) is:  1.23
SGN(number) is: -1

Number, please? _
```

FIGURE 7-2. Demonstration of the ABS and SGN functions

```
Number, please? 3.141583
Rounded value:  3.14

Number, please? -3.141593
Rounded value: -3.14

Number, please? 2.718282
Rounded value:  2.72

Number, please? -2.718282
Rounded value: -2.72

Number, please? 1.235
Rounded value:  1.24

Number, please? -1.235
Rounded value: -1.24

Number, please? _
```

FIGURE 7-3.   Numbers rounded to two decimal places

nmbr	ABS(nmbr)	FIX(100 * ABS(nmbr) + .5)	rounded
−3.554	3.554	355	−3.55
−3.555	3.555	356	−3.56
−.0055	.0055	6	−.01
.444	.444	44	.44
.445	.445	44	.44
.446	.446	45	.45
.044	.044	4	.04
.045	.045	5	.05
100.4545	100.4545	10045	100.45
100.5454	100.5454	10055	100.55

TABLE 7-1.   Producing Rounded Values

The SQR Numeric Function

SQR is a numeric function of a numeric argument. It returns the square root of a nonnegative argument. A negative argument causes an "Illegal function call" dialog box. In a right triangle, the length of the hypotenuse (c) can be computed from the lengths of the other two sides (a and b), as shown here:

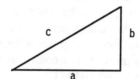

$$c^2 = a^2 + b^2$$
$$c = \sqrt{a^2 + b^2}$$

You can use the following program to compute the length of the hypotenuse for values of a and b entered from the keyboard:

```
CLS
DO
  INPUT "Length of side a"; a
  INPUT "Length of side b"; b
  PRINT "Length of hypotenuse:"; SQR(a ^ 2 + b ^ 2)
  PRINT
LOOP
```

Here is a sample run:

```
Length of side a? 3
Length of side b? 4
Length of hypotenuse: 5

Length of side a? _
```

STRING FUNCTIONS THAT REQUIRE ARGUMENTS

A string function name, like a string variable name, ends in a dollar sign ($). The value returned by a string function is a string. Earlier in this chapter, you learned how to use INKEY$, a string function that does not require an argument. Now you will learn how to use some string functions that require arguments.

The INPUT$ String Function

INPUT$ is a string function of a numeric argument. INPUT$(*n*) tells the computer to wait for a string of *n* characters to be entered from the keyboard. For example, INPUT$(1) tells the computer to wait for one character to be entered from the keyboard. You can press a letter key, a number key, or a punctuation key. SHIFT plus another key counts as one key.

Use the following program to learn more about INPUT$:

```
CLS
DO
  PRINT "Press a key"
  kbd$ = INPUT$(1)                 'Wait for one keypress
  PRINT "You pressed "; kbd$
  PRINT
LOOP WHILE kbd$ <> CHR$(27)        'Loop while ESC not pressed
PRINT "You pressed ESC, which ends the program."
```

Press the ESC key to end the program.

Figure 7-4 shows an annotated run of the program. Note that some keys, such as ENTER and the cursor control keys (arrow keys), are nonprinting keys. Try pressing these keys when you run the program, and see what happens.

The program line:

```
kbd$ = INPUT$(1)
```

tells the computer to wait for someone to enter one character by pressing one key or a key combination such as the SHIFT key and another key. The character entered is assigned as the value of the string variable *kbd$*.

The LCASE$ and UCASE$ String Functions

Suppose that you are writing a trivia program. One of the questions is, "What are the colors of a rainbow?" Red is one of the colors. People might enter it as **red** or **RED** or **Red**, or perhaps even as **ReD**. This could make it a bit

```
Press a key
You pressed a

Press a key
You pressed A          SHIFT A counts as one key

Press a key
You pressed 8

Press a key
You pressed *          SHIFT 8 counts as one key

Press a key
You pressed            Some keys are nonprinting

Press a key
You pressed <-         Press ESC to end the program

You pressed ESC, which ends the program


Press any key to continue
```

FIGURE 7-4.   The INPUT$ string function in action

difficult to determine if the answer is correct. You can use the LCASE$ and UCASE$ functions to solve this problem.

LCASE$ and UCASE$ are string functions of string arguments. LCASE$ returns a string with all of the letters converted to lowercase. UCASE$ returns a string with all of the letters converted to uppercase. For example:

Function	Value
LCASE$("ABC 123")	abc 123
LCASE$("Abc 123")	abc 123
UCASE$("abc 123")	ABC 123
UCASE$("Abc 123")	ABC 123

Use the following program to learn more about LCASE$ and UCASE$:

```
CLS
DO
  INPUT "String, please"; strng$
  PRINT "The LCASE$ is:  "; LCASE$(strng$)
  PRINT "The UCASE$ is:  "; UCASE$(strng$)
  PRINT
LOOP UNTIL strng$ = ""      'Loop until empty string is entered
```

To stop this program, press ENTER without typing any characters. This assigns the empty string ("") as the value of *strng$* and causes the DO . . . LOOP to end. Figure 7-5 shows a sample run of this program.

The MID$ String Function

MID$ is a string function of three arguments—one string argument and two numeric arguments. When a function has more than one argument, the

---

```
String, please? Agent 007
The LCASE$ is:  agent 007
The UCASE$ is:  AGENT 007

String, please? LCASE$ and ucase$ change only LeTTeRs!!!
The LCASE$ is:  lcase$ and ucase$ change only letters!!!
The UCASE$ is:  LCASE$ AND UCASE$ CHANGE ONLY LETTERS!!!

String, please?                    (ENTER was pressed)
The LCASE$ is:
The UCASE$ is:




Press any key to continue
```

FIGURE 7-5. Demonstration of LCASE$ and UCASE$ functions

arguments are separated by commas. You use MID$ to select a portion of a string (a *substring*) from within a string. For example, the word "proverb" contains these shorter words:

pro
prove
prover
rove
rover
over
verb

You can use MID$ to select these words within "proverb."

Here is a program to select and print two substrings of "proverb":

```
CLS
PRINT MID$("proverb", 1, 5), MID$("proverb", 2, 4)
```

Run this program to see the following on the Output screen:

```
prove           rove
```

The value returned by the MID$ function is a substring of the function's first argument. The second argument is numeric; it specifies the position within the string to begin selecting characters. The third argument is also numeric; it specifies how many characters to select, counting from where the substring begins, as illustrated here:

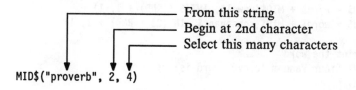

```
MID$("proverb", 2, 4)
```

Suppose that you want to name a new product, or even a new company. Perhaps you are writing a novel and want to create unusual names for characters or places. You can use your computer to help you invent names. How would you write a program to print names that are pronounceable, but seem exotic or even fantastic?

Program 7-1, WRDMKR01 (Word Maker), generates five-letter random words in this format: consonant, vowel, consonant, vowel, consonant (cvcvc). In this program, the letter "y" can appear as either a consonant or vowel. Here are some possible random words:

kobar
nigom
conan
zyypx
dufet

```
REM ** Word Maker **
' QBasic Made Easy, Chapter 7. Filename: WRDMKR01.BAS

REM ** Set up **
RANDOMIZE TIMER
consonant$ = "bcdfghjklmnpqrstvwxyz"        '21 consonants
vowel$ = "aeiouy"                           '6 vowels
CLS

REM ** DO...LOOP to make random words, ESC to exit **
DO

   BEEP: PRINT "Press a key for a word, ESC to quit"
   kbd$ = INPUT$(1): IF kbd$ = CHR$(27) THEN EXIT DO

   word$ = ""             'Start with the empty string ("")

   ' Add a consonant, vowel, consonant, vowel, consonant
   word$ = word$ + MID$(consonant$, INT(21 * RND) + 1, 1)
   word$ = word$ + MID$(vowel$, INT(6 * RND) + 1, 1)
   word$ = word$ + MID$(consonant$, INT(21 * RND) + 1, 1)
   word$ = word$ + MID$(vowel$, INT(6 * RND) + 1, 1)
   word$ = word$ + MID$(consonant$, INT(21 * RND) + 1, 1)

   ' Print the word
   PRINT "Your random 'cvcvc' word is: "; word$
   PRINT

LOOP
END
```

PROGRAM 7-1. Word Maker

Program WRDMKR01 uses MID$ to select random consonants from the value of *consonant$* and random vowels from the value of *vowel$*. The string variables *consonant$* and *vowel$* are assigned values during the setup block of the program.

The program line:

```
word$ = word$ + MID$(consonant$, INT(21 * RND) + 1, 1)
```

tells the computer to select one random letter from the value of *consonant$* and catenate (join) it to the value of *word$*. When used with strings, the plus sign (+) means catenate, or put together with, or attach to. The following MID$ function illustrates how this single letter is selected from *consonant$*:

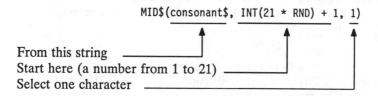

From this string
Start here (a number from 1 to 21)
Select one character

A similar program line selects a random vowel from *vowel$* and catenates it to the value of *word$*.

Here is a sample run:

```
Press a key for a word, ESC to quit
Your random 'cvcvc' word is: rudob

Press a key for a word, ESC to quit
Your random 'cvcvc' word is: cunan
```

When you run this program, the words generated will probably be different because the letters in the words are randomly selected. Press ESC to end the program.

Modify Program WRDMKR01 so that your new version prints random words of the form vccvcv. Examples of such words are athena, ursula, and othelo, although you probably won't see these when you run your program.

Modifying a program is a good way for you to make sure that you understand how the program works. The best way to learn how to program is to write programs and make them work. In programming, you can usually do things in more than one way. Try writing your own versions of programs that you see in this book.

The LEFT$ and RIGHT$ String Functions

You can think of the LEFT$ and RIGHT$ functions as specialized versions of the MID$ function. You can use LEFT$ to extract a substring from the left end of a string and RIGHT$ to obtain a substring from the right end of a string.

LEFT$ and RIGHT$ are both string functions of two arguments, a string argument followed by a numeric argument. Table 7-2 shows examples of both functions.

The value of LEFT$(*strng$, number*) is a string consisting of the leftmost *number* of characters of *strng$*. The value of RIGHT$(*strng$, number*) is a string consisting of the rightmost *number* of characters of *strng$*.

The following program uses LEFT$, RIGHT$, and MID$ to acquire a three-letter word and then prints it with the letters reversed.

```
CLS
DO
  INPUT "Enter a 3-letter word: ", wrd$
  rvrs$ = RIGHT$(wrd$, 1) + MID$(wrd$, 2, 1) + LEFT$(wrd$, 1)
  PRINT "The reverse word is:   "; rvrs$
  PRINT
LOOP
```

The sample run shown on the next page displays two *semordnilaps,* words whose reverses are also words:

Function	Value of function
LEFT$("abc", 1)	a
LEFT$("abc", 2)	ab
LEFT$("abc", 3)	abc
LEFT$("abc", 4)	abc
RIGHT$("abc", 1)	c
RIGHT$("abc", 2)	bc
RIGHT$("abc", 3)	abc
RIGHT$("abc", 4)	abc

TABLE 7-2.   Values of LEFT$ and RIGHT$ Functions

```
Enter a 3-letter word: pot
The reverse word is:    top

Enter a 3-letter word: won
The reverse word is:    now
```

ASCII CODES AND CHARACTERS

You can print many different characters on the screen. Some of these characters are visible on the keyboard, and you can use the keyboard to enter them. For example:

Uppercase letters	A	B	C	D
Lowercase letters	a	b	c	d
Digits	1	2	3	4
Punctuation	.	,	;	:
Special characters	@	#	$	*

There are also characters that you don't see on the keyboard. Some are shown here:

Card characters	♥	♦	♣	♠	
Greek letters	α	β	ε	π	Σ
Math symbols	√	±	≤	≡	≈
Graphics characters	⌐	⊥	╫	▐	

Every computer character has an *ASCII code*. An ASCII code is an integer in the range 0 to 255. ASCII stands for American Standard Code for Information Interchange. Here are some examples:

The ASCII code for A is 65
The ASCII code for B is 66

The ASCII code for a is 97
The ASCII code for b is 98
The ASCII code for * is 42
The ASCII code for ♥ is 3

You have probably guessed that the ASCII code for C is 67. For the uppercase letters A to Z, the ASCII codes are 65 to 90. For the lowercase letters "a" to "z," the ASCII codes are 97 to 122. Digits also have ASCII codes; the codes for the digits 0 to 9 are 48 to 57. ASCII codes from 128 to 255 are codes for special characters, such as foreign alphabets, graphics characters, and math symbols.

The CHR$ String Function

You can use the CHR$ string function to print ASCII characters on the screen. CHR$ is a string function of a numeric argument. The argument must be an ASCII code, an integer in the range 0 to 255. The value returned by CHR$ is the one-character string that corresponds to the ASCII code. See Appendix B for a list of ASCII codes and characters.

You can use Program 7-2, ASCII01 (ASCII Codes and Characters with CHR$ String Function), to print lots of ASCII codes and characters on the

```
REM ** ASCII Codes and Characters with CHR$ String Function **
' QBasic Made Easy, Chapter 7. Filename: ASCII01.BAS

REM ** Enter ASCII code range values **
CLS
INPUT "First ASCII code"; FirstCode
INPUT "Last ASCII code "; LastCode

REM ** Print characters and end **
CLS
FOR ascii = FirstCode TO LastCode
  PRINT ascii; CHR$(ascii); SPACE$(2);
  IF (ascii - FirstCode + 1) MOD 10 = 0 THEN PRINT : PRINT
NEXT ascii
END
```

═══════ **PROGRAM 7-2.** ASCII Codes and Characters with CHR$ String
Function

screen. You enter the first ASCII code and last ASCII code. The program then prints all ASCII codes and corresponding characters from your first code to your last code. Code and character pairs are printed ten to a line, and the lines are double spaced. Figure 7-6 is a sample run showing 100 codes and characters, from ASCII code 128 to ASCII code 227.

The program line:

```
PRINT ascii; CHR$(ascii); SPACE$(2);
```

prints the ASCII code (value of *ascii*), the ASCII character (value of CHR$(*ascii*), and two spaces. The value of *ascii* is printed with a leading and a trailing space. SPACE$ is a string function of a numeric argument. SPACE$(2) creates two spaces, which are then printed.

The program line:

```
IF (ascii - FirstCode + 1) MOD 10 = 0 THEN PRINT : PRINT
```

```
128 Ç  129 ü  130 é  131 â  132 ä  133 à  134 å  135 ç  136 ê  137 ë

138 è  139 ï  140 î  141 ì  142 Ä  143 Å  144 É  145 æ  146 Æ  147 ô

148 ö  149 ò  150 û  151 ù  152 ÿ  153 Ö  154 Ü  155 ¢  156 £  157 ¥

158 ₧  159 ƒ  160 á  161 í  162 ó  163 ú  164 ñ  165 Ñ  166 ª  167 º

168 ¿  169 ⌐  170 ¬  171 ½  172 ¼  173 ¡  174 «  175 »  176 ░  177 ▒

178 ▓  179 │  180 ┤  181 ╡  182 ╢  183 ╖  184 ╕  185 ╣  186 ║  187 ╗

188 ╝  189 ╜  190 ╛  191 ┐  192 └  193 ┴  194 ┬  195 ├  196 ─  197 ┼

198 ╞  199 ╟  200 ╚  201 ╔  202 ╩  203 ╦  204 ╠  205 ═  206 ╬  207 ╧

208 ╨  209 ╤  210 ╥  211 ╙  212 ╘  213 ╒  214 ╓  215 ╫  216 ╪  217 ┘

218 ┌  219 █  220 ▄  221 ▌  222 ▐  223 ▀  224 α  225 ß  226 Γ  227 π



Press any key to continue
```

FIGURE 7-6. ASCII codes and characters printed by Program ASCII01

causes two empty PRINT statements to occur after every ten pairs of codes and characters. This prints the lines double spaced so that you can read them easily. For the run shown in Figure 7-6, the value of *FirstCode* is 128 and the value of *ascii* runs from 128 to 227. The condition, (*ascii* − *FirstCode* + 1) MOD 10 = 0, is true for *ascii* = 137, 147, 157, and so on, up to 227.

The ASC Numeric Function

The ASC function is just the opposite of the CHR$ function. ASC is a numeric function of a string argument. ASC returns the ASCII code of a character. For example, ASC("A") is 65, and ASC("*") is 42. If the argument consists of two or more characters, the ASC function returns the ASCII code of the first character. For example, ASC("ABC") is 65, and ASC("abc") is 97. Note that ASC("") is illegal and causes an error. There is no ASCII code for the empty string.

Use the following program to print on the screen the ASCII codes of characters that you type on the keyboard:

```
CLS
DO
   INPUT "Enter a character: ", character$
   PRINT "The ASCII code is:"; ASC(character$) : PRINT
LOOP
```

Figure 7-7 shows an annotated run of the program. Entering the first two characters (a and A) is easy. However, it is a little more difficult to enter the tiny face (☺), the graphics character (╬), and the Greek letter pi (π). To type these characters, you use the ALT key with the numeric keypad on the right side of the keyboard.

To enter the tiny face (☺), hold down the ALT key, type **1** on the numeric keypad, and then release the ALT key. You should see the tiny face on the screen. If not, use BACKSPACE to erase any incorrect character and try again. When you see the tiny face, press ENTER.

To enter the graphics character (╬), hold down the ALT key, type **206** on the numeric keypad, and then release the ALT key. Press ENTER.

To enter the Greek letter pi (π), hold down the ALT key, type **227** on the numeric keypad, and then release the ALT key. Press ENTER.

In general, to display any ASCII character on the screen, hold down the ALT key, type the character's ASCII code on the numeric keypad, and then

```
Enter a character: a
The ASCII code is: 97

Enter a character: A
The ASCII code is: 65

Enter a character: ☺              (ALT-1 was pressed)
The ASCII code is: 1

Enter a character: ╬              (ALT-206 was pressed)
The ASCII code is: 206

Enter a character: π              (ALT-227 was pressed)
The ASCII code is: 227

Enter a character: _
```

FIGURE 7-7. ASCII codes for characters entered from the keyboard

release the ALT key. Try this with ASCII codes in the range 128 to 255, or the range 0 to 31. Some of the codes in the range 0 to 31 are nonprinting characters and will not display a character.

The STRING$ String Function

STRING$ is a string function of two numeric arguments or a numeric argument followed by a string argument. The value returned is a string of up to 255 characters, all the same character. Here are two ways to print a string of 23 asterisks (*). The ASCII code for the asterisk is 42.

```
PRINT STRING$(23, 42)

PRINT STRING$(23, "*")
```

The first argument is numeric and specifies the length of the value of STRING$ (the number of characters). The second argument can be string or numeric. It can be a single character or the ASCII code of a character. The value returned by STRING$ is this character repeated the number of times specified by the first argument.

For a colorful demonstration of the STRING$ function, run the following program:

```
CLS
FOR kolor = 1 TO 15
  COLOR kolor
  PRINT STRING$(80, 219);
NEXT kolor
```

The program displays color bars across the screen in the 15 colors numbered 1 through 15. Each color bar is 80 characters long, using the character whose ASCII code is 219—a solid block.

THE STR$ AND VAL FUNCTIONS

STR$ is a string function of a numeric argument; VAL is a numeric function of a string argument. These functions are opposites of each other. You use STR$ to obtain a string that corresponds to a number and VAL to obtain a number that corresponds to a string. Some values of the VAL numeric function are shown here:

Function	Value
VAL("123456789")	123456789
VAL("1E15")	1000000000000000
VAL("1E16")	1D+16
VAL("123abc")	123
VAL("abc123")	0

In these examples, note the following:

- The value of VAL is a double-precision number. If the value has more than 16 digits, it is printed as a floating-point number.

- If the string contains nonnumeric characters (such as "123abc"), VAL returns any number that appears on the left end of the string. If the first character of the string is nonnumeric, VAL returns 0.

Here are some examples of the STR$ string function. The value returned by the STR$ function is enclosed in quotation marks to remind you that it is a string.

Function	Value
STR$(123)	" 123"
STR$(-123.45)	"-123.45"
STR$(1E6)	" 1000000"

In these examples, note the following:

- The value returned by STR$ includes a leading space for nonnegative numbers or a minus sign (−) for negative numbers. For an integer argument, the length of the value of STR$ is one more than the number of digits in the argument.

- If the argument has a decimal point, it appears as a character in the value of STR$. The length of STR$(−123.45) is seven characters, two more than the number of digits in the argument.

The single-precision floating-point number, 1E6, was printed in ordinary notation. However, try 1E7 or 1E8 and see what happens. Also try numbers with more than seven digits and double-precision floating-point numbers such as 1D16.

Both VAL and STR$ appear in Program 7-3, SUMDGT01 (Sum of Digits of a Long Integer). This program computes and prints the sum of the digits of a long integer entered from the keyboard.

Following is a sample run:

```
Integer, please? 123456789
Sum of digits:  45

Integer, please? -123456789
Sum of digits:  45
```

Note that the sum of the digits is nonnegative even when the number entered is negative. Modify the program so that it will work for double-precision numbers that are integers or nonintegers.

```
REM ** Sum of Digits of a Long Integer **
' QBasic Made Easy, Chapter 7. Filename: SUMDGT02.BAS

REM ** Get number, add digits, and print result **
CLS
DO
  INPUT "Integer, please"; number&            'Long integer
  NmbrStrng$ = STR$(number&)                  'Change to a string

  SumDigits% = 0                              'Set sum to zero

  'Compute the sum of the digits, then print it
  FOR k% = 2 TO LEN(NmbrStrng$)
    SumDigits% = SumDigits% + VAL(MID$(NmbrStrng$, k%, 1))
  NEXT k%

  PRINT "Sum of digits: "; SumDigits%
  PRINT
LOOP
END
```

PROGRAM 7-3. Sum of Digits of a Long Integer

THE INSTR NUMERIC FUNCTION

INSTR is a numeric function of two string arguments. INSTR returns a numeric value that depends on whether the second argument is a substring of the first argument. If not, the value of INSTR is 0; if there is a match, the value of INSTR is the position in the first argument where the second argument matches. Table 7-3 shows values of INSTR for several pairs of arguments. INSTR appears in Program 7-4, RAINBOW1 (Rainbow Color Quiz).

Program RAINBOW1 is a simple quiz about the colors in a rainbow. You can enter the name of a color in any mixture of lowercase and uppercase letters. A sample run is shown here:

```
Enter a rainbow color: green
Yes, green is in my rainbow.

Enter a rainbow color: GREEN
Yes, GREEN is in my rainbow.

Enter a rainbow color: hot pink
Sorry, hot pink is not in my rainbow.
```

INSTR("abc","a") is 1	Match at position 1 of first argument
INSTR("abc","b") is 2	Match at position 2 of first argument
INSTR("abc","c") is 3	Match at position 3 of first argument
INSTR("abc","*") is 0	No match; no asterisk in first argument
INSTR("abc","A") is 0	No match; no A in first argument
INSTR("abc","ab") is 1	Match at position 1 of first argument
INSTR("abc","bc") is 2	Match at position 2 of first argument
INSTR("abc","abc") is 1	Match at first position of first argument
INSTR("ab","abc") is 0	No match; abc is not in first argument

TABLE 7-3. Values of INSTR for Several Pairs of Arguments

```
REM ** Rainbow Color Quiz **
' QBasic Made Easy, Chapter 7. Filename: RAINBOW1.BAS

REM ** Set up **
rainbow$ = "red orange yellow green blue violet"
CLS

REM ** Get a color and tell if correct **
DO
  INPUT "Enter a rainbow color: ", kolor$
  LookFor$ = LCASE$(kolor$)

  IF INSTR(rainbow$, LookFor$) <> 0 THEN
    PRINT "Yes, "; kolor$; " is in my rainbow."
  ELSE PRINT "Sorry, "; kolor$; " is not in my rainbow."
  END IF

  PRINT
LOOP
END
```

PROGRAM 7-4. Rainbow Color Quiz

USER-DEFINED FUNCTIONS

You can design your own user-defined functions and use them in the same ways that you use built-in functions. In this section, you will learn how to name, define, and use single-line user-defined functions. Later in this chapter you will learn how to name, define, and use multiline user-defined functions.

User-Defined Numeric Functions Without Arguments

To define and name your own function, use the DEF FN statement. Here is a user-defined function to "roll" one six-sided die (D6). This function, which does not have an argument, returns a random integer in the range 1 to 6.

```
DEF FNrollD6 = INT(6 * RND) + 1
```

The name of this function is FNrollD6. The name of a user-defined function always begins with FN. You may choose the part of the name following FN. The function name (FNrollD6) is followed by an equal sign (=) and a numeric expression (INT(6 * RND) + 1) that defines the function. The elements of this function definition are shown here:

```
DEF FNrollD6 = INT(6 * RND) + 1
```

Name of function   Equal sign   Definition of function

In Program 7-5, DICE01 (Roll Two Six-sided Dice (2D6)), the function FNrollD6 is called twice. Since the function must be defined before it can be used, the definition of the function appears near the beginning of the program.

In the following sample run, a key other than ESC was pressed twice to get two simulated rolls of two dice. The computer is waiting for another key-press.

```
REM ** Roll Two Six-Sided Dice (2D6) **
' QBasic Made Easy, Chapter 7. Filename: DICE01.BAS

REM ** Define FNroll D6, a function to 'roll' one die **
DEF FNroll D6 = INT(6 * RND) + 1

REM ** Set up **
RANDOMIZE TIMER
CLS

REM ** DO...LOOP to roll dice.  Press ESC to quit **
DO
  BEEP: PRINT "Press a key to roll, or ESC to quit"
  kbd$ = INPUT$(1): IF kbd$ = CHR$(27) THEN END
  PRINT "The roll is"; FNroll D6 + FNroll D6
  PRINT
LOOP
END
```

══════════ **PROGRAM 7-5.**   Roll Two Six-Sided Dice (2D6)

```
Press a key to roll, or ESC to quit
The roll is 6

Press a key to roll, or ESC to quit
The roll is 11

Press a key to roll, or ESC to quit
```

Press ESC to end the program.

Of course, you could define a function to simulate the rolling of two dice and then use it only once in your program. Modify the program to use the function FNroll2D6, shown here:

```
DEF FNRoll2D6 = INT(6 * RND) + INT(6 * RND) + 2
```

In role-playing games, such as *Dungeons & Dragons,* you might roll three six-sided dice several times to create a character to play in the game. The function FNroll3D6, which simulates rolling three six-sided dice, is defined here:

```
DEF FNRoll3D6 = INT(6 * RND) + INT(6 * RND) + INT(6 * RND) + 3
```

The functions FNrollD6, FNroll2D6, and FNroll3D6 are all single-precision numeric functions, even though their values are small integers. You can define them as integer or long integer functions by appending the appropriate type designator (% or &) to the function name. For example, the following are integer functions:

```
DEF FNrollD6% = INT(6 * RND) + 1
DEF FNroll2D6% = INT(6 * RND) + INT(6 * RND) + 2
DEF FNroll3D6% = INT(6 * RND) + INT(6 * RND) + INT(6 * RND) + 3
```

User-Defined String Functions Without Arguments

You can define a string function in much the same way that you define a numeric function. In a DEF FN statement, you write the name of the function, followed by an equal sign (=), followed by a string expression. The name of a string function must end in a dollar sign ($).

The function FNflip$, defined next, returns the value H or T, randomly selected. You can use it to simulate flipping a coin.

```
DEF FNflip$ = MID$("HT", INT(2 * RND) + 1, 1)
```

The FNFLIP$ function appears in Program 7-6, COIN01 (Flip a Fair Coin). Press a key other than ESC to simulate flipping a coin, or press ESC to quit. A sample run of Program COIN01 is shown here:

```
Press a key to flip, or ESC to quit
The flip is T

Press a key to flip, or ESC to quit
The flip is H

Press a key to flip, or ESC to quit
The flip is H
```

It is easy to define a function to simulate flipping an unfair coin. The following function returns H about 60% of the time and T about 40% of the time:

```
DEF FNflip$ = MID$("HHHTT", INT(5 * RND) + 1, 1)
```

```
REM ** Flip a Fair Coin **
' QBasic Made Easy, Chapter 7. Filename: COIN01.BAS

REM ** Define FNflip$, a string function to 'flip' one coin **
' Returns a string, "H" or "T", equally probable
DEF FNflip$ = MID$("HT", INT(2 * RND) + 1, 1)

REM ** Set up **
RANDOMIZE TIMER
CLS

REM ** DO...LOOP to flip coin.  Press ESC to quit **
DO
  BEEP: PRINT "Press a key to flip, or ESC to quit"
  kbd$ = INPUT$(1): IF kbd$ = CHR$(27) THEN END
  PRINT "The flip is "; FNflip$
  PRINT
LOOP
END
```

═══ **PROGRAM 7-6.** Flip a Fair Coin

The function FNLttr$ returns a random lowercase letter, any letter from "a" to "z." It appears in the first line of the following program, which prints random letters in random colors at random places on the screen:

```
DEF FNLttr$ = CHR$(INT(26 * RND) + 97)
RANDOMIZE TIMER: CLS
DO UNTIL INKEY$ = CHR$(27)
  COLOR FIX(15 * RND) + 1
  LOCATE FIX(24 * RND) + 1, FIX(80 * RND) + 1
  PRINT FNLttr$;
LOOP
```

Press ESC to stop the program.

You can modify the FNLttr$ function so that it returns an uppercase letter from A to Z. Also, try your hand at defining a function called FNchar$. This function should return random characters whose ASCII codes are in the range 123 to 254, inclusive. See Appendix B, "ASCII Codes," to see what these characters look like.

User-Defined Numeric Functions with Arguments

The user-defined functions that you have seen so far do not require arguments. You can also define functions that have arguments. As with built-in functions, the argument is enclosed in parentheses following the name of the function. The function FNran, shown next, is a function of one numeric argument, *n*. The value of FNran(*n*) is a random integer in the range 1 to *n*.

```
DEF FNran(n) = INT(n * RND) + 1
```

The argument *n* is a *local variable;* that is, the value of *n* has no meaning outside of the function definition. You may use *n* as a variable name elsewhere in the program without affecting its use as an argument name in the definition of FNran. The name for the argument (*n*) is chosen arbitrarily. You can replace *n* on both sides of the equal sign with any name, and the function will still operate as defined and will still produce the same result. For example:

```
DEF FNran(range) = INT(range * RND) + 1
```

Program 7-7, DRILL01 (Multiplication Drill), presents simple multiplication problems. The FNran function is used to obtain values of *a* and *b*. Each value is a random integer in the range 1 to 9. The sample run shown here shows a correct answer and an incorrect answer:

```
REM ** Multiplication Drill **
' QBasic Made Easy, Chapter 7. Filename: DRILL01.BAS

REM ** Set up **
DEF FNran (n) = INT(n * RND) + 1    'Random integer, 1 to n
RANDOMIZE TIMER: CLS

REM ** Present problems **
DO
  a = FNran(9)
  b = FNran(9)
  PRINT a; "x"; b; "= "; : INPUT answer
  IF answer = a * b THEN
    PRINT "Correct.  Good work!!!"
  ELSE PRINT "Oops.  The answer is"; a * b
  END IF
  PRINT
LOOP
END
```

PROGRAM 7-7. Multiplication Drill

```
 7 x 2 = ? 14
Correct.  Good work!!!

 4 x 9 = ? 38
Oops.  The answer is 36
```

A user-defined function can have more than one argument. The FNhyp function, defined next, computes the length of the hypotenuse of a right triangle, given the lengths of the other two sides, *a* and *b,* as arguments:

```
DEF FNhyp (a, b) = SQR(a ^ 2 + b ^ 2)
```

When a function has more than one argument, the arguments are separated by commas, as just shown. The FNran% function, shown next, is an integer function of two integer arguments, *Lo%* and *Hi%*:

```
DEF FNran% (Lo%, Hi%) = INT((Hi% - Lo% + 1) * RND) + Lo%
```

It returns random integers in the range *Lo%* to *Hi%,* inclusive. For example, if *Lo%* is 5 and *Hi%* is 10, then FNran% generates randomly one of the following integers: 5, 6, 7, 8, 9, 10.

User-Defined String Functions with Arguments

The FNranchr$ function, defined next, is a string function of a string argument. The value of FNranchr$ is a single character selected at random from its argument.

```
DEF FNranchr$ (s$) = MID$(s$, INT(LEN(s$) * RND) + 1, 1)
```

This definition uses the LEN function. LEN is a numeric function of a string argument. Its value is the number of characters, including spaces (if any), in a string argument. For example, LEN("abc") is 3, and LEN("a b c") is 5.

You can use FNranchr$ to select a random character from any string. Just use the string as the argument of FNranchr$. For example, perhaps the following program can write the great American novel, if you run it billions of times and do a great job of editing:

```
DEF FNranchr$ (s$) = MID$(s$, INT(LEN(s$) * RND) + 1, 1)
RANDOMIZE TIMER: CLS
alphabet$ = SPACE$(12) + "aaabcdeeefghiiijklmnooopqrstuuuvwxyz"
FOR k = 1 TO 1000
  PRINT FNranchr$(alphabet$);
NEXT k
```

Here is a different FNranchr$ function. It returns a random character defined by two numeric arguments, *Lo%* and *Hi%*. These arguments are ASCII codes for the "lowest" and "highest" possible characters.

```
DEF FNranchr$ (Lo%, Hi%) = CHR$(INT((Hi% - Lo% + 1) * RND) + Lo%)
```

This line defines FNranchr$ as a string function of two integer arguments, *Lo%* and *Hi%*. The first argument must be less than or equal to the second argument, and both arguments must be in the range for ASCII codes, 0 to 255.

Multiline User-Defined Functions

QBasic has two more ways to define functions. One is the FUNCTION ... END FUNCTION procedure, which is discussed in Chapter 8. The other is the multiline DEF FN ... END DEF function definition.

DEF FN ... END DEF evolved from the single-line DEF FN statement. It provides a way to define more complex function definitions that cannot be squeezed into a single line. Therefore, it is much more powerful than the single-line function definition.

A multiline function begins with a DEF FN statement, ends with an END DEF statement, and can have any number of lines between. Program 7-8, WRDMKR02 (Word Maker with Multiline Functions), has two multiline functions, FNc$ and FNv$. FNc$ returns a random consonant; FNv$ returns a random vowel.

The definition of FNv$ is shown here:

```
DEF FNv$
  ' Returns a random lowercase vowel
  vowel$ = "aeiou"
```

```
  ranvowel$ = MID$(vowel$, INT(5 * RND) + 1, 1)
  FNv$ = ranvowel$
END DEF
```

The first line is a DEF FN statement that contains the name of the function. The last line is an END DEF statement. In between are the lines that define the function and assign it as the value of FNv$.

```
REM ** Word Maker with Multiline Functions **
' QBasic Made Easy, Chapter 7. Filename: WRDMKR02.BAS

REM ** Define functions **
DEF FNc$
  ' Returns a random lowercase consonant
  consonant$ = "bcdfghjklmnpqrstvwxyz"
  rancon$ = MID$(consonant$, INT(21 * RND) + 1, 1)
  FNc$ = rancon$
END DEF

DEF FNv$
  ' Returns a random lowercase vowel
  vowel$ = "aeiou"
  ranvowel$ = MID$(vowel$, INT(5 * RND) + 1, 1)
  FNv$ = ranvowel$
END DEF

REM ** Set up **
RANDOMIZE TIMER: CLS

REM ** DO...LOOP to make random words, ESC to exit **
DO
  BEEP: PRINT "Press a key for a word, ESC to quit"
  kbd$ = INPUT$(1): IF kbd$ = CHR$(27) THEN EXIT DO

  word$ = FNc$ + FNv$ + FNc$ + FNv$ + FNc$

  PRINT "Your random 'cvcvc' word is: "; word$
  PRINT
LOOP
END
```

PROGRAM 7-8. Word Maker with Multiline Functions

The program line:

```
FNv$ = ranvowel$
```

assigns the value of *ranvowel$* as the value of the function. Every multiline defined function must have a statement of this type to actually define the value returned by the function. Enter and run Program WRDMKR02. Figure 7-8 shows a sample run.

If a multiline defined function requires an argument, the argument appears in the DEF FN statement, enclosed in quotation marks following the name of the function. Program 7-9, DICE02 (Demonstrate FNnD6% Multiline Defined Function), demonstrates a multiline defined function of one argument. A sample run is shown here:

6	12	7	9	7
12	7	11	12	15

The program line

```
DEF FNnD6% (n%)
```

```
Press a key for a word, ESC to quit
Your random 'cvcvc' word is: larey

Press a key for a word, ESC to quit
Your random 'cvcvc' word is: novef

Press a key for a word, ESC to quit
Your random 'cvcvc' word is: quqer

Press a key for a word, ESC to quit
Your random 'cvcvc' word is: kawon

Press a key for a word, ESC to quit
Your random 'cvcvc' word is: nipex

Press a key for a word, ESC to quit
Your random 'cvcvc' word is: vajov

Press a key for a word, ESC to quit
```

FIGURE 7-8. Output of Program WRDMKR02

```
REM ** Demonstrate FNnD6% Multiline Defined Function **
' QBasic Made Easy, Chapter 7. Filename: DICE02.BAS

REM ** FNnD6% is an integer function of an integer argument **
DEF FNnD6% (n%)
  ' Simulates rolling n 6-sided dice (nD6)
  DiceTotal% = 0
  FOR die% = 1 TO n%
    DiceTotal% = DiceTotal% + INT(6 * RND) + 1
  NEXT die%
  FNnD6% = DiceTotal%
END DEF

REM ** Roll 3D6 10 times **
RANDOMIZE TIMER: CLS
FOR k% = 1 TO 10
  PRINT FNnD6%(3),
NEXT k%
END
```

PROGRAM 7-9.   Demonstrate FNnD6% Multiline Defined Function

defines FNnD6% as an *integer* function of one *integer* argument. Both the function name and the argument end with the integer designator (%).

The program line

```
FNnD6% = DiceTotal%
```

assigns the value of *DiceTotal%* as the value of the function. Every multiline defined function must have a statement of this type that assigns the value to the name of the function.

RELAX WITH WORDSWORTH

This has been a long chapter, containing many new ideas and many programs. Now take some time for a recreational activity called Wordsworth. Assign a letter score to each letter of the alphabet, A through Z, as follows:

A=1	B=2	C=3	D=4	E=5	F=6	G=7
H=8	I=9	J=10	K=11	L=12	M=13	N=14
O=15	P=16	Q=17	R=18	S=19	T=20	U=21
V=22	W=23	X=24	Y=25	Z=26		

For any dictionary word you choose, compute two numbers, called *Wordsworth* + and *Wordsworth* *, as follows.

Wordsworth + is the numerical value of a word, obtained by adding the letter scores of all the letters in the word. For example:

hobbit is worth 8 + 15 + 2 + 2 + 9 + 20 = 56 points
dragon is worth 4 + 18 + 1 + 7 + 15 + 14 = 59 points

Wordsworth * is the numerical value of a word, obtained by multiplying the letter scores of all the letters in the word. For example:

hobbit is worth 8 * 15 * 2 * 2 * 9 * 20 = 86,400 points
dragon is worth 4 * 18 * 1 * 7 * 15 * 14 = 105,840 points

In other words, *Wordsworth* + is the sum of the letter scores of all the letters in a word; *Wordsworth* * is the product of the letter scores of all the letters in a word. You can use Program 7-10, WRDWRTH1 (Wordsworth), to compute and print *Wordsworth* + and *Wordsworth* * for a word entered from the keyboard. Figure 7-9 is an annotated run of Program WRDWRTH1. Note that words can be entered in all uppercase letters, all lowercase letters, or a mixture of both. The program ignores characters that are not letters.

Use Program WRDWRTH1 to help you answer one or more of the following questions. An answer must be a real dictionary word.

1. What three-letter word has the smallest *Wordsworth* +? Or *Wordsworth* *? Four-letter word?

2. What three-letter word has the largest *Wordsworth* +? Or *Wordsworth* *? Four-letter word?

3. What is the first word (alphabetically) to have a *Wordsworth* + of exactly 100? *Wordsworth* * of exactly 100?

4. What is the last word (alphabetically) to have a *Wordsworth* + of exactly 100? *Wordsworth* * of exactly 100?

5. In the entire dictionary, what word has the largest *Wordsworth* +? Or *Wordsworth* *?

6. What is the longest word (most letters) that has a *Wordsworth* + equal to the number of weeks in a year?

7. What word has a *Wordsworth* * closest to 1 million? The value can be less than 1 million or greater than 1 million.

Most of the work and play in answering these questions is people play: browsing through a dictionary, thinking about what to do, creating strategies—most enjoyable! People do this well. Some of the work, such as looking up letter scores and calculating, is tedious. Let the computer do those tasks.

```
To quit, press ENTER without first typing a word.

Your word? dragon        Word entered in all lowercase letters
Wordsworth + is 59
Wordsworth * is 105840

To quit, press ENTER without first typing a word.

Your word? DRAGON        Word entered in all uppercase letters
Wordsworth + is 59
Wordsworth * is 105840

To quit, press ENTER without first typing a word.

Your word? Dragon        Word entered in mixture of upper- and
Wordsworth + is 59        lowercase
Wordsworth * is 105840

To quit, press ENTER without first typing a word.

Your word? R2D2          Characters other than letters are
Wordsworth + is 22        ignored
Wordsworth * is 72
```

FIGURE 7-9.   An annotated run of Program WRDWRTH1

```
REM ** Wordsworth **
' QBasic Made Easy, Chapter 7. Filename: WRDWRTH1.BAS

REM ** Define Wordsworth + function, FNWWsum% **
DEF FNWWsum% (word$)
' Returns sum of letter scores (a = 1, b = 2, c = 3,...)
  sum% = 0
  FOR k% = 1 TO LEN(word$)
    Lttr$ = MID$(word$, k%, 1)
    IF Lttr$ >= "a" AND Lttr$ <= "z" THEN
      sum% = sum% + ASC(Lttr$) - 96
    END IF
  NEXT k%
  FNWWsum% = sum%
END DEF

REM ** Define Wordsworth * function, FNWWproduct# **
DEF FNWWproduct# (word$)
' Returns product of letter scores (a = 1, b = 2, c = 3, ...)
  product# = 1
  FOR k% = 1 TO LEN(word$)
    Lttr$ = MID$(word$, k%, 1)
    IF Lttr$ >= "a" AND Lttr$ <= "z" THEN
      product# = product# * (ASC(Lttr$) - 96)
    END IF
    FNWWproduct# = product#
  NEXT k%
END DEF

REM ** Get words, compute & print Wordsworths **
CLS
DO
  PRINT "To quit, press ENTER without first typing a word."
  PRINT
  INPUT "Your word"; word$
  IF word$ = "" THEN END                'END if empty string
  word$ = LCASE$(word$)
  PRINT "Wordsworth + is"; FNWWsum%(word$)
  PRINT "Wordsworth * is"; FNWWproduct#(word$)
  PRINT
LOOP
END
```

PROGRAM 7-10. Wordsworth

SUMMARY

QBasic has a rich repertoire of built-in functions and also allows you to create your own user-defined functions. When a function is used, a value is returned that is the result computed by the function. A string function returns a string value, and a numeric function returns a numeric value. Some functions require arguments; others do not.

- INKEY$, TIMER, and RND are examples of built-in QBasic functions that do not require arguments.

- FIX, INT, ABS, SGN, and SQR are built-in QBasic numeric functions that require arguments.

- INPUT$, LCASE$, UCASE$, MID$, LEFT$, and RIGHT$ are built-in QBasic string functions that require arguments.

ASC, CHR$, and STRING$ are built-in functions that use ASCII codes. STR$ and VAL are built-in functions that convert a string to number (VAL) or a number to a string (STR$). INSTR is a built-in function that returns a numeric value that depends on whether or not one string is a substring of another. All of these functions require arguments.

You can also define your own functions, with one or more arguments or without arguments. Such functions are called user-defined functions and begin with the keyword DEF. The function is assigned a name in the definition and is equated to an expression. The function's name must begin with the letters FN, as follows:

DEF FNname = expression

User-defined functions of this form are single-line functions.
Multiline functions use another form:

DEF FNname(argument list)
    .
    .   (Block of statements)
    .
    FNname = expression   (Assigns value to the function)
    END DEF

Multiline functions may have zero, one, or more arguments. The function's name (string or numeric) must match the type of value returned (string or numeric).

FUNCTION AND SUB
PROCEDURES

A QBasic program consists of one or more *modules*. Every QBasic program has a module called the *main program*. The main program contains the program's *entry point* — the place at which execution of the program begins.

As your programs become longer and more complex, you will want to develop general procedures that you can use in more than one program. In this chapter, you will learn:

- To use two types of QBasic procedures: FUNCTION and SUB

- To divide long, complex programs into several small parts

You can save these general-purpose procedures and build a library. Then you can use the copy and paste techniques of Chapter 6, "Editing and Dynamic Debugging," to copy the procedures from the library and paste them into other programs as needed.

Complex problems often require large programs. However, you can break up large problems into a series of small, simple subproblems. It is easier to write a complex program if you divide it into several small parts. Your programs are then *structured* into a series of small modules. Structured programs have a modular design and use only looping structures and structures that provide sequence and selection.

Using small modules makes your programs easy to read and modify. Each of these modules should perform a single, well-defined task. Your main program then becomes a traffic director to tell the computer which module to execute and when to execute it. The main program also provides the details for the more general modules.

Program modules should be as independent of each other as possible. QBasic has structures that allow you to write such modules. These modules are called procedures, defined by FUNCTION...END FUNCTION or SUB...END SUB. QBasic organizes these modules alphabetically and keeps them separate from the rest of the program.

QBASIC PROCEDURES

A *procedure* is either

- A function defined by a FUNCTION...END FUNCTION statement pair, or
- A subprogram defined by a SUB...END SUB statement pair

FUNCTION and SUB procedures are a part of a QBasic program but are external to the main program. You can look at the main part of a program (the main program) in the View window, or you can look at a FUNCTION or SUB in the View window. You can even split the View window into two parts and see two modules of a program at the same time. You can select what is seen in the View window from the View menu, as you will see later in this chapter.

You enter a new FUNCTION or SUB procedure from the Edit menu. Once they are entered, these procedures are accessible from the View menu.

FUNCTION PROCEDURES

A FUNCTION...END FUNCTION procedure is similar to the DEF FN...END DEF function discussed in Chapter 7, "Function Junction." However, a FUNCTION has a number of advantages over the older style

DEF FN function definition structure. Four of the major benefits of programming with FUNCTION . . . END FUNCTION are listed here:

- You can break your programs into discrete logical units. You can test and correct each unit more easily than you can an entire program that does not use such procedures.

- Once a FUNCTION has been debugged (tested and corrected), you can use it as a building block in programs other than the one in which it was created.

- Programs using procedures are generally more reliable than those that do not because a procedure has one and only one entry point and because any variables declared inside them are, by default, local to that particular procedure.

- Complete arrays (discussed in Chapter 10, "Arrays") may be passed to a FUNCTION procedure.

A FUNCTION procedure begins with the keyword FUNCTION followed by its name and an optional parameter list containing the variables to be passed from the main program to the FUNCTION. The FUNCTION is then defined by a block of statements that describe the steps to be performed. The result is then assigned to the name of the FUNCTION so that it can be passed back to the main program. A FUNCTION ends with the keywords END FUNCTION.

The Roll Dice FUNCTION

In Chapter 7, "Function Junction," you used the multiline DEF FN to simulate rolling a number of six-sided dice. This DEF FN is repeated here:

```
DEF FNnD6% (n%)
  ' Simulates rolling n 6-sided dice (nD6)
  DiceTotal% = 0
  FOR die% = 1 to n%
    DiceTotal% = DiceTotal% + INT(6 * RND) + 1
  NEXT die%
  FNnD6% = DiceTotal%
END DEF
```

This DEF FN was used in Program DICE02 (FNnD6% Multiline Defined Function). You will now convert that program to one that uses a FUNCTION procedure.

First, select the New option from the File menu and enter the following lines, which compose the main program:

```
REM ** Demonstrate FNnD6% FUNCTION Procedure **
' QBasic Made Easy, Chapter 8.  Filename: DICE03.BAS

REM ** Roll 3D6 10 times **
RANDOMIZE TIMER: CLS
FOR k% = 1 TO 10
   PRINT nD6%(3),              'call the FUNCTION
NEXT k%
END
```

That's all there is to the main program. Notice that you call the FUNCTION by using its name in the PRINT statement. Only one value can be returned from a FUNCTION to the main program that called it. That value is assigned to nD6%(3) in the FUNCTION procedure.

Entering the Roll Dice FUNCTION

Now add the FUNCTION procedure. First, access the Edit menu and move the highlight down to the New FUNCTION. . . option, as shown here:

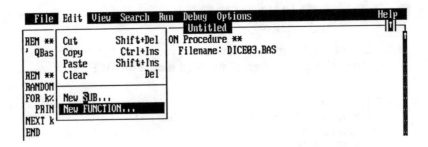

With the highlight on New FUNCTION,

Press: ENTER

```
 File  Edit  View  Search  Run  Debug  Options                    Help
                         Untitled
REM ** Demonstrate nD6% FUNCTION Procedure **
' QBasic Made Easy, Chapter 8.  Filename: DICE03.BAS

REM ** Roll 3D6 10 times **
RANDOMIZE TIMER: CLS
FOR k% = 1 TO 10
   PRINT n6%(3)        ┌─────── New FUNCTION ───────┐
NEXT k%                │                            │
END                    │ Name: _                    │
                       │                            │
                       │                            │
                       │  < OK >  < Cancel >  < Help > │
                       └────────────────────────────┘




                         ──── Immediate ────
 F1=Help   Enter=Execute   Esc=Cancel   Tab=Next Field   Arrow=Next Item
```

FIGURE 8-1. The New FUNCTION dialog box

The New FUNCTION dialog box appears, as shown by the screen in
Figure 8-1. The cursor is blinking in the Name box under the New FUNC-
TION title. The computer is waiting for you to name the FUNCTION.

Type: **nD6%**
and press ENTER

The main program is cleared from the View window and is replaced by
the first and last lines of the New FUNCTION, as shown here:

```
 File  Edit  View  Search  Run  Debug  Options                    Help
                        Untitled:nD6
FUNCTION nD6%_
END FUNCTION
```

Notice the title under the menu bar. It shows the title of the main
program and the title of the FUNCTION currently in the View window:

```
Untitled:  nD6
```

Main program   FUNCTION

Since you haven't named the main program yet, it is temporarily called "Untitled." The title shown for the FUNCTION is "nD6." Notice that QBasic does not include the type declaration character (%) in the name of nD6 in the title bar. The cursor is blinking at the end of the first line of the FUNCTION.

Complete the first line and press ENTER so that the screen looks like this:

```
FUNCTION nD6% (n%)
_
END FUNCTION
```

Continue entering the lines of the FUNCTION shown here:

```
FUNCTION nD6% (n%)
  'Simulates rolling n 6-sided dice (nD6)
  FOR die% = 1 TO n%
    DiceTotal% = DiceTotal% + INT(6 * RND) + 1
  NEXT die%
  nD6% = DiceTotal%_
END FUNCTION
```

When you have typed the line

```
nD6% = DiceTotal%_
```

the FUNCTION is complete. Notice that this line assigns the value of *DiceTotal%* to the name of the FUNCTION, nD6%, before an exit is made at END FUNCTION, the last statement of the FUNCTION.

 Only one value can be passed from a FUNCTION to the main program.

Using the View Window

You have entered the main program in the View window and named a new FUNCTION. QBasic cleared the View window, and you created the New

FUNCTION in the View window. Now put the main program back in the View window. To do so, access the View menu:

Press: ALT-V

When the View menu appears, the highlight is on the SUBs... option, as shown here:

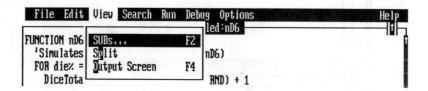

Notice that the status bar at the bottom of the screen reads, "Displays a loaded SUB or FUNCTION." (Of course, you can also use the View menu to load the main program module.) The second option on the View menu allows you to split the View window into two parts. You will use that option later in this chapter. You have already used the Output Screen (F4) option to toggle between the View window and the Output screen. While the highlight is on SUBs...,

Press: ENTER

The large dialog box shown by the screen in Figure 8-2 displays two options in the large rectangle headed by "Choose program item to edit." The highlight is on Untitled. Just below the rectangle is a status message, "Untitled is the Main Module." If you select the Untitled option, the main program is displayed in the View window. Do not select it yet. Instead,

Press: ↓

The highlight moves down to nD6, as shown here:

Notice that QBasic does not include a type declaration character (%) in the name of the FUNCTION nD6 or the status message. The status message

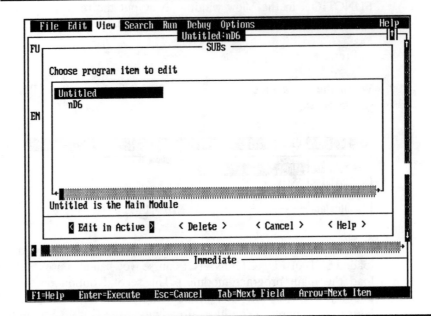

FIGURE 8-2. Choose program item to edit

now reads, "nD6 is a FUNCTION in Untitled." If you select this option, the FUNCTION nD6 is displayed in the View window. Do not select this option; the FUNCTION is already in the View window.

Instead,

Press: ↑

to move the highlight back to Untitled. Then,

Press: ENTER

The main program is displayed in the View window again. If you want to edit (or view) any one of the program's modules, put the module to be edited (or viewed) in the View window. Use the SUBs... option in the View menu to select the desired module.

Practice moving each module into the View window. Instead of pressing ALT, V, ENTER, you can use the shortcut keypress F2. As your final step, move the main program into the View window.

You can also split the View window into two parts from the View menu. Access the Split option in the View menu and

　　Press: ENTER

Now the View window is split into two parts. The main program shows in both parts, as shown by the screen in Figure 8-3. The cursor is blinking and the scroll bars appear in the top half of the View window.

　　Press: F6

The cursor moves to the bottom half of the View window, and the scroll bars appear in this half of the View window.

　　Press: F6

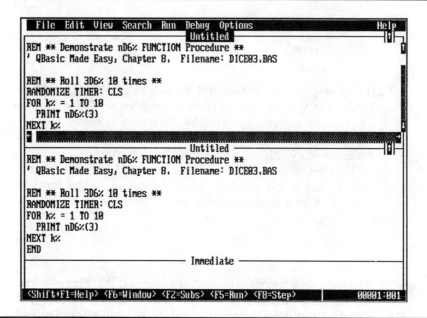

FIGURE 8-3. Split screen

The cursor moves to the Immediate window. You can move to any part of
QBasic Control (either half of the View window or the Immediate window)
by pressing the F6 key the appropriate number of times.

Press: F6

until the cursor is in the bottom half of the View window. Then access the
View menu (press ALT-V). While the SUBs... option is highlighted,

Press: ENTER

The SUBs dialog box appears. Move the highlight to the name of the
FUNCTION, nD6, as shown here:

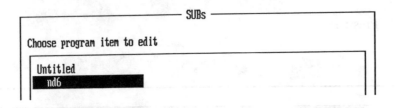

Press: ENTER

The dialog box disappears, and the nD6% FUNCTION appears in the lower
half of the View window. The main program is still displayed in the top half
of the View window, as shown by the screen in Figure 8-4.

You can use the F6 key to move the cursor to either part of the program
(main or FUNCTION) and edit it if necessary.

To remove the FUNCTION from the View window and remove the
second half of the window, move the cursor to the top half of the View
window. Access the Split option in the View menu. Then

Press: ENTER

The main program stays in the View window, the View window is enlarged to
full size, and the FUNCTION is no longer displayed. The Split option in the
View menu toggles between a full View window display and a split View
window display.

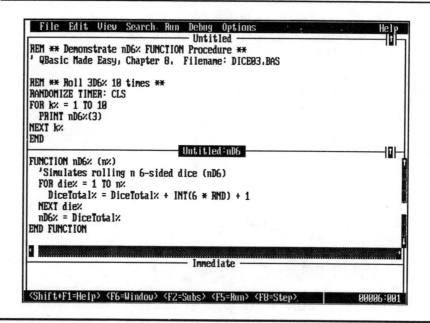

```
 File  Edit  View  Search  Run  Debug  Options                    Help
──────────────────────────── Untitled ─────────────────────────────┤↑├─
REM ** Demonstrate nD6% FUNCTION Procedure **
' QBasic Made Easy, Chapter 8.  Filename: DICE03.BAS

REM ** Roll 3D6% 10 times **
RANDOMIZE TIMER: CLS
FOR k% = 1 TO 10
  PRINT nD6%(3)
NEXT k%
END
──────────────────────────── Untitled:nD6 ─────────────────────────┤↑├─
FUNCTION nD6% (n%)
  'Simulates rolling n 6-sided dice (nD6)
  FOR die% = 1 TO n%
    DiceTotal% = DiceTotal% + INT(6 * RND) + 1
  NEXT die%
  nD6% = DiceTotal%
END FUNCTION

◀▓▓▓▓▓▓▓▓▓▓▓▓▓▓▓▓▓▓▓▓▓▓▓▓▓▓▓▓▓▓▓▓▓▓▓▓▓▓▓▓▓▓▓▓▓▓▓▓▓▓▓▓▓▓▓▓▓▓▓▓▓▓▓▓▓▶
──────────────────────────── Immediate ─────────────────────────────


<Shift+F1=Help> <F6=Window> <F2=Subs> <F5=Run> <F8=Step>      00006:001
```

═══ **FIGURE 8-4.**   Split screen, untitled and nD6

DECLARE Statement Added

Save Program 8-1, DICE03 (Demonstrate nD6% FUNCTION Procedure), with the file name DICE03.BAS. When the save is complete, notice that QBasic has added a line to the beginning of the program:

```
DECLARE FUNCTION nD6% (n%)
```

The DECLARE statement gives the type of procedure (FUNCTION, in this example), the name of the procedure, and a list of parameters that are passed between the two modules of the program. DECLARE is placed at the beginning of the program so that the program can call procedures that are defined later in the program. The computer checks the DECLARE statement to be sure that the variables in the parameter list agree with the number and type of parameters passed to the procedure.

As a precaution, you should always make a final check to be sure that a DECLARE statement exists for each FUNCTION that you have entered.

```
DECLARE FUNCTION nD6% (n%)
REM ** Demonstrate nD6% FUNCTION Procedure **
' QBasic Made Easy, Chapter 8.  Filename: DICE03.BAS

REM ** Roll 3D6 10 times **
RANDOMIZE TIMER: CLS
FOR k% = 1 TO 10
  PRINT nD6%(3)              'call the FUNCTION
NEXT k%
END

FUNCTION nD6% (n%)
  'Simulates rolling n 6-sided dice (nD6)
  FOR die% = 1 TO n%
    DiceTotal% = DiceTotal% + INT(6 * RND) + 1
  NEXT die%
  nD6% = DiceTotal%
END FUNCTION
```

PROGRAM 8-1. Demonstrate nD6% FUNCTION Procedure

Now that you have saved the program, run it. The FUNCTION is called each time the statement

```
PRINT nD6%(3)              'call the FUNCTION
```

is executed in the FOR . . . NEXT loop in the main program. The value 3 is passed from the main program and assigned to the variable *n%* in the FUNCTION. The value of nD6%(3) is passed back to the main program from the FUNCTION so that it can be printed.

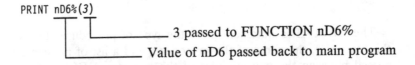

```
PRINT nD6%(3)
```
             3 passed to FUNCTION nD6%
             Value of nD6 passed back to main program

Printing Programs with Procedures

You may want to make a paper copy of Program DICE03. The Print dialog box that appears when you select the Print. . . option from the File menu displays three options for doing this:

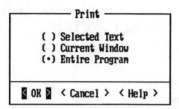

Since you have not selected any text, do not select the first option. If you want to print only the module currently in the View window, select the second option. If you want to print the entire program, select the third option.

You can print each module separately by moving the desired module into the View window from the View menu and then printing only the text in the View window. You then move the next module that you want to print into the View window from the View menu and print it.

Using Two FUNCTION Procedures in One Program

The following program is another version of WRDMKR02 from Chapter 7, "Function Junction." The multiline DEF FN functions of WRDMKR02 are replaced by two FUNCTION . . . END FUNCTION structures.

Follow the same steps in entering WRDMKR03 that you used with Program DICE03. First, enter the main program:

```
REM ** Word Maker with Two FUNCTIONs **
' QBasic Made Easy, Chapter 8.  Filename: WRDMKR03.BAS

REM ** Main Program **
' DO...LOOP to make random words, ESC to exit **
CLS
DO
   BEEP: PRINT "Press a key for a word, ESC to quit"
   kbd$ = INPUT$(1): IF kbd$ = CHR$(27) THEN EXIT DO

   word$ = c$ + v$ + c$ + v$ + c$

   PRINT "Your random 'cvcvc' word is: "; word$
   PRINT
LOOP
END
```

Next, select New FUNCTION... from the Edit menu, use c$ for the FUNCTION's name, and enter the following FUNCTION:

```
FUNCTION c$
  ' Returns a random lowercase consonant
  consonant$ = "bcdfghjklmnpqrstvwxyz"
  rancon$ = MID$(consonant$, INT(21 * RND) + 1, 1)
  c$ = rancon$
END FUNCTION
```

When you have entered the first FUNCTION, select the New FUNC-TION... option again from the Edit menu. Use v$ as the name of the FUNCTION, and then enter the second FUNCTION, shown here:

```
FUNCTION v$
  'Returns a random lowercase vowel
  vowel$ = "aeiou"
  ranvowel$ = MID$(vowel$, INT(5 * RND) + 1, 1)
  v$ = ranvowel$
END FUNCTION
```

When both FUNCTIONs have been entered, save your finished product, Program 8-2, WRDMKR03 (Word Maker with Two FUNCTIONs), with the file name WRDMKR03.BAS. Then you should select the main program from the SUBs... option of the View menu.

Note that the following DECLARE statements are added at the beginning of the program when it is saved:

```
DECLARE FUNCTION c$ ()
DECLARE FUNCTION v$ ()
```

Notice that a pair of parentheses follows the name of each FUNCTION. QBasic includes the empty parentheses to indicate that no parameters are being passed to the FUNCTIONs.

The two FUNCTIONs are alternately called from the main program when the following assignment is made to the variable *word$:*

```
word$ = c$ + v$ + c$ + v$ + c$
```

```
DECLARE FUNCTION c$ ()
DECLARE FUNCTION v$ ()
REM ** Word Maker with Two FUNCTIONs **
' QBasic Made Easy, Chapter 8.  Filename: WRDMKR03.BAS

REM ** Main Program **
' DO...LOOP to make random words, ESC to exit
CLS
DO
  BEEP: PRINT "Press a key for a word, ESC to quit"
  kbd$ = INPUT$(1): IF kbd$ = CHR$(27) THEN EXIT DO

  word$ = c$ + v$ + c$ + v$ + c$

  PRINT "Your random 'cvcvc' word is: "; word$
  PRINT
LOOP
END

FUNCTION c$
  ' Returns a random lowercase consonant
  consonant$ = "bcdfghjklmnpqrstvwxyz"
  rancon$ = MID$(consonant$, INT(21 * RND) + 1, 1)
  c$ = rancon$
END FUNCTION

FUNCTION v$
  'Returns a random lowercase vowel
  vowel$ = "aeiou"
  ranvowel$ = MID$(vowel$, INT(5 * RND) + 1, 1)
  v$ = ranvowel$
END FUNCTION
```

═════ **PROGRAM 8-2.**   Word Maker with Two FUNCTIONs

Each of the variables calls one of the FUNCTIONs in turn. Each *c$* calls
FUNCTION c$, and each *v$* calls FUNCTION v$. As the functions are
called, the values are catenated to form the final value of *word$,* making a
five-letter word of the form cvcvc. A sample run is shown by the screen in
Figure 8-5.

```
Press a key for a word, Esc to quit
Your random 'cvcvc' word is: siqej

Press a key for a word, Esc to quit
Your random 'cvcvc' word is: vatus

Press a key for a word, Esc to quit
Your random 'cvcvc' word is: bixok

Press a key for a word, Esc to quit
Your random 'cvcvc' word is: zucuk

Press a key for a word, Esc to quit
Your random 'cvcvc' word is: pocin

Press a key for a word, Esc to quit
Your random 'cvcvc' word is: joreh

Press a key for a word, Esc to quit
Your random 'cvcvc' word is: wuquy

Press a key for a word, Esc to quit
```

FIGURE 8-5.   Output of Program WRDMKR03

Access the SUBs... option from the View menu. You can select one of three modules to display in the View window. The three modules are the main program (WRDMKR03), FUNCTION c, and FUNCTION v.

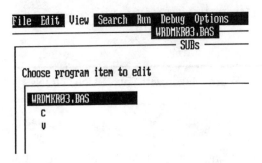

You can also use the Split option from the View menu to put any two of the three modules in a split View window.

SUB PROCEDURES

The SUB ... END SUB procedure has a syntax that is similar to that of the FUNCTION ... END FUNCTION procedure. The following program uses a SUB procedure to produce a time delay. Enter this part of the program now, but don't save it yet:

```
REM ** Draw Triangles with Time Delay SUB **
' QBasic Made Easy, Chapter 8.  Filename: GRAFIX05.BAS

REM ** Main Program **
SCREEN 1: CLS
PRINT "Press ESC to quit"
seconds! = .5
' Draw triangles until ESC key is pressed
DO WHILE INKEY$ <> CHR$(27)
  col = RND * 292 + 18: row = RND * 191 + 8
  PSET (col, row), 3
  DRAW "R16; H8; G8; BR4; BU2; P2,3"
  CALL Delay(seconds!)
LOOP
END
```

A defined subprogram (SUB) is called in a different way than a defined function procedure (FUNCTION). There are two ways to call a SUB:

- You can put its name in a CALL statement, such as in this program:

```
CALL Delay(seconds!)
```

- You can use its name as a statement by itself, as in

```
Delay seconds!
```

where Delay is the subprogram's name and *seconds!* is the argument passed between the main program and the subprogram (SUB).

If the CALL keyword is used (as in the first example), you must place parentheses around the list of arguments being passed. If CALL is omitted (as in the second example), do not place parentheses around the arguments. In the rest of this book, all calls to subprograms use a CALL statement to indicate clearly that a subprogram is being used.

Entering the Delay Subprogram

You access the Edit menu to enter a SUB, just as you would to access a FUNCTION. However, you select the New SUB... option to enter the subprogram, as shown here:

When New SUB... is highlighted and you press ENTER, a SUB Name dialog box appears:

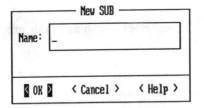

For this program, enter the name **Delay**. When you have done so, press ENTER, and the first and last statements of the SUB appear:

```
SUB Delay_
END SUB
```

Finish the first line of the SUB; then enter the one-line body of the subprogram:

```
SUB Delay (seconds!)
  start! = TIMER: DO WHILE TIMER < start! + seconds!: LOOP
END SUB
```

The SUB statement marks the beginning of the SUB procedure. It includes the subprogram's name (Delay) and a list of the variables being passed between the main program and the subprogram. In this case the list includes only the variable *seconds!,* which is passed from the main program to the subroutine. No value is passed back to the main program. More variables could be exchanged if necessary.

 The same procedure name cannot be used for both SUB and a FUNCTION. In addition, SUB and FUNCTION names must be different from those of any variables used.

END SUB marks the end of the SUB procedure and causes an exit from the SUB. A return is made to the statement immediately following the statement that called the SUB.

You have now completed Program 8-3, GRAFIX05 (Draw Triangles with Time Delay SUB). Save it as GRAFIX05.BAS. Then run it.

A random point is selected for the variables *col* and *row.* Then a PSET statement places a white (color number 3) point at that position (column and row).

```
col = RND * 292 + 18: row = rnd * 191 + 8
PSET(col, row), 3
```

A DRAW statement is used to draw the white triangle and paint its interior magenta. DRAW statements use short commands to do a series of specified graphic actions. Here is how the DRAW statement works in this program:

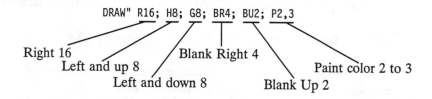

```
DRAW" R16; H8; G8; BR4; BU2; P2,3
```

Right 16
Left and up 8
Left and down 8
Blank Right 4
Blank Up 2
Paint color 2 to 3

The letters used in the DRAW commands may be upper- or lowercase.

Follow the directions at the top of the screen when you have seen enough triangles—press ESC to quit.

```
DECLARE SUB Delay (seconds!)
REM ** Draw Triangles with Time Delay SUB **
' QBasic Made Easy, Chapter 8.  Filename: GRAFIX05.BAS

REM ** Main Program **
SCREEN 1: CLS
PRINT "Press ESC to quit"
seconds! = .5
'Draw triangles until ESC key is pressed
DO WHILE INKEY$ <> CHR$(27)
  col = RND * 292 + 18: row = RND * 191 + 8
  PSET (col, row), 3
  DRAW "R16; H8; G8; BR4; BU2; P2,3"
  CALL Delay(seconds!)
LOOP
END

SUB Delay (seconds!)
  start! = TIMER: DO WHILE TIMER < start! + seconds!: LOOP
END SUB
```

═══════ **PROGRAM 8-3.** Draw Triangles with Time Delay SUB

HOW THE TIME DELAY WORKS The number of seconds for the length of the time delay (*seconds!*) is passed to the SUB in the opening line:

```
SUB Delay (seconds!)
```

The current value of TIMER is assigned to the variable *start!* before the DO . . . LOOP delay is entered. The computer stays in the DO . . . LOOP until the specified condition (TIMER < *start!* + *seconds!*) is satisfied:

```
start! = TIMER: DO WHILE TIMER < start! + seconds!: LOOP
```

As described in Chapter 7, "Function Junction," the value of TIMER at midnight is 0. At high noon, the value of TIMER is 43200. At one minute before midnight, the value of TIMER is 86340. At one second before midnight, the value of TIMER is 86399. At midnight, TIMER is reset to 0.

The value of TIMER is usually printed with one or two decimal places to the right of the decimal point. The value of TIMER is precise to 1 clock tick.

Since there are 18.2 clock ticks in 1 second, the value is precise to 1/18.2 second, or approximately 0.055 second. When the value of TIMER changes, it changes by either .05 or .06.

What if the computer's time is very close to midnight and you enter a time delay that will include the change of TIMER from its high numbers through 0? For example, consider these conditions:

start!	= 86399.94	(Value of TIMER entering loop)
seconds!	= 3	(Length of time delay in seconds)
start! + seconds!	= 86402.94	

The condition in SUB Delay (*seconds!*) in Program GRAFIX05 will always be true. The computer will be in an infinite loop; you must interrupt the program with CTRL-BREAK to stop it. This condition will seldom happen unless you work the night shift.

Going Through Midnight

Here is a modification to the time delay subroutine that will work even if midnight occurs during the time delay:

```
SUB Delay (seconds!)
  start! = TIMER                        'get TIMER value
  IF start! + seconds! < 86400 THEN
    DO WHILE TIMER < start! + seconds!: LOOP
  ELSE
    DO UNTIL TIMER = 0: LOOP
    DO WHILE TIMER < start! + seconds! - 86400: LOOP
  END IF
END SUB
```

If the value of *start!* + *seconds!* is less than 86400, midnight will not come about during the time delay. Therefore, the IF condition is true and the normal time delay is used.

If midnight occurs during the time delay, the IF condition is false and the ELSE block is executed. The DO UNTIL...LOOP in the ELSE block is executed until midnight is reached (TIMER = 0); then the DO WHILE...LOOP is executed for the balance of the delay.

A typical example with this time delay uses the following values:

Original values:

seconds!	= 5
start!	= 86398
start! + seconds!	= 86403

Time in loops:

DO ... UNTIL LOOP	= 2 sec.	−TIMER from 86398 to 86400
DO ... WHILE LOOP	= 3 sec.	−TIMER from 0 to (86403 − 86400)
Total delay time	= 5 sec.	

Passing Variable Values to a SUB

The next program has a main module that illustrates the use of passing variable values between the main program and a subprogram. The main program produces an output that is similar to that of WRDWRTH1 in Chapter 7, "Function Junction."

One subprogram is used in place of the two DEF FN functions of WRDWRTH1. Enter the following opening program lines, making the third line a blank line:

```
REM ** Wordsworth with SUB **
' QBasic Made Easy, Chapter 8.  Filename: WRDWRTH2.BAS
```

Now enter this main program:

```
REM ** Main Program **
' Get words, compute & print Wordsworths
CLS
DO
  PRINT "To quit, press ENTER without typing a word"
  PRINT
  INPUT "Your word"; word$
  IF word$ = "" THEN EXIT DO
  word$ = LCASE$(word$)
  CALL TallyWord(word$, Total%, Times#)
  PRINT "Wordsworth + is"; Total%
  PRINT "Wordsworth * is"; Times#
  PRINT
LOOP
END
```

```
To quit, press ENTER without typing a word

Your word? words
Wordsworth + is 79
Wordsworth * is 471960

To quit, press ENTER without typing a word

Your word? worth
Wordsworth + is 84
Wordsworth * is 993600

To quit, press ENTER without typing a word

Your word? Wordsworth
Wordsworth + is 163
Wordsworth * is 468939456000

To quit, press ENTER without typing a word

Your word? _
```

FIGURE 8-6. Output of Program WRDWRTH2

Notice that the CALL keyword is used to access the subprogram, Tally-Word(*word$, Total%, Times#*). Three parameters are specified. The first (*word$*) is passed from the main program module to the SUB. The next two (*Total%*) and (*Times#*) are passed back from the SUB to the main program. The main program then prints the values of Wordsworth.

When you have entered the main program, access the Edit menu and select the New SUB. . . option, as you did with Program GRAFIX05.

   Type: **Tallyword**
   and press ENTER

Enter the following subprogram when its first and last lines appear:

```
SUB TallyWord (word$, Total%, Times#)
  ' Returns sum of letter scores (a = 1, b = 2, c = 3, ...)
  Times# = 1: Total% = 0
  FOR k% = 1 TO LEN(word$)
    Lttr$ = MID$(word$, k%, 1)
    IF Lttr$ >= "a" AND Lttr$ <= "z" THEN
      Total% = Total% + ASC(Lttr$) - 96
```

```
        Times# = Times# * (ASC(Lttr$) - 96)
      END IF
   NEXT k%
END SUB
```

This completes Program 8-4, WRDWRTH2 (Wordsworth with SUB). Save it with the file name WRDWRTH2.BAS; then run it. The screen in Figure 8-6 (see previous page) shows the results of some sample entries. The results are the same as they would be with WRDWRTH1.

```
DECLARE SUB TallyWord (word$, Total%, Times#)
REM ** Wordsworth with SUB **
' QBasic Made Easy, Chapter 8.  Filename: WRDWRTH2.BAS

REM ** Main Program **
' Get words, compute & print Wordsworths
CLS
DO
  PRINT "To quit, press ENTER without typing a word"
  PRINT
  INPUT "Your word"; word$
  IF word$ = "" THEN EXIT DO
  word$ = LCASE$(word$)
  CALL TallyWord(word$, Total%, Times#)
  PRINT "Wordsworth + is"; Total%
  PRINT "Wordsworth * is"; Times#
  PRINT
LOOP
END

SUB TallyWord (word$, Total%, Times#)
  ' Returns product of letter scores (a = 1, b = 2, c = 3, ...)
  Times# = 1: Total% = 0
  FOR k% = 1 TO LEN(word$)
    Lttr$ = MID$(word$, k%, 1)
    IF Lttr$ >= "a" AND Lttr$ <= "z" THEN
      Total% = Total% + ASC(Lttr$) - 96
      Times# = Times# * (ASC(Lttr$) - 96)
    END IF
  NEXT k%
END SUB
```

═══ **PROGRAM 8-4.** Wordsworth with SUB

When the program is saved, a DECLARE statement is automatically added at the beginning of the program:

```
DECLARE SUB TallyWord (word$, Total%, Times#)
```

If you select the Print option from the file menu to send a copy of the program to your printer, the main program is printed first, and the procedure follows. If there were more than one procedure, the procedures would be printed in alphabetical order.

Although not shown in this chapter, you can mix user-defined FN functions, FUNCTIONs, and SUBs in the same program.

SUMMARY

This chapter has emphasized modular programming by using the procedures SUB . . . END SUB and FUNCTION . . . END FUNCTION. Procedures are part of the entire program but are external to the main program. QBasic organizes procedures alphabetically and keeps them separate from the rest of the program.

Procedures are entered from the Edit menu and can be viewed from the View menu. A DECLARE statement is necessary for each SUB and FUNCTION procedure used in a program. The DECLARE statement must specify any variables being passed. The number and type of variables passed must match those specified in the DECLARE statement.

You can view two modules from the same program in the View window by using the Split option in the View window.

Only one value is returned by a FUNCTION procedure, but more than one value may be passed between the main program and a SUB procedure.

DATA STRUCTURES

In this chapter, you will learn another way to store numbers and strings and read them as values of variables. You will learn how to use:

- DATA statements to store lists of numbers and strings as part of your program

- READ statements to read these numbers and strings as values of variables

- RESTORE statements to place the DATA pointer at the beginning of a desired DATA statement

USING READ AND DATA TO ACQUIRE VALUES OF VARIABLES

The first program in this chapter introduces two new statements: the *DATA statement* and the *READ statement*. A DATA statement stores number or string values to be assigned to a variable. A READ statement accesses one or more items from a DATA statement and assigns each item to a variable. You use numeric variables for numeric data items, and you use string variables for string data items.

Reading Numeric Values

A DATA statement can contain one numeric value or two or more values, separated by commas. You use a READ statement to read the data stored in DATA statements as values of a variable. If the variable in the READ statement is a numeric variable, values in the DATA statement must be valid numbers, as shown here:

```
CLS
DO
  READ number
  DATA 1, 22, 333
  PRINT number
LOOP
```

The program line

```
READ number
```

tells the computer to read one number from a DATA statement as the value of *number*. Because this line is in a DO ... LOOP, it is executed repeatedly. Each time through the loop, the line reads the next value in the DATA statement and assigns it as the value of *number*. The value is printed by the line

```
PRINT number
```

Then a return is made to the top of the DO ... LOOP to read the next number.

Run the program. As the DO ... LOOP is executed, the data items are read and printed as follows:

	READ	PRINT
First pass	1	1
Second pass	22	22
Third pass	333	333
Fourth pass	— Out of DATA —	

The program stops with the Out of DATA dialog box, shown by the screen in Figure 9-1.

While the OK option is highlighted,

Press: ENTER

to remove the dialog box. Then

Press: F4

to see the output screen, which shows

```
1
22
333
```

The program reads and prints the three values in the DATA statement and then tries to read another value. Because there are only three values in the DATA statement, the Out of DATA dialog box appears.

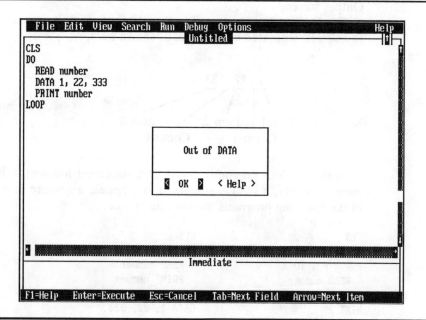

FIGURE 9-1. Out of DATA dialog box

You can avoid the Out of DATA dialog box by reading only as many values as are contained in the DATA statement, or fewer values. Do this by using a FOR ... NEXT loop to read and print the data. For example, try this program:

```
CLS
FOR k = 1 TO 3
  READ number
  DATA 1, 22, 333
  PRINT number
NEXT k
```

The FOR ... NEXT loop causes exactly three values to be read from the DATA statement and printed. After the third value is read and printed, the program ends. No Out of DATA dialog box appears, as you can see from this sample run:

```
1
22
333
```

The familiar "Press any key to continue" is displayed at the bottom of the Output screen.

The DATA statement used in the previous example contains three items (numbers), separated by commas, as shown here:

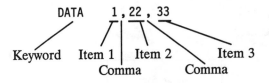

In the previous programs, the DATA statement follows the READ statement. However, a DATA statement may appear anywhere in a program, as in the following programs, shown side by side:

```
CLS
DATA 1, 22, 333
FOR k = 1 TO 3
  READ number
  PRINT number
NEXT k
```

```
CLS
FOR k = 1 TO 3
  READ number
  PRINT number
NEXT k
DATA 1, 22, 333
```

The location of DATA statements within a program is a personal choice. Some people like to place them near the beginning of a program. Others like to place them near the READ statement that uses them. Still others like to place them at the end of the program. In this book, most DATA statements are placed after the end of the main program module.

Reading String Values

You can also store strings in DATA statements and then use a READ statement to read a string as the value of a string variable. When the variable used in the READ statement is a string variable, the items in the DATA statement are interpreted as strings. Try this program:

```
CLS
DO
  READ strng$
  PRINT strng$
LOOP
DATA one, two, three
```

Run the program. Once again, the Out of DATA dialog box appears.

Press: ENTER, F4

to remove the dialog box and see the following on the Output screen:

```
one
two
three
```

Items in a DATA statement are separated by commas. Therefore, if a string contains a comma, it must be enclosed in quotation marks, as shown in the DATA statement in the following program:

```
CLS
DO
  READ strng$
  IF strng$ = "last" THEN EXIT DO
  PRINT strng$
LOOP
DATA "Stardrake, Laran", "April 1, 1991", last
```

The DATA statement contains three strings. Each of the first two strings is enclosed in quotation marks. Commas separate the strings. The third string acts as a flag so that the IF ... THEN statement causes an exit from the DO ... LOOP.

```
IF strng$ = "last" then EXIT DO
```

Run the program to see the results shown here:

```
Stardrake, Laran
April 1, 1991
```

Multiple DATA Statements

You can put two, three, or more DATA statements in a program—as many as you want. For example, the following program has three DATA statements, each containing one string:

```
CLS
DO
  READ strng$
  IF strng$ = "last" then EXIT DO
  PRINT strng$
LOOP
DATA "Stardrake, Laran"
DATA "April 1, 1991"
DATA last
```

When you run a program that has two or more DATA statements, the computer begins at the first item in the first DATA statement. After reading all the data in the first DATA statement, it continues with the first item in the second DATA statement, and so on. Therefore, the result is the same as if the items were all in one long DATA statement. When you have a long list of items that you want to read into a program, this feature allows you to break the DATA into smaller parts. The DATA statements are then easier to read; you don't have to scroll the View window right and left to see the DATA being used.

Examples

1. You can mix strings and numbers in a DATA statement as long as their positions in the statement match the order in which the strings and numbers

are accessed by the matching READ statement. The READ statement shown in the following program reads two values from DATA statements. The first value must be a string, the value of the string variable *note$*. The second value must be a number, the value of the numeric variable *frequency*. Run the program to see what you hear and hear what you see.

```
CLS
DO
  READ note$, frequency
  IF note$ = "last" THEN EXIT DO
  SOUND frequency, 9
  PRINT note$
LOOP
END
DATA DO, 262, RE, 294, MI, 330, FA, 349
DATA SOL, 392, LA, 440, TI, 494, DO, 523, last, 0
```

As mentioned, the values in the DATA statement must match the variables in the READ statement—a string value for a string variable and a numeric value for a numeric variable. Therefore, the data appears in pairs (one string and one number), as shown here:

```
DATA DO, 262, RE, 294, MI, 330, FA, 349
        |         |         |         |
      Pair 1    Pair 2    Pair 3    Pair 4
```

2. Have you ever used flash cards to study a language or to learn something else? You can use Program 9-1, FLSHCD01 (Flash Card with Japanese-English Data), to learn some Japanese words and phrases. Run the program. It begins like this:

```
Press a key for Japanese word or phrase
```

    Press: a key

to see the Japanese word in the first DATA statement, as well as instructions on what to do next. Pronounce the Japanese words. Then

    Press: a key

to see the corresponding English words. The screen now looks like this:

```
Press a key for Japanese word or phrase

Nihon'go
```

Press a key for English word or phrase

Japanese language

Press a key to continue

You have now seen both "sides" of the first "flash card," the information in the first DATA statement.

Press: a key

```
REM ** Flash Card with Japanese-English Data **
' QBasic Made Easy, Chapter 9. Filename: FLSHCD01.BAS

REM ** Read and print Japanese, then English **
DO
  READ Japanese$, English$ 'Get two strings from DATA statement

  CLS
  LOCATE 1, 1: PRINT "Press a key for Japanese word or phrase"
  kbd$ = INPUT$(1)
  LOCATE 3, 1: PRINT Japanese$

  LOCATE 5, 1: PRINT "Press a key for English word or phrase"
  kbd$ = INPUT$(1)
  LOCATE 7, 1: PRINT English$

  LOCATE 9, 1: PRINT "Press a key to continue"
  kbd$ = INPUT$(1)
  IF English$ = "Goodbye" THEN EXIT DO
LOOP
END

REM ** Data: Japanese, English **
DATA Nihon'go, Japanese language
DATA Ohayo gozaimasu, Good morning
DATA Kon'nichi wa, Hello or Good day
DATA Kon'ban wa, Good evening
DATA Oyasumi nasai, Good night
DATA "Jaa, mata ashita", "Well, I'll see you again tomorrow"
DATA Sayonara, Goodbye
```

PROGRAM 9-1. Flash Card with Japanese-English Data

to see "side A" of the next card, using information from the second DATA statement. Keep pressing keys, and eventually you will see the information in the next-to-last and the last DATA statement, as follows:

```
Press a key for Japanese word or phrase

Sayonara

Press a key for English word or phrase

Goodbye

Press a key to continue
```

Now press a key. The IF statement that follows causes an exit from the DO...LOOP when the "Goodbye" string is read. Therefore, you don't see the Out of DATA dialog box that appeared in previous programs.

```
IF English$ = "Goodbye" THEN EXIT DO
```

The program ends. For more practice, run the program again.

Use commas in DATA statements to separate the items to be read. If you need a comma in a string item, enclose the string in quotation marks.

3. Run the following program as a reminder of what will happen when items containing commas are not included in quotation marks:

```
CLS
DO UNTIL strng$ = "last"
  READ strng$
  PRINT strng$
LOOP
DATA Stardrake, Laran
DATA April 1, 1991, last
```

When you run the program, you should see

```
Stardrake
Laran
April 1
1991
```

The commas (called *delimiters*) separate items in the DATA statement. Therefore, the DATA statements are interpreted to contain five data items—four that are printed and one that causes an exit from the loop.

If only three data items are desired, you should modify the DATA statements to include quotation marks, as shown here:

```
DATA "Stardrake, Laran"
DATA "April 1, 1991", last
```

Using Null Items in a Data List

Null data items (those with nothing in them) can appear in a data list, like this:

```
DATA 5, 7, , 3
```

           \
               Null item

When a null item is read into a numeric variable, the variable is assigned a value of 0. For example, enter and run this program:

```
CLS
DATA 5, 7, , 3              '4 items, including null item
FOR k% = 1 TO 4
  READ number%
  PRINT number%,
NEXT k%
PRINT
```

When the program is run, the Output screen shows

```
5          7          0          3
```

As you can see, a 0 is displayed as the value of the null item in the DATA statement.

When a null item is read into a string variable, the variable is assigned the null string (""), as in the following program:

```
CLS
DATA alpha, beta, , gamma
FOR k% = 1 TO 4
  READ strng$
  PRINT strng$,
NEXT k%
PRINT
```

When you run this program, the Output screen shows

```
alpha          beta                        gamma
```

Nothing is printed (except blank spaces) as the value of the null item. When the next string (gamma) is read, it is printed as if it were the fourth string on the line.

 You may not want to use a null item in a DATA statement very often. However, be careful not to include any extra commas in DATA statements; if you do, the computer will assume that a null item is intended.

You can also use the null string ("") explicitly in the string, as shown here:

```
DATA alpha, beta, "", gamma
```

Using READ in External Modules

READ statements can appear anywhere in a program, even in a FUNCTION or SUB procedure. However, DATA statements can appear only in the main program module.

As an example, enter the following as a main program:

```
CLS
CALL TryIt
END
```

Then access the New SUB. . . option on the Edit menu, press ENTER, and enter **TryIt** as the name of the SUB procedure. Then enter the following SUB:

```
SUB TryIt
  FOR k% = 1 TO 3
    READ strng$
    DATA apples, bananas, oranges
```

```
      PRINT strng$,
   NEXT k%
END SUB
```

When you have entered the SUB, run the program.

The program does not execute. Instead, the following error dialog box appears:

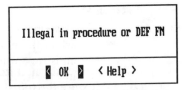

Press ENTER to clear the dialog box. Then use your editing skills, as follows:

1. Highlight the DATA statement.

2. Use Cut from the Edit menu to remove the DATA statement from the program and send it to the clipboard.

3. Access the SUBs. . . option in the View menu.

4. Access the main program (Untitled) from the SUBs dialog box.

5. Move the cursor below the END statement.

6. Paste the DATA statement from the clipboard to the main program.

You now have this main program:

```
CLS
CALL TryIt
END
DATA apples, bananas, oranges
```

Use the View menu to access the SUB TryIt to make sure that it is also correct. It should look like this:

```
SUB TryIt
   FOR k% = 1 TO 3
     READ strng$
     PRINT strng$,
   NEXT k%
END SUB
```

Now run the program again. This time it executes and prints the data as follows:

apples   bananas   oranges

USING RESTORE TO RESET THE DATA POINTER

Sometimes, you will want to use the items in DATA statement more than once in a program. An internal *DATA pointer* keeps track of the next DATA item to be accessed by a READ statement. As one item is read, the pointer moves to the next item. You can reset the DATA pointer to the first item in the first DATA statement by executing the keyword RESTORE.

The following program uses the RESTORE statement:

```
RANDOMIZE TIMER: CLS
DO WHILE INKEY$ <> CHR$(27)
  RESTORE
  FOR k = 1 TO INT(3 * RND) + 1
    READ strng$
  NEXT k
  PRINT strng$,
LOOP
DATA one, two, three
```

This program prints strings selected from the DATA statement in random order, as shown in the following sample run. The ESC key is pressed to end the program.

two	one	three	one	two
three	two	three	one	three
three	three	two	one	

The following lines are inside a DO ... LOOP that continues until you press ESC:

```
  RESTORE
  FOR k = 1 TO INT(3 * RND) + 1
    READ strng$
  NEXT k
  PRINT strng$,
```

These lines read one, two, or three strings from the DATA statement. The DATA pointer is reset by the RESTORE statement to the first item in the DATA statement.

In the FOR statement, the value of INT(3 * RND) + 1 is 1, 2, or 3. Therefore, the FOR...NEXT loop is executed 1, 2, or 3 times. Each value that is read replaces the previous value of *strng$*. When the FOR...NEXT loop is exited, the final value of *strng$* is printed.

Examples

1. Program 9-2, FLSHCD02 (Random Flash Card with READ, DATA, RESTORE), presents randomly selected Japanese and English words and phrases. After each pair of phrases, you can press ESC to quit or press another key to see another pair of phrases. The phrase pairs are selected randomly from the DATA statements.

Run the program. There is one chance in seven that the first phrase pair will be the one shown here:

```
Press a key for Japanese word or phrase

Kon'ban wa

Press a key for English word or phrase

Good evening

Press a key to continue, or ESC to quit
```

When you are ready to quit, press the ESC key.

2. Programs FLSHCD01 and FLSHCD02 are designed to work with exactly seven flash cards. This is inconvenient. It would be better to be able to use a variable number of flash cards. Program 9-3, FLSHCD03 (A More General Random Flash Card Program), reads the number of flash cards (data pairs) from the first DATA statement as the value of *NmbrCards*. The data block is shown here:

```
REM ** Data: Japanese, English **
DATA 7
DATA Nihon'go, Japanese language
DATA Ohayo gozaimasu, Good morning
DATA Kon'nichi wa, Hello or Good day
DATA Kon'ban wa, Good evening
DATA Oyasumi nasai, Good night
DATA "Jaa, mata ashita", "Well, I'll see you again tomorrow"
DATA Sayonara, Goodbye
```

```
REM ** Random Flash Card with READ, DATA, RESTORE **
' QBasic Made Easy, Chapter 9. Filename: FLSHCD02.BAS

REM ** Set up **
RANDOMIZE TIMER
CLS

REM ** Get random flash card **
DO
  RESTORE
  FOR k = 1 TO INT(7 * RND) + 1
    READ Japanese$, English$
  NEXT k

  REM ** Print side A, then side B **
  CLS
  LOCATE 1, 1: PRINT "Press a key for Japanese word or phrase"
  kbd$ = INPUT$(1)
  LOCATE 3, 1: PRINT Japanese$

  LOCATE 5, 1: PRINT "Press a key for English word or phrase"
  kbd$ = INPUT$(1)
  LOCATE 7, 1: PRINT English$

  REM ** Continue practice or quit **
  LOCATE 9, 1: PRINT "Press a key to continue, or ESC to quit"
  kbd$ = INPUT$(1)
  IF kbd$ = CHR$(27) THEN EXIT DO
LOOP
END

REM ** Data: Japanese, English **
DATA Nihon'go, Japanese language
DATA Ohayo gozaimasu, Good morning
DATA Kon'nichi wa, Hello or Good day
DATA Kon'ban wa, Good evening
DATA Oyasumi nasai, Good night
DATA "Jaa, mata ashita", "Well, I'll see you again tomorrow"
DATA Sayonara, Goodbye
```

═══ **PROGRAM 9-2.** Random Flash Card with READ, DATA, RESTORE

```
REM ** A More General Random Flash Card Program **
' QBasic Made Easy, Chapter 9. Filename: FLSHCD03.BAS

REM ** Set up **
RANDOMIZE TIMER
CLS

REM ** Get random flash card **
DO
  RESTORE
  READ NmbrCards
  FOR k = 1 TO INT(NmbrCards * RND) + 1
    READ Japanese$, English$
  NEXT k

  REM ** Print side A, then side B **
  CLS
  LOCATE 1, 1: PRINT "Press a key for Japanese word or phrase"
  kbd$ = INPUT$(1)
  LOCATE 3, 1: PRINT Japanese$

  LOCATE 5, 1: PRINT "Press a key for English word or phrase"
  kbd$ = INPUT$(1)
  LOCATE 7, 1: PRINT English$

  REM ** Continue practice or quit **
  LOCATE 9, 1: PRINT "Press a key to continue, or ESC to quit"
  kbd$ = INPUT$(1)
  IF kbd$ = CHR$(27) THEN EXIT DO
LOOP
END

REM ** Data: Japanese, English **
DATA 7
DATA Nihon'go, Japanese language
DATA Ohayo gozaimasu, Good morning
DATA Kon'nichi wa, Hello or Good day
DATA Kon'ban wa, Good evening
DATA Oyasumi nasai, Good night
DATA "Jaa, mata ashita", "Well, I'll see you again tomorrow"
DATA Sayonara, Goodbye
```

PROGRAM 9-3. A More General Random Flash Card Program

The first DATA statement contains the number of flash cards stored in the remaining DATA statements (each flash card is a pair of strings). This value (7) is read as the value of *NmbrCards* in the following block:

```
REM ** Get random flash card **
RESTORE
READ NmbrCards
FOR k = 1 TO INT(NmbrCards * RND) + 1
  READ Japanese$, English$
NEXT k
```

If you go to a sushi bar, you might like to know the Japanese names of some of the things you eat. Use the following data in Program FLSHCD03. Each DATA statement, except the first one, contains two data pairs, for a total of eight pairs, as specified in the first DATA statement.

```
REM ** Data: Japanese, English **
DATA 8
DATA buri, yellowtail, kaki, oyster
DATA tako, octopus, anago, sea eel
DATA maguro, tuna, kurumaebi, prawn
DATA saba, mackerel, tamago, egg
```

RESTORE to a Label

Although line numbers are not a requirement for QBasic programs, you may use a line number or a label as a marker to locate a particular part of a program. A label is helpful in some programming situations. For example, the RESTORE keyword, when used by itself as a statement, moves the DATA pointer to the beginning of the first DATA statement in a program.

Problem: What if you want to use some DATA statements once and other DATA statements repeatedly?

Solution: If a label is appended to a RESTORE statement, the RESTORE statement moves the DATA pointer to the line following the label. In Program 9-4, SOUND04 (RESTORE DATA Pointer to a Label), a READ statement uses all items (frequency and duration pairs of data) from the following DATA statement to sound three tones:

```
DATA 100, 10,  150, 10,  200, 10
```

```
REM ** RESTORE DATA Pointer to a Label **
' QBasic Made Easy, Chapter 9. Filename: SOUND04.BAS

REM ** Opening sounds **
CLS
FOR k% = 1 TO 3
  READ frequency, duration
  SOUND frequency, duration
NEXT k%
start! = TIMER: DO WHILE TIMER < start! + 1.5: LOOP
DATA 100, 10, 150, 10, 200, 10

REM ** Repeated sounds using RESTORE **
WIDTH 40
LOCATE 12, 10: PRINT "Press ESC to quit"
DO WHILE INKEY$ <> CHR$(27)
  FOR k% = 1 TO 14
    READ frequency
    SOUND frequency, 2
  NEXT k%
  RESTORE scale
LOOP
scale: DATA 262, 294, 330, 349, 392, 440, 494, 523
DATA 494, 440, 392, 349, 330, 294

REM ** End program **
WIDTH 80
END
```

PROGRAM 9-4. RESTORE DATA Pointer to a Label

The program uses data from a second and a third DATA statement over and over to make a series of short notes. A label is placed in front of the second DATA statement so that these two lines of DATA can be read repeatedly until you press the ESC key. The two lines provide sounds that run up, down, up, down, and so on.

```
scale: DATA 262, 294, 330, 349, 392, 440, 494, 523
DATA 494, 440, 392, 349, 330, 294
```

Enter and run the program. A short time delay is used after the opening sounds to separate them from the repeated sounds.

```
start! = TIMER: DO WHILE TIMER < start! + 1.5: LOOP
```

Experiment by changing the frequencies and durations in the DATA statements.

You may notice that the message "Press ESC to quit" is displayed near the center of the Output screen in letters that are twice the normal width. You accomplish this by using the WIDTH statement:

```
WIDTH 40
```

This statement selects a 40-characters-per-line size for the printed characters. The number of characters is reset to the normal 80-characters-per-line size just before the program ends:

```
WIDTH 80
END
```

SUMMARY

DATA and READ are used as a pair of statements. Numeric values in a DATA statement are assigned to numeric variables in a READ statement, and strings in a DATA statement are assigned to string variables in a READ statement. Once the assignments have been made, you can use the variables in QBasic statements for calculations, printing, and other functions.

You can use more than one DATA statement in a program. Data is accessed sequentially from a DATA statement. When all of the items of one DATA statement have been used, data is acquired from the next DATA statement in the program. A DATA pointer keeps track of the next item of data to be acquired.

You can use a RESTORE statement to move the DATA pointer to the beginning of the first DATA statement or to the beginning of any other DATA statement that is preceded by a label.

A READ statement can appear anywhere in a program, but a DATA statement can appear only in the main program.

chapter 10

ARRAYS

This chapter introduces a new way to store and process large amounts of data. Related data can be stored as a large group, or family, of items in what is called an *array*. All members of an array family have the same name, but the position of each element, or member, in the array is important. Therefore, each member of an array is assigned a number, called a *subscript*.

In this chapter you will learn that

- An array is a set of array variables

- String arrays have string variable names

- Numeric arrays have numeric variable names

- Arrays may have more than one dimension

- An array must be dimensioned before it is used

ARRAYS AND ARRAY VARIABLES

You have used simple numeric and string variables. For example:

Numeric variables:	*number*	*k*	*Pop1990*	*Value#*
String variables:	*kbd$*	*vowel$*	*word$*	*Naym$*

Now you will learn about *arrays* and *array variables*. An array is a set, or collection, of array variables. Each individual array variable in an array is called an *element* of the array. Every array has a name. An array variable consists of the name of the array followed by a subscript. The subscript is enclosed in parentheses.

All elements in an array have the same variable name, which is also the name of the entire array. An array variable can be numeric or string. For example:

Numeric array variables:	*temperature(3)*	*AcctBalance#(5)*
String array variables:	*StateName$(50)*	*word$(23)*

Note that a string array variable name ends in a dollar sign. A numeric array variable name may end in a numeric type designator (%, &, !, or #), which designates the array as an integer array, a long integer array, a single-precision array, or a double-precision array. These numeric type designators were discussed in Chapter 3, "Number Crunching."

The subscript of an array variable is the number enclosed in parentheses following the variable name, as shown here:

```
        Price(12)                      SideA$(7)
        /      \                        /      \
    Name     Subscript             Name     Subscript
```

A subscript can be a number, a numeric variable, or a numeric expression consisting of any legal combination of numbers, numeric variables, and numeric functions, as in the following:

Number:	*temperature(7)*
Variable:	*word$(index%)*
Numeric expression:	*SideA$(INT(7 * RND) + 1)*

Subscripts must be integers. If you use a subscript that is not an integer,
QBasic will round it to the nearest integer.

 An array variable consists of these parts, in this order:

	Numeric	**String**
A variable name	*number*	*word$*
Left parenthesis	*number(*	*word$(*
A numeric subscript	*number(3*	*word$(3*
Right parenthesis	*number(3)*	*word$(3)*

An array is a list of array variables. A numeric array with four array variables
follows. Note that the subscripts begin with 0, followed by 1, 2, and 3.

```
number(0)    number(1)    number(2)    number(3)
```

A string array with three array variables is shown next. The subscripts are 0,
1, and 2.

```
word$(0)    word$(1)    word$(2)
```

Unless you tell it otherwise, QBasic assumes that an array has 11 elements,
with subscripts 0 through 10. These are QBasic's default values for the
smallest (0) to the largest (10) subscripts.

You can set the lower bound to one (1) for an array by using the
OPTION BASE statement:

```
OPTION BASE 1
```

If you use OPTION BASE 1, there is no element in the array with a
subscript of 0.

The OPTION BASE statement can only be used once in a program, and
the statement must appear before the array is used or referenced in any way.

The default value for the lower bound is 0. You can use the OPTION
BASE statement to change the lower bound to 1 if you wish.

However, using OPTION BASE is unnecessary. The TO clause in a dimension statement allows you to control both the lower bound and the upper bound of an array, as you will see in the next section.

Dimensioning Arrays

You can use the DIM statement to specify a maximum subscript that is different than 10. The keyword DIM is a shortened form of the word "dimension." In this book, all programs that use arrays contain a DIM statement. Some examples of DIM statements are

```
DIM temperature(7)
DIM DaysInMonth%(12)
DIM AcctBalance#(1000)
DIM StateName$(50)
```

The statement DIM *temperature(7)* defines a single-precision numeric array of eight elements, *temperature(0)* through *temperature(7)*. You could also use an exclamation point (!) to define this array: DIM *temperature!(7)*.

The statement DIM *DaysInMonth%(12)* defines an integer array of 13 elements, *DaysInMonth%(0)* through *DaysInMonth%(12)*. Elements 1 through 12 might be the number of days in each month, January through December.

The statement DIM *AcctBalance#(1000)* defines a double-precision numeric array composed of 1001 elements, that is, *AcctBalance#(0)* through *AcctBalance#(1000)*.

The statement DIM *StateName$(50)* defines a string array of 51 elements, *StateName$(0)* through *StateName$(50)*. The values of elements 1 through 50 might be the names of the 50 states.

In this book, an array name followed by an empty set of parentheses refers to an entire array. This convention is used to help you distinguish an array from a simple, nonsubscripted variable or a single array variable, as demonstrated here:

	Numeric	String
Simple variables	*number*	*word$*
Single array variables	*number(7)*	*word$(7)*
Entire array	*number( )*	*word$( )*

The DIM statement reserves memory for the specified number of array elements and clears this space to 0's for numeric arrays or to null strings for string arrays. You can use a TO clause in a DIM statement to declare the upper and lower bounds of an array. This allows greater flexibility for the range of array subscripts. For example, the statement

DIM *DaysInMonth%(1 TO 12)*

allocates memory for 12 integer array variables, from *DaysInMonth%(1)* through *DaysInMonth%(12)*. An integer requires 2 bytes of memory. Therefore, 24 bytes are reserved.

The statement

DIM *Tally&(3 TO 18)*

allocates memory for 16 long integer array variables, *Tally&(3)* through *Tally&(18)*. A long integer number requires 4 bytes of memory. Therefore, 64 bytes are reserved.

The statement

DIM *temperature!(0 TO 7)*

allocates memory for 8 single-precision array variables, *temperature!(0)* through *temperature!(7)*. A single-precision number requires 4 bytes of memory. Therefore, 32 bytes are reserved.

The statement

DIM *LotsaBucks#(1 TO 1000)*

allocates memory for 1000 double-precision array variables, *LotsaBucks#(1)* through *LotsaBucks#(1000)*. A double-precision number requires 8 bytes of memory. Therefore, 8000 bytes are reserved.

The statement

DIM *word$(0 TO 100)*

tells the computer that *word$( )* is a string array with 101 elements, *word$(0)* through *word$(100)*. Strings are variable in length, from no bytes (an empty string) to a maximum of 32,767 bytes. The DIM statement allocates a 3-byte string pointer for each array variable. Additional memory is allocated later when string array variables are assigned values.

The statement

DIM *TicTacToe%(1 TO 3, 1 TO 3)*

tells the computer that *TicTacToe%( )* is a two-dimensional integer array with 9 elements.

You can think of a two-dimensional array as a matrix of rows and columns. See the section "Adding Another Dimension" later in this chapter.

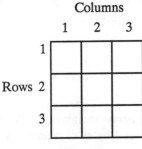

TicTacToe Array

The DIM statement allocates memory for 9 integer array variables. Each integer requires 2 bytes of memory. Therefore, 18 bytes are reserved.

Instead of using a symbol (%, &, !, #, or $), the DIM statement may specify the variable type declaration as follows:

DIM *DaysInMonth(1 TO 12)* AS INTEGER
DIM *Tally(3 TO 18)* AS LONG
DIM *temperature(0 TO 7)* AS SINGLE
DIM *LotsaBucks(1 TO 1000)* AS DOUBLE
DIM *word(0 TO 100)* AS STRING

The DIM statement determines whether an array is *static* (dimensions allocated when the program is translated) or *dynamic* (dimensions allocated when the program is run). Arrays that are dimensioned with numeric constants are static. Arrays that are dimensioned with variables are dynamic. Table 10-1 shows some examples of both types of arrays.

USING ARRAYS IN PROGRAMS

Arrays add a new dimension to your ability to make the computer do what you want it to do, the way you want it done. You can use arrays in programs that would be impractical, or even impossible, to write without arrays.

Statement	Description
DIM price(100)	Static, single-precision, elements price(0) through price(100)
DIM price!(nmbr!)	Dynamic, single-precision, elements price!(0) through price!(nmbr!)
DIM Days%(1 TO 12)	Static, integer, elements Days%(1) through Days%(12)
DIM Tally&(3 TO 18)	Static, long integer, elements Tally&(3) through Tally&(18)
DIM word(1 TO n) AS STRING	Dynamic, string, elements word(1) through word(n)
DIM TTToe%(1 TO 3, 1 TO 3)	Static, two-dimensional, integer, elements TTToe%(1, 1) through TTToe%(3, 3)

TABLE 10-1. Examples of DIM Statements

The following program reads values for array variables *frequency(0)* through *frequency(7)* and then prints all the values in the entire array:

```
CLS: DIM frequency(0 TO 7) AS INTEGER
FOR k% = 0 TO 7
  READ frequency(k%)
NEXT k%
DATA 262, 294, 330, 349, 392, 440, 494, 523

FOR k% = 0 to 7
  PRINT frequency(k%);
NEXT k%
END
```

Since the PRINT statement in the second FOR...NEXT loop ends in a semicolon (;) the values of *frequency(0)* through *frequency(7)* are printed on a single line (each value with a leading and a trailing blank space), like this:

```
262  294  330  349  392  440  494  523
```

If you omit the semicolon, the values are printed in a column, one value on each line.

If you try to use a subscript greater than 7, you will see a "Subscript out of range" dialog box. To see this dialog box, enter the following PRINT statement in the Immediate window:

```
PRINT frequency(8)
```

When you enter the PRINT statement, the following dialog box appears:

```
┌─────────────────────────────┐
│                             │
│  Subscript out of range     │
│                             │
│  ▌ OK ▐   < Help >          │
│                             │
└─────────────────────────────┘
```

Press: ENTER

to remove the dialog box.

It is good programming practice to use a DIM statement to define an array used in a program even if the largest subscript is less than or equal to 10. The DIM statement should be near the beginning of the program, before the array is used.

Examples

1. The random flash card programs shown previously access data sequentially to obtain the selected data. Suppose that the DATA statements contained 1000 sets of data. To get the 997th set, the computer would first read, but not use, the first 996 pairs of values. This could take a few seconds. Each time you access a set of data, you must read each set that precedes it.

Program 10-1, FLSHCD04 (Random Flash Card with Arrays and Time Delay), solves this problem. It reads the flash card data into the arrays *SideA$( )* and *SideB$( )* and then selects randomly from the arrays.

```
DECLARE SUB ShowSides (SideA$(), SideB$(), CardNmbr!)
DECLARE FUNCTION Delay! (seconds!)
REM ** Random Flash Card with Arrays and Time Delay **
' QBasic Made Easy, Chapter 10.  Filename: FLSHCD04.BAS

REM ** Set up **
RANDOMIZE TIMER

REM ** Read data, dimension string arrays **
READ NmbrCards      1
DIM SideA$(1 TO NmbrCards), SideB$(1 TO NmbrCards)
FOR card = 1 TO NmbrCards
  READ SideA$(card), SideB$(card)
NEXT card

REM ** Get random card: Show sides A and B in SUB **
DO
  CLS
  CardNmbr = INT(NmbrCards * RND) + 1      'Random subscript
  CALL ShowSides(SideA$(), SideB$(), CardNmbr)

  'Continue practice or quit
  LOCATE 5, 1: PRINT "Press a key to continue, or ESC to quit"
  kbd$ = INPUT$(1)
  IF kbd$ = CHR$(27) THEN EXIT DO
LOOP
END

REM ** Data: NmbrCards, SideA$, SideB$ **
DATA 7
DATA Nihon'go, Japanese language
DATA Ohayo gozaimasu, Good morning
DATA Kon'nichi wa, Hello or Good day
DATA Kon'ban wa, Good evening
DATA Oyasumi nasai, Good night
DATA "Jaa, mata ashita", "Well, I'll see you again tomorrow"
DATA Sayonara, Goodbye

FUNCTION Delay (seconds!)
  start! = TIMER: DO WHILE TIMER < start! + seconds!: LOOP
END FUNCTION
```

PROGRAM 10-1. Random Flash Card with Arrays and Time Delay

```
SUB ShowSides (SideA$(), SideB$(), CardNmbr)
  LOCATE 1, 1: PRINT SideA$(CardNmbr)      'Show side A
  seconds! = 5: a = Delay(seconds!)        'Delay FUNCTION called
  LOCATE 3, 1: PRINT SideB$(CardNmbr)      'Show side B
END SUB
```

PROGRAM 10-1. Random Flash Card with Arrays and Time Delay *(continued)*

The following program block reads the flash card data into the arrays:

```
REM ** Read data, dimension string arrays **
READ NmbrCards
DIM SideA$(1 TO NmbrCards), SideB$(1 TO NmbrCards)
FOR card = 1 TO NmbrCards
  READ SideA$(card), SideB$(card)
NEXT card
```

The first READ statement in the block reads the number of flash cards as the value of *NmbrCards*. The DIM statement uses the value of *NmbrCards* to dimension both *SideA$( )* and *SideB$( )* as dynamic arrays. A single DIM statement allocates space for both arrays. A comma (,) is used to separate the arrays in the DIM statement.

The READ statement inside the FOR ... NEXT loop reads the values of the array variables *SideA$(1)*, *SideB$(1)*, *SideA$(2)*, *SideB$(2)*, and so on. There are no array variables *SideA$(0)* and *SideB$(0)* because the arrays were dimensioned with the TO clause, as follows:

```
DIM SideA$(1 TO NmbrCards), SideB$(1 TO NmbrCards)
```

Therefore, both *SideA$( )* and *SideB$( )* are dynamic arrays, not static arrays.

The following block contains the beginning of a DO ... LOOP that clears the screen, picks a random flash card, and then calls a SUB procedure named ShowSides to display the sides of the selected card:

```
REM ** Get random card: Show sides A and B in SUB **
DO
  CLS
  CardNmbr = INT(NmbrCards * RND) + 1     'Random subscript
  CALL ShowSides(SideA$(), SideB$(), CardNmbr)
```

Notice in the next block that both arrays, *SideA$( )* and *SideB$( ),* and the value of *CardNmbr* are passed to the SUB procedure. The SUB displays the first side of the selected card, calls a FUNCTION procedure that contains a five-second delay, and then displays the second side of the card. If you think five seconds is too long, change the delay to a smaller value.

```
SUB ShowSides (SideA$(), SideB$(), CardNmbr)
   LOCATE 1, 1: PRINT SideA$(CardNmbr)     'Show side A
   seconds! = 5: a = Delay(seconds!)       'Delay FUNCTION called
   LOCATE 3, 1: PRINT SideB$(CardNmbr)     'Show side B
END SUB
```

The time delay is contained in the following FUNCTION procedure:

```
FUNCTION Delay (seconds!)
   start! = TIMER: DO WHILE TIMER < start! + seconds!: LOOP
END FUNCTION
```

When the end of the procedure is reached, control returns to the main program, at the statement following the CALL statement, where you have the choice of selecting another card or quitting:

```
   'Continue practice or quit
   LOCATE 5, 1: PRINT "Press a key to continue, or ESC to quit"
   kbd$ = INPUT$(1)
   IF kbd$ = CHR$(27) THEN EXIT DO
LOOP
END
```

A block of DATA statements follows the end of the program. The block contains the number of cards as the first data item and also contains pairs of data strings for *SideA$* and *SideB$* of the cards.

The flash cards are selected randomly. The value of *CardNmbr* will be in the range of 1 to the value of *NmbrCards.*

The program is generalized, using dynamic dimensioning of the arrays. Therefore, if you want to change the data, you need to change only the DATA statement block that contains the value of *NmbrCards* and pairs of strings for the flash card data. All other parts of the program can remain unchanged.

If you plan to be studying near midnight, you may want to change the time delay. Remember, the short time delay will not work if midnight occurs during the delay. Instead, use the following Delay FUNCTION, which was discussed in Chapter 8, "FUNCTION and SUB Procedures":

```
FUNCTION Delay (seconds!)
  start! = TIMER
  IF start! + seconds! < 86400 THEN
    DO WHILE TIMER < start! + seconds!: LOOP
  ELSE
    DO UNTIL TIMER = 0: LOOP
    DO WHILE TIMER < start! + seconds! - 86400: LOOP
  END IF
END FUNCTION
```

2. Program 10-2, STAT01 (High, Low, and Average Temperatures Using FUNCTIONs), is a simple statistics program. Arrays are very useful for this type of application.

The "Set up" program block includes a CLS statement to clear the Output screen and a DIM statement to dimension *temperature!( )* as a static array with elements *temperature!(1)* through *temperature!(7)*:

```
CLS: DIM temperature!(1 TO 7)      'Dimension static array
```

The program is designed to process temperature data for one week, Sunday through Saturday. The "Read data into array" block reads the temperatures from the DATA statement into array variables *temperature!(1)* through *temperature!(7)*.

```
DECLARE FUNCTION Bottom! (temperature!())
DECLARE FUNCTION Top! (temperature!())
DECLARE FUNCTION Avg! (temperature!())
REM ** High, Low, and Average Temperatures Using FUNCTIONs **
' QBasic Made Easy, Chapter 10.  Filename: STAT01.BAS

REM ** Set up **
CLS : DIM temperature!(1 TO 7)      'Dimension static array

REM ** Read data into array **
FOR day% = 1 TO 7
  READ temperature!(day%)
NEXT day%

REM ** Find high, low, and average temperatures **
High! = Top!(temperature!())
```

PROGRAM 10-2. High, Low, and Average Temperatures Using FUNCTIONs

```
Low! = Bottom!(temperature!())
Average! = Avg!(temperature!())

REM ** Print day of week and temperature for each day **
FOR day% = 1 TO 7
  READ DayOfWeek$
  PRINT DayOfWeek$, temperature!(day%)
NEXT day%

REM ** Print high, low, and average temperatures **
PRINT
PRINT "High:", High!: PRINT "Low:", Low!
PRINT "Average:", : PRINT USING "###.#"; Average!
END

DATA 68.8, 67.6, 70.4, 72.2, 75, 80.5, 77
DATA Sunday, Monday, Tuesday, Wednesday
DATA Thursday, Friday, Saturday

FUNCTION Avg! (temperature!())
  Total! = 0
  FOR day% = 1 TO 7
    Total! = Total! + temperature!(day%)
  NEXT day%
  Average! = Total! / 7
  Avg! = Average!
END FUNCTION

FUNCTION Bottom! (temperature!())
  Lo! = temperature!(1)
  FOR day% = 2 TO 7
    IF temperature!(day%) < Lo! THEN Lo! = temperature!(day%)
  NEXT day%
  Bottom! = Lo!
END FUNCTION

FUNCTION Top! (temperature!())
  Hi! = temperature!(1)
  FOR day% = 2 TO 7
    IF temperature!(day%) > Hi! THEN Hi! = temperature!(day%)
  NEXT day%
  Top! = Hi!
END FUNCTION
```

PROGRAM 10-2. High, Low, and Average Temperatures Using FUNCTIONs *(continued)*

```
REM ** Read data into array **
FOR day% = 1 TO 7
  READ temperature!(day%)
NEXT day%
```

The "Find high, low, and average temperatures" block calls three functions, in this order: Top!(*temperature!( )*), Bottom!(*temperature!( )*), and Avg!(*temperature!( )*).

```
REM ** Find high, low, and average temperatures **
High! = Top!(temperature!())
Low! = Bottom!(temperature!())
Average! = Avg!(temperature!())
```

The Top! FUNCTION searches the *temperature!( )* array for the highest temperature in the array:

```
FUNCTION Top! (temperature!())
  Hi! = temperature!(1)
  FOR day% = 2 TO 7
    IF temperature!(day%) > Hi! THEN Hi! = temperature!(day%)
  NEXT day%
  Top! = Hi!
END FUNCTION
```

The value of *Hi!* is set equal to the first number in the array, the value of *temperature!(1)*. The FOR . . . NEXT loop then searches the rest of the array (subscripts 2 through 7). If any value in the array is higher than the value of *Hi!*, it is assigned as the new *Hi!* value. The final value of *Hi!* is assigned to the FUNCTION name (*Top!*) to be passed back to the main program.

The Bottom! FUNCTION uses a similar method to search the *temperature!( )* array for the lowest temperature in the array:

```
FUNCTION Bottom! (temperature!())
  Lo! = temperature!(1)
  FOR day% = 2 TO 7
    IF temperature!(day%) < Lo! THEN Lo! = temperature!(day%)
  NEXT day%
  Bottom! = Lo!
END FUNCTION
```

The lowest value is assigned to the name of the FUNCTION (Bottom!) to be passed back to the main program.

The Avg! FUNCTION adds the seven temperatures and then divides the result by 7 to obtain the average temperature. A FOR...NEXT loop is used to add the temperatures. When the division is made, the result (*Average!*) is assigned to the name of the FUNCTION (*Avg!*) to be passed back to the main program.

```
FUNCTION Avg! (temperature!())
  Total! = 0
  FOR day% = 1 TO 7
    Total! = Total! + temperature!(day%)
  NEXT day%
  Average! = Total! / 7
  Avg! = Average!
END FUNCTION
```

After each of these FUNCTIONs is called, the day of the week is read and its name and the temperature for that day are printed:

```
REM ** Print day of week and temperature for each day **
FOR day% = 1 TO 7
  READ DayOfWeek$
  PRINT DayOfWeek$, temperature!(day%)
NEXT day%
```

In the last program block the high, low, and average temperatures are printed:

```
REM ** Print high, low, and average temperatures **
PRINT
PRINT "High:", High!: PRINT "Low:", Low!
PRINT "Average:", : PRINT USING "###.#"; Average!
END
```

Data statements contain the temperatures and names of the days:

```
DATA 68.8, 67.6, 70.4, 72.2, 75, 80.5, 77
DATA Sunday, Monday, Tuesday, Wednesday
DATA Thursday, Friday, Saturday
```

Enter and run the program. Figure 10-1 shows the results of a run. The program is suitable for a small set of data. Because a FUNCTION can return only one value, three FUNCTION procedures are required, one for each calculation. The program could be more flexible if the user were allowed to enter the data from the keyboard and if one SUB procedure combined the calculations that required the three FUNCTIONs.

3. Program 10-3, STAT02 (High, Low, and Average Temperatures Using a SUB), is more flexible than STAT01. It is also more compact. One SUB procedure is able to handle the work performed by the three FUNCTIONs used in STAT01. More than one value can be passed from the SUB procedure back to the main program.

The program is able to dynamically dimension the *temp( )* array by using the number of array elements that you enter from the keyboard. After the array is dimensioned, you enter each value from the keyboard.

```
REM ** Enter data into array **
INPUT "How many elements in array"; NmbrDays%
DIM temp(1 TO NmbrDays%) AS SINGLE
FOR day% = 1 TO NmbrDays%
  PRINT "Element"; day%;
  INPUT temp(day%)
NEXT day%
```

With this program, your array can have many elements (up to the maximum value for integers). The value you enter for *NmbrDays%* is used to dynamically dimension the temperature array. You then enter that number of temperatures. Sample entries for a 14-day period are shown in Figure 10-2.

After the entries are made, a SUB procedure named Calc is called. The complete *temp( )* array is passed to the SUB:

```
CALL Calc(temp(), High!, Low!, Average!)
```

Sunday	68.8
Monday	67.6
Tuesday	70.4
Wednesday	72.2
Thursday	75
Friday	80.5
Saturday	77
High:	80.5
Low:	67.6
Average:	73.1

FIGURE 10-1. Output of Program STAT01

```
DECLARE SUB Calc (temp!(), High!, Low!, Average!)
REM ** High, Low, and Average Temperatures Using a SUB **
' QBasic Made Easy, Chapter 10.  Filename: STAT02.BAS

REM ** Set up **
CLS                                     'Clear screen

REM ** Enter data into array **
INPUT "How many elements in array"; NmbrDays%
DIM temp(1 TO NmbrDays%) AS SINGLE
FOR day% = 1 TO NmbrDays%
  PRINT "Element"; day%;
  INPUT temp(day%)
NEXT day%
CALL Calc(temp(), High!, Low!, Average!)

REM ** Print temperatures entered **
CLS
FOR day% = 1 TO NmbrDays%
  PRINT USING "##.#"; temp(day%); SPC(3);
  IF day% MOD 7 = 0 THEN PRINT
NEXT day%

REM ** Print high, low, and average temperatures **
PRINT : PRINT
PRINT "High:", High!
PRINT "Low:", Low!
PRINT "Average:", : PRINT USING "###.#"; Average!
END

SUB Calc (temp(), High!, Low!, Average!)
  Total! = temp(1): Low! = temp(1): High! = temp(1)
  FOR day% = LBOUND(temp) + 1 TO UBOUND(temp)
    IF temp(day%) < Low! THEN Low! = temp(day%)
    IF temp(day%) > High! THEN High! = temp(day%)
    Total! = Total! + temp(day%)
  NEXT day%
  Average! = Total! / (UBOUND(temp) - LBOUND(temp) + 1)
END SUB
```

PROGRAM 10-3. High, Low, and Average Temperatures Using a SUB

```
How many elements? 14
Element 1 ? 68.8
Element 2 ? 67.6
Element 3 ? 70.4
Element 4 ? 72.2
Element 5 ? 75
Element 6 ? 80.5
Element 7 ? 77
Element 8 ? 73.5
Element 9 ? 72
Element 10 ? 69
Element 11 ? 67.8
Element 12 ? 65.3
Element 13 ? 69.5
Element 14 ? 70
```

FIGURE 10-2. Entries of Program STAT02

Notice that *High!, Low!,* and *Average!* are included in the parameter list. This is done so that the Calc SUB can pass these values back to the main program. The number and type of parameters appended to the name of the SUB in the CALL statement must match the number and type of parameters appended to the name of the SUB, as shown here:

```
SUB Calc (temp(), High!, Low!, Average!)
  Total! = temp(1): Low! = temp(1): High! = temp(1)
  FOR day% = LBOUND(temp) + 1 TO UBOUND(temp)
    IF temp(day%) < Low! THEN Low! = temp(day%)
    IF temp(day%) > High! THEN High! = temp(day%)
    Total! = Total! + temp(day%)
  NEXT day%
  Average! = Total! / (UBOUND(temp) - LBOUND(temp) + 1)
END SUB
```

Two new QBasic keywords (LBOUND and UBOUND) appear in the Calc SUB.

LBOUND is a QBasic function that returns the lowest (Lower) subscript of the array the name of which is used as an argument of LBOUND. Thus, LBOUND(*temp*) is the lowest subscript of the *temp( )* array (1 in this program).

UBOUND is a QBasic function that returns the highest (Upper) subscript of the array the name of which is used as an argument of UBOUND. Thus,

UBOUND(*temp*) is the highest subscript of the *temp( )* array (whose value depends on your entry for the number of elements in the array).

By using LBOUND and UBOUND, you can write program modules in a general way so that SUB procedures can be used in more than one program. The determination of the values returned by the SUB is independent of the number of items entered.

After the calculations are completed, the main program finishes its task by printing all the temperatures that you entered and then printing the calculated values. First the temperatures that were entered are printed:

```
REM ** Print temperatures entered **
CLS
FOR day% = 1 TO NmbrDays%
  PRINT USING "##.#"; temp(day%); SPC(3);
  IF day% MOD 7 = 0 THEN PRINT
NEXT day%
```

Seven values are printed on each line. The MOD function in the IF...THEN statement causes printing to begin on the next line after each group of seven values is printed.

The final program block prints the high, low, and average temperatures that were calculated and passed back to the main program from the SUB:

```
REM ** Print high, low, and average temperatures **
PRINT : PRINT
PRINT "High:", High!
PRINT "Low:", Low!
PRINT "Average:", : PRINT USING "###.#"; Average!
END
```

Enter and run STAT02. Figure 10-3 shows the output produced from the entries that were shown in Figure 10-2.

```
68.8   67.6   70.4   72.2   75.0   80.5   77.0
73.5   72.0   69.0   67.8   65.3   69.5   70.0

High:        80.5
Low:         65.3
Average:     71.3
```

FIGURE 10-3. Output of Program STAT02

USING ARRAYS TO COUNT THINGS

Arrays are useful for counting occurrences of various types of events. One use is for counting votes in a poll. Here is a questionnaire used for a recent survey by The People's Poll:

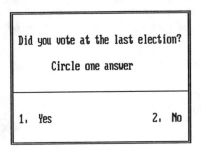

Program 10-4, POLL01 (The People's Poll), uses a simple array with two elements: the array variable *Tally%(1)* to count "Yes" answers and the array variable *Tally%(2)* to count "No" answers. The "Set tallies to zero" block shown here sets these variables to 0:

```
REM ** Set tallies to zero **
Tally%(1) = 0                    'Tally for 'Yes' answers
Tally%(2) = 0                    'Tally for 'No' answers
```

This block is not really necessary. The DIM statement in the "Set up" block dimensions the array and also sets all of its variables to 0. However, you can include this block to remind yourself that before any answers are entered, the tallies are 0.

The "Tell what to do" block gives instructions for using the survey questionnaire:

```
REM ** Tell what to do **
LOCATE 1, 1: PRINT "Did you vote at the last election?"
LOCATE 3, 1: PRINT "1 = Yes    2 = No"
LOCATE 5, 1: PRINT "To quit, enter zero (0) as your answer."
```

The "Get answers and count them" block calls a SUB procedure that is the heart of the program and does most of the work. The parameter list includes the *Tally%( )* array and the *Oop$* string variable. This allows the initial values (0) of *Tally%(1)* and *Tally%(2)* to be passed to the SUB and the final

```
DECLARE SUB Count (Tally%(), Oop$)
REM ** The People's Poll **
' QBasic Made Easy, Chapter 10.  Filename: POLLO1.BAS

REM ** Set up **
DIM Tally%(1 TO 2)
Oop$ = "Oops!  Please enter 1, 2, or 0."
CLS

REM ** Set tallies to zero **
Tally%(1) = 0                       'Tally for 'Yes' answers
Tally%(2) = 0                       'Tally for 'No' answers

REM ** Tell what to do **
LOCATE 1, 1: PRINT "Did you vote at the last election?"
LOCATE 3, 1: PRINT "1 = Yes    2 = No"
LOCATE 5, 1: PRINT "To quit, enter zero (0) as your answer."

REM ** Get answers and count them **
CALL Count(Tally%(), Oop$)

REM ** Print the final tallies **
PRINT
PRINT "Total 'Yes' answers:"; Tally%(1)
PRINT "Total 'No' answers: "; Tally%(2)
END

SUB Count (Tally%(), Oop$)
  DO
    PRINT
    INPUT "Answer 1, 2, or 0 to quit"; answer
    SELECT CASE answer
      CASE 0
        EXIT DO
      CASE 1
        Tally%(1) = Tally%(1) + 1
      CASE 2
        Tally%(2) = Tally%(2) + 1
      CASE ELSE
        PRINT Oop$
    END SELECT
  LOOP
END SUB
```

PROGRAM 10-4. The People's Poll

values of the two elements to be returned. In addition, the *Oop$* string variable is passed so that it can be used in the SUB:

```
REM ** Get answers and count them **
CALL Count(Tally%(), Oop$)
```

The SUB procedure named Count contains a DO . . . LOOP that begins with a PRINT statement and an INPUT statement to get an answer to the question posed by the poll.

```
DO
  PRINT
  INPUT "Answer 1, 2, or 0 to quit"; answer
```

Then, SELECT CASE determines what to do with the answer:

```
SELECT CASE answer
  CASE 0
      EXIT DO
  CASE 1
      Tally%(1) = Tally%(1) + 1
  CASE 2
      Tally%(2) = Tally%(2) + 1
  CASE ELSE
      PRINT Oop$
END SELECT
```

If the answer is 0, CASE 0 is executed. The loop is exited and the end of the SUB is reached. Control then passes to the "Print the final tallies" block of the main program.

If the answer is one (1), CASE 1 is executed. The value of *Tally%(1)* is increased by one. If the answer is two (2), CASE 2 is executed. The value of *Tally%(2)* is increased by one. If the answer is not 0, not 1, and not 2, an invalid response has been made. CASE ELSE is executed, printing the *Oop$* message.

For any entry, only one of the four cases is executed. Tallies are increased only if the answer is equal to 1 or 2. No tallies are made if the answer is 0 or an invalid value.

Execution of the DO . . . LOOP continues until a 0 is entered and the first case executed. The main program then prints the final results, and the program ends:

```
REM ** Print the final tallies **
PRINT
PRINT "Total 'Yes' answers:"; Tally%(1)
PRINT "Total 'No' answers: "; Tally%(2)
END
```

Enter and run Program POLL01 to tally some fictitious answers to the questionnaire. A test run is shown in the screen in Figure 10-4. No valid answers were entered. This test run merely tests for invalid answers and for the entry of 0 to end the data entry part of the program to make sure that the SELECT CASE structure is working properly.

The screen in Figure 10-5 shows another test run. Seven valid responses were entered, then zero to end the data entry.

Example

1. If you roll three six-sided dice, you could get many possible values (3 through 18) for the roll's total. If you rolled these three dice 5000 times, you might expect to see each possible three-dice total come up about the same

```
Did you vote at the last election?

1 = Yes   2 = No

To quit, enter zero (0) as your answer.

Answer 1, 2, or 0 to quit? 3
Oops!  Please enter 1, 2, or 0.

Answer 1, 2, or 0 to quit? 1.5
Oops!  Please enter 1, 2, or 0.

Answer 1, 2, or 0 to quit? 0

Total 'Yes' answers: 0
Total 'No' answers: 0




Press any key to continue
```

FIGURE 10-4. Invalid entry results, Program POLL01

```
1 = Yes   2 = No

To quit, enter zero (0) as your answer.

Answer (1, 2, or 0 to quit)? 1

Answer (1, 2, or 0 to quit)? 2

Answer (1, 2, or 0 to quit)? 1

Answer (1, 2, or 0 to quit)? 1

Answer (1, 2, or 0 to quit)? 2

Answer (1, 2, or 0 to quit)? 1

Answer (1, 2, or 0 to quit)? 2

Answer (1, 2, or 0 to quit)? 0

Total 'Yes' answers: 4
Total 'No' answers:  3

Press any key to continue
```

FIGURE 10-5. Test run, Program POLL01

number of times. Then again, you might be surprised at the results. If you rolled four six-sided dice, you could get values in the range 4 through 24. The range of possibilities for rolling any number (n) of six-sided dice is n to $6 * n$.

Program 10-5, DICE04 (Tally Results of Dice Rolls), allows you to choose any number of six-sided dice and to simulate throwing them any number of times. A long integer array named *Tally&( )* is used to hold the number of times each result is obtained. You enter the number of dice to be used and the number of rolls that you want to make. An integer variable, *NmbrDice%,* is used for the number of dice, and a long integer variable, *NmbrRolls&,* is used for the number of rolls. A DIM statement uses *NmbrDice%* to dimension the array only for the necessary subscripts of the elements in the array.

```
INPUT "How many dice to be used for each roll"; NmbrDice%
INPUT "How many rolls"; NmbrRolls&
DIM Tally&(NmbrDice% TO 6 * NmbrDice%)
```

A SUB procedure named TallyRolls is then called to simulate the throws and tally the results. The *Tally&( )* array, *NmbrRolls&* variable, and *NmbrDice%* variables are passed to the SUB:

```
DECLARE SUB TallyRolls (Tally&(), NmbrRolls&, NmbrDice%)
DECLARE FUNCTION nD6% (n%)
REM ** Tally Results of Dice Rolls **
' QBasic Made Easy, Chapter 10.  Filename: DICE04.BAS

REM ** Set up **
RANDOMIZE TIMER: CLS : WIDTH 80

REM ** Get Initial values and dimension array **
INPUT "How many dice to be used for each roll"; NmbrDice%
INPUT "How many rolls"; NmbrRolls&
DIM Tally&(NmbrDice% TO 6 * NmbrDice%)

REM ** Call SUB for rolls **
CALL TallyRolls(Tally&(), NmbrRolls&, NmbrDice%)

REM ** Print results and end **
CLS
LOCATE 2, 1: PRINT "Dice Total    Frequency"
VIEW PRINT 4 TO 24
row% = 3
FOR k% = NmbrDice% TO 6 * NmbrDice%
  row% = row% + 1
  IF row% = 23 THEN
    LOCATE 24, 1: PRINT "Press a key to see more";
    kbd$ = INPUT$(1): row% = 4: CLS
  END IF
  LOCATE row%, 1: PRINT k%, Tally&(k%);
NEXT k%
LOCATE 24, 1: PRINT "Press a key to clear screen";
kbd$ = INPUT$(1): VIEW PRINT: WIDTH 80
END

FUNCTION nD6% (n%)
  'Simulates rolling n 6-sided dice (nD6)
  FOR die% = 1 TO n%
    DiceTotal% = DiceTotal% + INT(6 * RND) + 1
  NEXT die%
  nD6% = DiceTotal%
END FUNCTION
```

PROGRAM 10-5. Tally Results of Dice Rolls

```
SUB TallyRolls (Tally&(), NmbrRolls&, NmbrDice%)
  WIDTH 40
  FOR roll% = 1 TO NmbrRolls&
    count% = nD6%(NmbrDice%)
    LOCATE 12, 15: PRINT "Roll"; roll%
    Tally&(count%) = Tally&(count%) + 1
  NEXT roll%
END SUB
```

PROGRAM 10-5. Tally Results of Dice Rolls *(continued)*

```
CALL TallyRolls(Tally&(), NmbrRolls&, NmbrDice%)
```

The TallyRolls SUB sets the character width to 40 characters per line. A FOR...NEXT loop calls FUNCTION nD6% to simulate the dice rolls. The loop also displays the changing roll count. The appropriate element of the *Tally&( )* array is increased to tally each result:

```
SUB TallyRolls (Tally&(), NmbrRolls&, NmbrDice%)
  WIDTH 40
  FOR roll% = 1 TO NmbrRolls&
    count% = nD6%(NmbrDice%)
    LOCATE 12, 15: PRINT "Roll"; roll%
    Talley&(count%) = Talley&(count%) + 1
  NEXT roll%
END SUB
```

If the number of rolls is large, you can see the number of the roll that is currently being made. This value is displayed on the Output screen (near its center). The LOCATE statement displays the roll count at the same position on the screen each time. This number changes rapidly, but you can see the progress of the dice rolls when the number of rolls is large. Here is a count made when the program was interrupted:

```
Roll 1229
```

The FUNCTION nD6%, which was introduced in Chapter 8, "FUNCTION and SUB Procedures," is used to obtain the value of each three-dice roll:

```
FUNCTION nD6% (n%)
  'Simulates rolling n 6-sided dice (nD6)
  FOR die% = 1 to n%
    DiceTotal% = DiceTotal% + INT(6 * RND) + 1
  NEXT die%
  nD6% = DiceTotal%
END FUNCTION
```

Variables used in a FUNCTION are *local variables*. This means that they have no meaning outside the FUNCTION. Values of local variables are allocated each time the FUNCTION is invoked. The nD6% FUNCTION may be called many times, but each time, the value of the *DiceTotal%* variable is reset to 0 and gives the correct total for the roll.

After all rolls have been made, the results of the simulation are displayed in table form. The headings for the table are printed on the second line of the screen, and a VIEW PRINT statement is used to reserve an area on the screen for the table items:

```
REM ** Print results and end **
CLS
LOCATE 2, 1: PRINT "Dice Total     Frequency"
VIEW PRINT 4 TO 24
```

VIEW PRINT sets the boundaries of a screen text viewport. The top line (4) and the bottom line (24) determine where subsequent printing may take place. Text within the viewport may scroll, but the text in the first three lines is undisturbed. Therefore, the headings for the data remain on the screen even if a CLS statement is entered. CLS will clear only the viewport. If you want to remove the restrictions set by a VIEW PRINT statement, you execute a VIEW PRINT statement without specifying the top and bottom lines.

Items in the table are printed until line 23 is reached. The program is then halted until you press a key. This allows you to scan a screenful of items before going on. Pressing a key clears the viewport and prints the next block of data.

```
row% = 3
FOR k% = NmbrDice% TO 6 * NmbrDice%
  row% = row% + 1
  IF row% = 23 THEN
```

```
   LOCATE 24, 1: PRINT "Press a key to see more";
   kbd$ = INPUT$(1): row% = 4: CLS
 END IF
 LOCATE row%, 1: PRINT k%, Talley&(k%);
NEXT k%
```

When the last item has been displayed, the FOR . . . NEXT loop is exited. The message "Press a key to clear screen" is displayed, and the program halts again. When you press a key, a VIEW PRINT statement removes the restriction of the viewport. The screen width is reset to 80 characters per line, and the program ends:

```
LOCATE 24, 1: PRINT "Press a key to clear screen";
kbd$ = INPUT$(1): VIEW PRINT: WIDTH 80
END
```

A simulation of 5000 rolls of three six-sided dice is displayed in Figure 10-6. Of course, you could modify the program to print the results on your printer.

```
Dice Total        Frequency

  3                 30
  4                 68
  5                139
  6                225
  7                349
  8                488
  9                559
 10                613
 11                618
 12                622
 13                491
 14                366
 15                244
 16                124
 17                 64
 18                 18




Press a key to clear screen
```

FIGURE 10-6.   Output of Program DICE05

ADDING ANOTHER DIMENSION

Original Dartmouth BASIC had one-dimensional and two-dimensional arrays. In the documentation, one-dimensional arrays were called lists or vectors, and two-dimensional arrays were called tables or matrices. QBasic arrays can have one, two, or even more dimensions. You have already used one-dimensional arrays. Now you will learn about two-dimensional arrays. A two-dimensional array variable has two subscripts, separated by a comma. Some two-dimensional array variables are shown here:

```
Tally(1, 2)      Chess$(8, 3)      Go(13, 17)
```

It is sometimes convenient to think of a two-dimensional array arranged as rows and columns of array variables, with the first subscript denoting the row and the second subscript the column. For example:

```
TicTacToe(1, 1)      TicTacToe(1, 2)      TicTacToe(1, 3)

TicTacToe(2, 1)      TicTacToe(2, 2)      TicTacToe(2, 3)

TicTacToe(3, 1)      TicTacToe(3, 2)      TicTacToe(3, 3)
```

This array has nine elements. It is dimensioned like this:

```
DIM TicTacToe(1 TO 3, 1 TO 3)
```

The *TicTacToe( )* array is a *square array;* it has the same number of rows and columns, three of each.

The following array has 12 elements arranged in three rows and four columns:

```
array(1, 1)    array(1, 2)    array(1, 3)    array(1, 4)

array(2, 1)    array(2, 2)    array(2, 3)    array(2, 4)

array(3, 1)    array(3, 2)    array(3, 3)    array(3, 4)
```

You would dimension the array called *array( )* like this:

```
DIM array(1 TO 3, 1 TO 4)
```

Examples

1. The results of the previous "Did you vote at the last election" survey was very interesting. Some people said yes and some said no. Does age make a difference? Here is the latest questionnaire:

Did you vote at the last election? Circle one answer	What is your age? Circle one answer
1. Yes 2. No	1. 40 or under 2. 41 to 60 3. Over 60

The first question has two possible answers (1 or 2). The second question has three possible answers (1, 2, or 3). Each completed questionnaire provides a pair of numbers that can be used as subscripts to select the appropriate two-dimensional array variables, as shown here:

	40 or under	41 to 60	Over 60
Yes	Tally(1, 1)	Tally(1, 2)	Tally(1, 3)
No	Tally(2, 1)	Tally(2, 2)	Tally(2, 3)

Answers from 32 questionnaires are shown in the following DATA statements. There are 32 pairs of answers followed by an "end of data" pair (0,0). A comma, but no space, separates the two numbers of each pair. A comma and a space follow each pair so that you can more easily distinguish between pairs. The computer ignores this space.

```
REM ** Data: answer to question 1, answer to question 2 **
DATA 1,2, 2,1, 2,3, 1,1, 2,2, 2,2, 1,1, 2,1, 1,2, 2,2
DATA 2,2, 1,3, 2,2, 1,1, 1,1, 2,2, 1,2, 2,3, 2,2, 2,1
DATA 1,1, 1,1, 1,1, 1,2, 1,1, 1,2, 2,1, 1,2, 2,2, 1,1
DATA 1,3, 1,1, 0,0
```

```
DECLARE SUB Count (Tally!())
REM ** The People's Poll #2 **
' QBasic Made Easy, Chapter 10.  Filename: POLL02.BAS

REM ** Set up **
DIM Tally(1 TO 2, 1 TO 3)                'Two-dimensional static array
CLS

REM ** Get answers and count them **
CALL Count(Tally())

REM ** Print the final tallies and end **
PRINT
PRINT "Answer    "; "40 or under", "41 to 60", "Over 60"
PRINT
PRINT "Yes"; TAB(12); Tally(1, 1), Tally(1, 2), Tally(1, 3)
PRINT "No"; TAB(12); Tally(2, 1), Tally(2, 2), Tally(2, 3)
END

REM ** Data: answer to question 1, answer to question 2 **
DATA 1,2, 2,1, 2,3, 1,1, 2,2, 2,2, 1,1, 2,1, 1,2, 2,2
DATA 2,2, 1,3, 2,2, 1,1, 1,1, 2,2, 1,2, 2,3, 2,2, 2,1
DATA 1,1, 1,1, 1,1, 1,2, 1,1, 1,2, 2,1, 1,2, 2,2, 1,1
DATA 1,3, 1,1, 0,0

SUB Count (Tally())
  DO
    READ ans1, ans2
    IF ans1 = 0 THEN EXIT DO                  'Exit if zero
    Tally(ans1, ans2) = Tally(ans1, ans2) + 1 'Count answer
  LOOP
END SUB
```

≡≡≡ **PROGRAM 10-6.** The People's Poll #2

Program 10-6, POLL02 (The People's Poll #2), calls a SUB procedure named Count to process the data that is passed as the array named *Tally( )*, as shown here:

```
SUB Count (Tally())
  DO
    READ ans1, ans2
```

```
      IF ans1 = 0 THEN EXIT DO              'Exit if zero
      Tally(ans1, ans2) = Tally(ans1, ans2) + 1   'Count answer
   LOOP
END SUB
```

When the processing is finished, control passes back to the main program, where the following summary report is printed:

Answer	40 or under	41 and 60	Over 60
Yes	10	6	2
No	4	8	2

This program does not perform a validity check on the data to ensure that only valid values (0, 1, 2, or 3) are read. You may add this, if you wish.

2. Program 10-7, SCORES01 (Mean and Deviation of Student Scores), allows you to enter scores for a class of students. It calculates the mean (average) of the scores and the difference of each student's score from the mean (the deviation). It places these values in a two-dimensional array with the student score in column 1 and the deviation from the mean of that score in column 2.

```
DECLARE SUB Calc ()
REM ** Mean and Deviation of Student Scores **
' QBasic Made Easy, Chapter 10.  Filename: SCORES01.BAS

REM ** Set up **
CLS
INPUT "How many student scores"; Nmbr%
DIM SHARED Scores(1 TO Nmbr%, 1 TO 2) AS SINGLE

REM ** Get scores **
FOR student% = 1 TO Nmbr%
  PRINT "Student #"; student%;
  INPUT Scores(student%, 1)
NEXT student%

REM ** Make calculations **
CLS : CALL Calc
```

PROGRAM 10-7. Mean and Deviation of Student Scores

```
REM ** Print results **
PRINT "Mean:"; : PRINT USING "###.#"; Mean!; SPC(5);
PRINT "High:"; High!, "Low:"; Low!: PRINT
PRINT "Student"; TAB(10); "Score"; TAB(20); "Deviation"
PRINT
VIEW PRINT 4 TO 24
row% = 4
FOR student% = 1 TO Nmbr%
  row% = row% + 1
  IF row% = 23 THEN
    LOCATE 24, 1: PRINT "Press a key to see more";
    kbd$ = INPUT$(1): CLS : row% = 5
  END IF
  LOCATE row%, 2:
  PRINT student%; TAB(10); Scores(student%, 1);
  PRINT TAB(20); : PRINT USING "###.#"; Scores(student%, 2);
NEXT student%
END

SUB Calc
  SHARED Nmbr%, High!, Low!, Mean!
  Total! = 0: High! = 0: Low! = 100
  FOR num% = 1 TO Nmbr%
    IF Scores(num%, 1) < Low! THEN Low! = Scores(num%, 1)
    IF Scores(num%, 1) > High! THEN High! = Scores(num%, 1)
    Total! = Total! + Scores(num%, 1)
  NEXT num%
  Mean! = Total! / Nmbr%
  FOR num% = 1 TO Nmbr%
    Scores(num%, 2) = Scores(num%, 1) - Mean!
  NEXT num%
END SUB
```

PROGRAM 10-7. Mean and Deviation of Student Scores
(continued)

When you run the program, the screen is cleared and you enter the number of student scores. Then the *Scores( )* array is dimensioned:

```
REM ** Set up **
CLS
```

```
INPUT "How many student scores"; Nmbr%
DIM SHARED Scores(1 TO Nmbr%, 1 TO 2) AS SINGLE
```

Notice the SHARED keyword in the DIM statement. When the SHARED keyword is used in this way, the array *Scores( )* is shared between the main module and all procedures, eliminating the need to include it in the list of parameters passed to the procedure.

Scores are input from the keyboard. A prompt (the student's number) is printed for each student:

```
REM ** Get scores **
FOR student% = 1 TO Nmbr%
  PRINT "Student #"; student%;
  INPUT Scores(student%, 1)
NEXT student%
```

Then the Calc SUB is called to make the calculations:

```
REM ** Make calculations **
CLS : CALL Calc
```

Notice that there is no parameter list. The *Scores( )* array is shared because of the DIM SHARED statement in the main program. The SHARED keyword in a dimension statement shares variables among all procedures in a module. The SUB includes a SHARED statement that allows the main program to share the specified variable values in this particular procedure:

```
SUB Calc
  SHARED Nmbr%, High!, Low!, Mean!
```

The scores are totaled, and the lowest score and the highest score are found and assigned to *Low!* and *High!* within the Calc SUB:

```
Total! = 0: High! = 0: Low! = 100
FOR num% = 1 TO Nmbr%
  IF Scores(num%, 1) < Low! THEN Low! = Scores(num%, 1)
  IF Scores(num%, 1) > High! THEN High! = Scores(num%, 1)
  Total! = Total! + Scores(num%, 1)
NEXT num%
```

The mean is then calculated and assigned to the *Mean!* variable. The SUB concludes with a FOR ... NEXT loop that calculates the deviations from the

mean for each score and places this value in the second column of the
Scores() array:

```
Mean! = Total! / Nmbr%
FOR num% = 1 TO Nmbr%
  Scores(num%, 2) = Scores(num%, 1) - Mean!
NEXT num%
END SUB
```

The values of the variables *Mean!, High!,* and *Low!* are printed along with a
table consisting of the student's number, the student's score, and the deviation of that score from the mean.

Enter Program SCORES01. Then run it. A sample of 28 entries is shown
in Figure 10-7.

```
How many student scores? 28
Student # 1 ? 85
Student # 2 ? 72
Student # 3 ? 78
Student # 4 ? 88
Student # 5 ? 76
Student # 6 ? 60
Student # 7 ? 90
Student # 8 ? 86
Student # 9 ? 75
Student # 10 ? 72
Student # 11 ? 88
Student # 12 ? 80
Student # 13 ? 76
Student # 14 ? 84
Student # 15 ? 84
Student # 16 ? 76
Student # 17 ? 72
Student # 18 ? 84
Student # 19 ? 78
Student # 20 ? 82
Student # 21 ? 86
Student # 22 ? 70
Student # 23 ? 75
Student # 24 ? 84
Student # 25 ? 80
Student # 26 ? 98
Student # 27 ? 92
Student # 28 ? 85
```

FIGURE 10-7. Entries for Program SCORES01

When you run the program with these entries, it takes two display screens to show the results for the entire class. The program halts when a screen is filled with results, as shown in Figure 10-8. When you press a key, the screen is cleared and the information for the next group of scores is displayed, as shown in Figure 10-9. At the top of the screen, you see the mean, the highest score, and the lowest score. A table follows, showing the number of each student, the student's score, and the difference between the student's score and the mean (Deviation).

SUMMARY

An array is a group of related values that are assigned a common array name. Elements (members) of the array are distinguished by unique subscripts. Arrays may be either string or numeric type. A string array variable name ends with a dollar sign ($). A numeric array variable name may end with a numeric type designator (%, &, !, or #).

```
Mean: 80.6     High: 98     Low: 60

Student  Score     Deviation

  1       85          4.4
  2       72         -8.6
  3       78         -2.6
  4       88          7.4
  5       76         -4.6
  6       60        -20.6
  7       90          9.4
  8       86          5.4
  9       75         -5.6
 10       72         -8.6
 11       88          7.4
 12       80         -0.6
 13       76         -4.6
 14       84          3.4
 15       84          3.4
 16       76         -4.6
 17       72         -8.6
 18       84          3.4

Press a key to see more
```

FIGURE 10-8. First screen, output of Program SCORES01

```
┌──────────────────────────────────────────────────────────┐
│Mean: 80.6    High: 98    Low: 60                           │
│                                                            │
│Student  Score    Deviation                                 │
│                                                            │
│   19      78       -2.6                                    │
│   20      82        1.4                                    │
│   21      86        5.4                                    │
│   22      70      -10.6                                    │
│   23      75       -5.6                                    │
│   24      84        3.4                                    │
│   25      80       -0.6                                    │
│   26      98       17.4                                    │
│   27      92       11.4                                    │
│   28      85        4.4                                    │
│                                                            │
│                                                            │
│                                                            │
│                                                            │
│                                                            │
│                                                            │
│Press any key to continue                                   │
└──────────────────────────────────────────────────────────┘
```

FIGURE 10-9.   Second screen, output of Program SCORES01

Default values for array subscripts start with the smallest (0) and end with the largest (10). You may use a DIM statement to specify larger arrays or to specify the range of subscripts to be used for the array. The DIM statement also initializes all elements of numeric arrays to 0 and all elements of string arrays to null ("").

DIM *temperature!(7)*	(Elements 0 to 7)
DIM *Tally&(3 TO 18)*	(Elements 3 to 18)

A DIM statement may use either a type declaration character or an AS clause to specify the data type:

DIM *number%(1 TO 7)*	(Type declaration %)
DIM *number(1 TO 7)* AS INTEGER	(AS clause)

Arrays may be dimensioned as static arrays or as dynamic arrays:

DIM *temp!(1 TO 7)*	(Static)
DIM *temp!(1 TO NmbrDays%)*	(Dynamic)

The LBOUND function returns the lowest subscript for which an array has been dimensioned, and UBOUND returns the highest subscript for which an array has been dimensioned.

You use VIEW PRINT to set the boundary lines for a text viewport. Text within the viewport may scroll, but text outside the viewport remains where it was originally displayed.

READ and DATA statements are often used to assign values to the elements of an array. However, you can also input data for an array from the keyboard.

Arrays may have one or more dimensions. One-dimensional arrays are often considered to be lists of data, and two-dimensional arrays can be thought of as a table, or a matrix of rows and columns.

chapter 11

SEQUENTIAL FILES

I n this chapter you will read about the different types of data files: sequential and random-access. You will learn about unstructured sequential files and structured sequential files and how to create and access records from each. In particular, you will learn how to

- Create and scan structured and unstructured sequential files

- Use the file statements OPEN, INPUT #, LINE INPUT #, PRINT #, WRITE #, and CLOSE

- Create and read the NOTES.DOC file, an unstructured sequential file of free-form notes

- Create and scan the JAPANESE.DOC file, a structured sequential file of Japanese and English words and phrases

- Use the file functions EOF and LOF

- Delete a file by using the KILL statement

- Change the name of a file by using the NAME statement

TYPES OF FILES

A *file* is a collection of information; the information contained in a file can be on any topic and organized in any way you choose. Think of a computer file as a file in a file cabinet: The file contains information and notes that you want to save, about one or several topics.

There are several kinds of computer files, including program files and data files. You have already used and created many different program files in previous chapters; each program you saved is a program file. In this chapter and in the next chapter, you will learn to create and use two kinds of files: sequential files and random-access files.

Sequential Files

A file is usually organized as a collection of records. A *sequential file* is a file in which the records must be accessed sequentially; that is, to read the fifth record in a sequential file, records 1 through 4 must be accessed first. You might think of a cassette tape that contains popular songs as a kind of sequential file. To hear the third song on the tape, you have to play or fast-forward past the first and second songs on the tape. This sequential file structure is depicted in Figure 11-1.

Because each record in a sequential file must be accessed in order, using such files can be cumbersome—but they do have some advantages. A record in a sequential file can be of variable length, from very short to very long, and the record uses only as much space as the data being stored. If a record is only 15 characters long, only 15 bytes (plus any special characters that identify the end of the record) are used to store it.

Sequential files also have some disadvantages. Although the data stored in a sequential file is stored in a minimum of space, the process of searching for

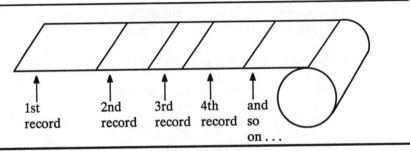

FIGURE 11-1. Diagram of sequential file structure

a given record, especially in a large file, can be slow. Modifying, inserting, and deleting records in a sequential file can also be time consuming, usually requiring that the file be rewritten. In addition, sorting a large sequential file can be awkward, often considerably more difficult than sorting a random-access file.

For example, imagine how difficult it would be to delete a song from a cassette tape, or add one, or change the length of one, without leaving gaps or deleting parts of other songs. You would need to make an entirely new tape. Imagine trying to create a tape in which the songs appear in an entirely different order. This is the dilemma with sequential files.

Random-access Files

A *random-access file* is one in which any record can be accessed immediately, without regard to any other record. You can access record 17, then record 4, then record 235, then record 2, and so on. A record can be accessed regardless of whether the previous records have already been accessed. This is similar to the way that songs can be accessed on a compact disc.

All records in a random-access file are the same length, which means that random-access files can be somewhat wasteful of storage space. Modifying a record in a random-access file, however, is much easier than modifying a record in a sequential file. Only the record being changed, rather than the entire file, needs to be rewritten. You will learn more about random-access files in Chapter 12.

UNSTRUCTURED SEQUENTIAL FILES

An *unstructured sequential file* is a sequential file in which each record is a single string of characters. One record is one string. A record can be very short or very long, up to the maximum length of a QBasic string, 32,767 characters. You can even have an empty string ("") as a record.

In contrast, a *structured sequential file* is a file in which each record has two or more parts, called *fields*. All records in a file have the same number of fields. Fields can be numeric or string. String fields can be any length up to the maximum length for a QBasic string (32,767 characters). Numbers are also stored as strings. You will learn more about structured sequential files later in this chapter.

Reading and Displaying an Unstructured Sequential File

When you save a QBasic program, it is saved to the disk as an unstructured sequential file. Each program line is a record in the file. If the program contains blank lines, they are also stored as records ("empty" records) in the file.

The following program introduces two file statements: OPEN and LINE INPUT #. This program reads a file named READFIL1.BAS and displays it in the Output screen.

```
CLS

OPEN "READFIL1.BAS" FOR INPUT AS #1

DO
  LINE INPUT #1, Record$
  PRINT Record$
LOOP
```

This program has eight program lines, including two blank lines. When saved to a disk, the program will be an unstructured sequential file with eight records, one for each program line.

Enter the program as a new program in the View window, and then save it under the file name READFIL1.BAS. After you do so, the program is on the disk and also in the View window, ready to run. Program READFIL1 is designed to "read itself" as a data file from the disk and display the file in the Output screen.

An OPEN statement is *required* before a file can be read from or written to. When you open a file, you must declare the kind of access for which it is opened: input, output, or append. You must also assign a file number.

The statement

```
OPEN "READFIL1.BAS" FOR INPUT AS #1
```

opens the file named READFIL1.BAS for input as file 1. Because no disk drive is specified, QBasic looks for READFIL1.BAS on the default drive or directory. If the file exists, it is opened for input and records can be read from it. If the file does not exist, you will see a "File not found" dialog box.

You can open a file on a designated disk drive by including the drive letter in the OPEN statement. For example, if READFIL1.BAS is on disk drive B, write the OPEN statement like this:

```
OPEN "B:READFILE1.BAS" FOR INPUT AS #1
```

You can use any integer from 1 to 255 as the file number. One (1) is a good choice if only one file is open.

The LINE INPUT # statement is well suited for entering a record from an unstructured sequential file. It reads a complete record, including commas and quotation marks, as a single string, and assigns the record as the value of the string variable in the statement.

The statement

```
LINE INPUT #1, Record$
```

reads one record from file 1 and assigns it as the value of the string variable *Record$*.

In Program READFIL1, the following DO ... LOOP reads all records in file 1 and prints them on the Output screen:

```
DO
  LINE INPUT #1, Record$
  PRINT Record$
LOOP
```

Run the program. You will immediately see an "Input past end of file" dialog box, as shown by the screen in Figure 11-2. This dialog box occurs because the DO...LOOP is never ending. It read all the records in the READFIL1.BAS file and then tried to read more records, past the end of the file. Because there were no more records, an error occurred. Remove this dialog box:

Press: ENTER

Now look at the Output screen:

Press: F4

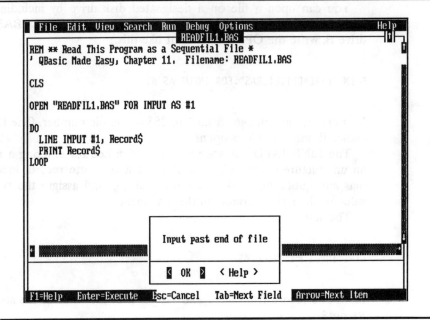

FIGURE 11-2. "Input past end of file" dialog box

The READFIL1.BAS file should appear in the Output screen, as shown here:

```
CLS

OPEN "READFIL1.BAS" FOR INPUT AS #1

DO
  LINE INPUT #1, Record$
  PRINT Record$
LOOP
```

The program successfully read and displayed the file and then tried to read past the end of the file, causing an error condition. You will soon fix the program by adding an end-of-file detector, but first,

Press: F4   (to return to the View window)

The program is still in the View window. Also, the READFIL1.BAS file is still open. Before continuing, go to the Immediate window and close any open files:

    Press: F6   (to go to the Immediate window)

    Type: **CLOSE**   (to close all open files)
    and press ENTER

    Press: F6   (to return to the View window)

When you are finished using a file, you should close it. The preceding CLOSE statement closes *all* open files. You can also close a single file by including the file number in a CLOSE statement. For example, close file 1 as follows:

```
CLOSE #1
```

Adding an End-of-file Detector

Program 11-1, READFIL1 (Read This Program as a Sequential File), uses the EOF function to detect the end-of-file and terminate the DO...LOOP that reads and displays records. After ending the DO...LOOP, the program closes the open file. You can modify the program shown previously to obtain Program READFIL1.

```
REM ** Read This Program as a Sequential File *
' QBasic Made Easy, Chapter 11.  Filename: READFIL1.BAS

CLS

OPEN "READFIL1.BAS" FOR INPUT AS #1

DO UNTIL EOF(1)
  LINE INPUT #1, Record$
  PRINT Record$
LOOP

CLOSE #1
END
```

PROGRAM 11-1. Read This Program as a Sequential File

Run the program. It "reads itself" as a data file and displays the file in the Output screen, as shown in Figure 11-3. An "Input past end of file" error does not occur.

The DO ... LOOP in Program READFIL1 is shown here:

```
DO UNTIL EOF(1)
  LINE INPUT #1, Record$
  PRINT Record$
LOOP
```

The statement

```
DO UNTIL EOF(1)
```

tells the computer to continue the DO ... LOOP until the end of file 1 is reached. EOF is a function. The argument (1) refers to file 1. The value of EOF(1) is 0 if the end of file 1 has not been reached. At the end of file 1, the value of EOF(1) becomes −1, recognized as a true condition in the DO UNTIL statement.

To verify this, change the PRINT statement so that the DO ... LOOP looks like this:

```
DO UNTIL EOF(1)
  LINE INPUT #1, Record$
  PRINT Record$; TAB(60); EOF(1)
LOOP
```

```
REM ** Read This Program as a Sequential File *
' QBasic Made Easy, Chapter 11.  Filename: READFIL1.BAS

CLS

OPEN "READFIL1.BAS" FOR INPUT AS #1

DO UNTIL EOF(1)
  LINE INPUT #1, Record$
  PRINT Record$
LOOP

CLOSE #1
END
```

FIGURE 11-3. The READFIL1.BAS file displayed in the Output screen

Run the program again. Now the program prints the value of EOF(1) on each line, to the right of the value of *Record$,* as shown by the screen in Figure 11-4. Note that the value of EOF(1) is 0 until the end of the file is reached and then becomes −1.

The original DO...LOOP can be written in several other ways. One example is shown here:

```
DO WHILE NOT EOF(1)
  LINE INPUT #1, Record$
  PRINT Record$
LOOP
```

This DO...LOOP continues WHILE the end of file 1 has NOT been reached. DO WHILE NOT EOF(1) and DO UNTIL EOF(1) are equivalent statements.

On reaching the end of file 1, the DO...LOOP terminates and the program closes file 1, as follows:

```
CLOSE #1
```

The program ends with the file displayed in the Output screen and the file properly closed.

```
REM ** Read This Program as a Sequential File *        0
' QBasic Made Easy, Chapter 11.  Filename: READFIL1.BAS 0
                                                        0
CLS                                                     0
                                                        0
OPEN "READFIL1.BAS" FOR INPUT AS #1                     0
                                                        0
DO UNTIL EOF(1)                                         0
  LINE INPUT #1, Record$                                0
  PRINT Record$                                         0
LOOP                                                    0
                                                        0
CLOSE #1                                                0
                                                       -1
```

FIGURE 11-4.   Value of EOF(1) shown to right of each record

A More General Program

Program READFILE1 is designed to read only the file called READFIL1.BAS. If you want to use the program to read and display a different file, you must change the file name in the OPEN statement. The next program allows you to enter from the keyboard the name of the file that you want to read and display.

Program 11-2, READFIL2 (Read and Display an Unstructured Sequential File), asks for keyboard entry of the name of a file. After acquiring the file name, the program opens the file, reads and prints the records to the Output screen, and then closes the file.

Enter this program, save it, and run it. The program begins like this:

```
File name? _
```

Use Program READFIL2 to read and display the READFIL1.BAS file:

Type: **READFIL1.BAS**   (or type **readfil1.bas**)
and press ENTER

```
REM ** Read and Display an Unstructured Sequential File *
' QBasic Made Easy, Chapter 11.  Filename: READFIL2.BAS

CLS

INPUT "File name"; filename$        'Acquire name of file
PRINT

OPEN filename$ FOR INPUT AS #1      'Open the file as file #1

DO UNTIL EOF(1)                     'Do until end of file
   LINE INPUT #1, Record$           'Read one record
   PRINT Record$                    'Print the record
LOOP

CLOSE #1                            'Close file #1
END
```

PROGRAM 11-2. Read and Display an Unstructured Sequential File

The program should read and display the file, as shown by the screen in Figure 11-5. If you want to read and display a file from a designated disk drive, include the drive letter as part of your keyboard entry. For example, to read and display the READFIL1.BAS file from disk drive B,

Type: **B:READFIL1.BAS**
and press ENTER

Use Program READFIL2 to read and display files that appeared in previous chapters. Be sure to try some program files that have more than 24 lines. For these, you will see only the last 24 lines in the Output screen. The top part of the program will have scrolled off the Output screen.

Creating the NOTES.DOC File

You will now create and use NOTES.DOC, an unstructured sequential file. This file consists of free-form records that are notes. A record in this file can be anything you wish, as long as it is typed as a single string. It might

```
File name? READFIL1.BAS

REM ** Read This Program as a Sequential File *
' QBasic Made Easy, Chapter 11.  Filename: READFIL1.BAS

CLS

OPEN "READFIL1.BAS" FOR INPUT AS #1

DO UNTIL EOF(1)
  LINE INPUT #1, Record$
  PRINT Record$
LOOP

CLOSE #1
```

FIGURE 11-5. The READFIL1.BAS file as read and displayed by Program READFIL2

contain, for example, notes on how to use QBasic. Or, as in Figure 11-6, it might hold notes on QBasic, your appointments for April, and your favorite quote from a book you're reading.

NOTES.DOC is a data file, not a program file. The file name extension (.DOC) is chosen to indicate that it is a document file. This choice is arbitrary. Here are some other possibilities for the file name extension:

.TXT   To indicate a text file

.DAT   To indicate a data file

.SEQ   To indicate a sequential file

Use the file name extension that suits *your* style.

To create this file, you will

- Open the file so that information can be written into it.

- Enter records from the keyboard and write them to the file.

- Close the file after all records have been entered.

Record 1: This is the NOTES.DOC file.

Record 2: NOTES.DOC is an unstructured sequential file.

Record 3: Each record is one string, up to 32767 characters.

Record 4: Use NOTES.DOC for notes of any kind.

Record 5: Meet with Jester at noon on 4/1.

Record 6: Library books due 4/15 -- also mail tax return.

Record 7: Reality expands to fill the available fantasies.

FIGURE 11-6. The NOTES.DOC file with seven records

To do this, you will use the following QBasic statements:

```
OPEN         (To open the file)
LINE INPUT   (To obtain a string (record) from the
              keyboard)
PRINT #      (To print a record (string) to the file)
CLOSE        (To close the file)
```

Program 11-3, MAKEFIL1 (Create an Unstructured Sequential File), first asks for the name of the new file to be created. You then enter the records from the keyboard. Each record can have up to 255 characters, the number

---

```
REM ** Create an Unstructured Sequential File **
' QBasic Made Easy, Chapter 11.  Filename: MAKEFIL1.BAS

REM ** Set up and acquire name of file to create **
CLS
PRINT "Create an unstructured sequential file"
PRINT
INPUT "Name of file"; filename$

REM ** Open the file for output as file #1 **
OPEN filename$ FOR OUTPUT AS #1

REM ** Obtain records from keyboard and print to file **
DO
  PRINT : PRINT "Press a key to enter a record, or ESC to quit"
  kbd$ = INPUT$(1): IF kbd$ = CHR$(27) THEN EXIT DO

  PRINT : LINE INPUT ">"; Record$    'Obtain record from keyboard
  PRINT #1, Record$                  'Print record to file #1
LOOP

CLOSE #1
PRINT
PRINT "You pressed ESC.  The "; filename$; " file is closed."
END
```

PROGRAM 11-3. Create an Unstructured Sequential File

of characters allowed by the LINE INPUT statement. Enter the program and save it as MAKEFIL1.BAS. Then use the program to create the NOTES.DOC file. When run, the program begins like this:

```
Create an unstructured sequential file

Name of file? _
```

    Type: **NOTES.DOC**
    and press ENTER

The program opens the NOTES.DOC file and prompts you as follows:

```
Create an unstructured sequential file

Name of file? NOTES.DOC

Press a key to enter a record, or ESC to quit
```

If you press the ESC key, the computer exits the DO . . . LOOP and closes the file. In this case, NOTES.DOC will be an empty file—a file with a name but with no records. Don't press ESC. Instead, press another key (the SPACEBAR is a good choice). You will see a greater-than symbol (>) and the cursor (_) as shown here:

```
Press a key to enter a record, or ESC to quit

>_
```

Type the first record of the NOTES.DOC file, make sure that it is correct, and then press ENTER. You should then see the following in the Output screen:

```
>This is the NOTES.DOC file.

Press a key to enter a record, or ESC to quit
```

Go ahead and enter the other six records of the NOTES.DOC file, as shown in Figure 11-6. After entering the seventh record, you will see

```
>Reality expands to fill the available fantasies.

Press a key to enter a record, or ESC to quit
```

You can end with this or add additional records of your choice. To end the program,

     Press: ESC

Pressing the ESC key causes an exit from the DO...LOOP. The program closes the file and ends with the following information on the bottom part of the Output screen:

```
>Reality expands to fill the available fantasies.

Press a key to enter a record, or ESC to quit

You pressed ESC.  The NOTES.DOC file is closed.

Press any key to continue
```

You have created the NOTES.DOC file. Now use Program READFIL2 to read the NOTES.DOC file and display it on the Output screen. Use the Open... option on the File menu to load Program READFIL2 into the View window, and then run it. When asked for the name of the file, type **NOTES.DOC** and press ENTER. You should then see the NOTES.DOC file displayed in the Output screen, as shown by the screen in Figure 11-7.

```
File name? NOTES.DOC

This is the NOTES.DOC file.
NOTES.DOC is an unstructured sequential file.
Each record is one string, up to 32767 characters.
Use NOTES.DOC for notes of any kind.
Meet with Jester at noon on 4/1.
Library books due 4/15 -- also mail tax return.
Reality expands to fill the available fantasies.
```

FIGURE 11-7. NOTES.DOC file displayed by Program READFIL2

Although the NOTES.DOC file is not a QBasic program, you can load it into the View window and view it, but you cannot edit it. To load the file, use the Open... choice in the File menu to obtain the Open dialog box. In the File Name box,

Type: **NOTES.DOC**
and press ENTER

You should see the NOTES.DOC file displayed in the View window, as shown by the screen in Figure 11-8.

Go ahead and try to edit a line. Change a letter or add something, and then move the cursor off the line that you changed. You will probably see some type of error dialog box. Since the NOTES.DOC file is not a QBasic program, you cannot edit it in the View window. You can, however, load NOTES.DOC into your word processor and treat it as you would an ASCII file.

In Program MAKEFIL1, the statement

```
OPEN filename$ FOR OUTPUT AS #1
```

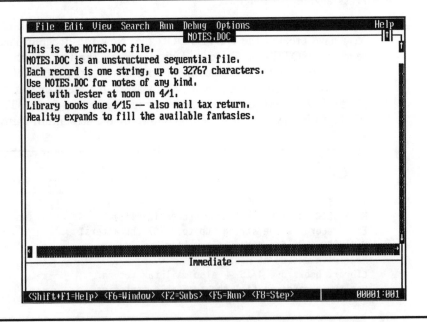

FIGURE 11-8. The NOTES.DOC file in the View window

opens a file for output and designates it as file 1. If the file already exists, it is immediately emptied—all records are erased. Therefore, before you use an OPEN . . . FOR OUTPUT statement, check the directory of the disk you are using to be sure that you will not erase the contents of a file that you wish to keep.

Instead of using an OPEN . . . FOR OUTPUT statement, you can use an OPEN . . . FOR APPEND statement. A file opened for appending, like a file opened for output, can only be written to. However, the file's contents are not erased before any records are written to it. Also, as the term "append" implies, any records written to a file opened for appending are added to the bottom of the file.

The statement

```
OPEN filename$ FOR APPEND AS #1
```

opens a file for appending as file 1 and allows you to append records to the bottom of the file. The appended file contains all the old records plus any new records you add.

You can easily modify Program MAKEFIL1 to obtain Program 11-4, APPEND1 (Append to an Unstructured Sequential File). Try using this new program to add records to the NOTES.DOC file.

Programs MAKEFIL1 and APPEND1 both use a LINE INPUT statement to acquire a string entered from the keyboard. LINE INPUT accepts all characters entered, including commas and quotation marks, as a single string. A LINE INPUT statement without a number symbol (#) and file number automatically selects the keyboard as the input device. Note the difference between LINE INPUT, which accepts a string entered from the keyboard, and LINE INPUT #, which reads a record from a file.

You can use Program APPEND1 to create a new file. If the file named in the OPEN . . . FOR APPEND statement does not already exist, QBasic creates a new file with that name. Therefore, you can use Program APPEND1 either to create a new file or to add records to an existing file.

Use Program APPEND1 to create a new file called DOODLE.DOC. This is a temporary file that you will use for doodling, in order to learn more about how records are stored in files. Run the program. It begins like this:

```
Append to an unstructured sequential file

Name of file? _
```

Type: **DOODLE.DOC**
and press ENTER

```
REM ** Append to an Unstructured Sequential File **
' QBasic Made Easy, Chapter 11.  Filename:  APPEND1.BAS

REM ** Set up and acquire name of file to append to **
CLS
PRINT "Append to an unstructured sequential file"
PRINT
INPUT "Name of file"; filename$

REM ** Open the file for append as file #1
OPEN filename$ FOR APPEND AS #1

REM ** Obtain records frorm keyboard and append to file **
DO
  PRINT : PRINT "Press a key to enter a record, or ESC to quit"
  kbd$ = INPUT$(1):  IF kbd$ = CHR$(27) THEN EXIT DO

  PRINT : LINE INPUT ">"; Record$      'Obtain record from keyboard
  PRINT #1, Record$                    'Print record to file #1
LOOP

REM ** Print number of bytes in file, close file, end program **
PRINT
PRINT "The "; filename$; " file has"; LOF(1); "bytes."
CLOSE #1
PRINT "The file is closed."
END
```

PROGRAM 11-4. Append to an Unstructured Sequential File

Since the DOODLE.DOC file does not already exist, a new file with that name is created. You are prompted to enter a record or to press ESC to quit, as follows:

```
Append to an unstructured sequential file

Name of file? DOODLE.DOC

Press a key to enter a record, or ESC to quit
```

The DOODLE.DOC file has been opened and is empty. Press a key other than ESC (the SPACEBAR is a good choice); then enter **qwerty** as the first record, as shown here, and press ENTER:

```
?qwerty
```

```
Press a key to enter a record, or ESC to quit
```

The DOODLE.DOC file now has one record. Do not enter more records. Instead,

Press: ESC

This causes an exit from the DO ... LOOP. The program prints the size of the file (number of bytes), closes the file, and ends. The screen should appear as shown in Figure 11-9. Before closing the file, the program prints the size of the file (number of bytes), as shown here:

```
The DOODLE.DOC file has 8 bytes.
```

The DOODLE.DOC file has one record with 8 bytes. This record consists of the string you entered (qwerty), which has 6 bytes, plus two *end-of-record* characters. These are the CR (Carriage Return) and LF (Line Feed) characters. Every record ends with these two characters. The ASCII code for CR is 13, and the ASCII code for LF is 10.
    The statement

```
PRINT "The "; filename$; " file has"; LOF(1); "bytes."
```

```
Append to an unstructured sequential file

Name of file? DOODLE.DOC

Press a key to enter a record, or ESC to quit

>qwerty

Press a key to enter a record, or ESC to quit

The DOODLE.DOC file has 8 bytes.
The file is closed.
```

═══ **FIGURE 11-9.**   The DOODLE.DOC file has one record and is 8 bytes long

uses the LOF function to print the length of the file. LOF(1) is the length (number of bytes) of file 1. You can use the LOF function to obtain the length of any open file.

At this point, run Program APPEND1 again and append a record to the DOODLE.DOC file. Enter **abc** as the record. The screen should look like this:

```
Append to an unstructured sequential file

Name of file? DOODLE.DOC

Press a key to enter a record, or ESC to quit

>abc

Press a key to enter a record, or ESC to quit
```

Do not enter more records. Instead,

Press: ESC

The program prints the length of the file, as shown here:

```
The DOODLE.DOC file has 13 bytes.
```

The file now has two records and a total of 13 bytes. The first record consists of six characters (qwerty) followed by the two end-of-record characters, CR and LF. The second record consists of three characters (abc) followed by the two end-of-record characters, CR and LF. If you could look into the file, you would see something like this:

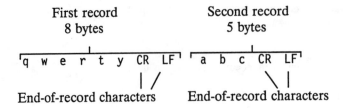

If you wish, run the program again and append records of your choice. When you are finished doodling in DOODLE.DOC, use a KILL statement in the Immediate window to delete the file from the disk, as follows:

Press: F6   (to go to the Immediate window)

Type: **KILL "DOODLE.DOC"**
and press ENTER

Press: F6   (to return to the View window)

STRUCTURED SEQUENTIAL FILES

In a structured sequential file, each record consists of at least two fields. Each field in a record is a variable-length string; that is, a field can be any length, up to the maximum length allowed for a string (32,767 characters).

For example, consider a file called JAPANESE.DOC, which contains Japanese words and phrases and their English equivalents. Each record in this file has two fields: *Japanese$* and *English$*. Sample records from this file are shown in Table 11-1. The spelling conventions in Table 11-1 are consistent with those in *Learn Japanese* by John Young and Kimiko Nakajima-Okano (Honolulu: University of Hawaii Press, 1984).

Record Number	First Field (*Japanese$*)	Second Field (*English$*)
1	Nihon'go	Japanese language
2	Ohayo gozaimasu	Good morning
3	Kon'nichi wa	Hello or Good day
4	Kon'ban wa	Good evening
5	Oyasumi nasai	Good night
6	Jaa, mata ashita	Well, see you again tomorrow
7	Sayonara	Goodbye

TABLE 11-1. Sample Records from JAPANESE.DOC, a Structured Sequential File

Another example of a structured sequential file is inspired by a catalog of camping equipment. In this file, each record has five fields, as follows:

Page%	Page number, a numeric field
CatNum$	Catalog number, a string field
Item$	Brief description of item, a string field
Price!	Price, a numeric field
Ounces!	Weight in ounces, a numeric field

Table 11-2 shows sample records from the CAMPING.CAT file.

Creating a Structured Sequential File

Program 11-5, MAKEFIL2 (Create a Structured Sequential File), creates a sequential file in which each record consists of two string fields called *FieldA$* and *FieldB$*. The program has a main program and a SUB procedure called CreateFile.

Page%	CatNum$	Item$	Price!	Ounces!
5	33-972	Backpack	129.95	72
10	47-865	Tent	199.95	96
19	50-336	Sleeping bag	99.95	53
25	40-027	Stove	41.95	13
27	40-115	Cooking kit	29.95	32
31	45-820	Compass	25.95	3
44	47-322	Swiss army knife	13.95	2

≡≡ **TABLE 11-2.** Sample Records from CAMPING.CAT

```
DECLARE SUB CreateFile (filename$)
REM ** Create a Structured Sequential File **
' QBasic Made Easy, Chapter 11.  Filename: MAKEFIL2.BAS

REM ** Set up and acquire name of file to create **
CLS
PRINT "Create a sequential file with two string fields"
PRINT
INPUT "Name of file"; filename$

REM ** Use the CreateFile SUB procedure to create the file **
CALL CreateFile(filename$)
END

SUB CreateFile (filename$)
  ' Create a sequential file with two fields, FieldA$ & FieldB$

  OPEN filename$ FOR OUTPUT AS #1

  ' Obtain records from keyboard and write to file
  DO
    CLS : PRINT "Creating "; filename$; " file."
    PRINT : PRINT "Press a key to enter a record, or ESC to quit"
    kbd$ = INPUT$(1): IF kbd$ = CHR$(27) THEN EXIT DO

    PRINT : PRINT "Enter first field"
    PRINT : LINE INPUT ">"; FieldA$

    PRINT : PRINT "Enter second field"
    PRINT : LINE INPUT ">"; FieldB$

    WRITE #1, FieldA$, FieldB$
  LOOP

  ' Print number of bytes in file and close file
  PRINT
  PRINT "The "; filename$; " file has"; LOF(1); "bytes."
  CLOSE #1
  PRINT "The file is closed."

END SUB
```

══ **PROGRAM 11-5.** Create a Structured Sequential File

Use the program to create the JAPANESE.DOC file with the records shown in Table 11-1. When you run the program, it begins like this:

```
Create a sequential file with two string fields

Name of file? _
```

Type: **JAPANESE.DOC**
and press ENTER

You are then prompted as follows:

```
Creating JAPANESE.DOC file.

Press a key to enter a record, or ESC to quit
```

Press a key other than ESC and enter the first record shown in Table 11-1. Just before you press ENTER after typing the second field, the screen will look like this:

```
Enter first field

>Nihon'go

Enter second field

>Japanese language_
```

Press ENTER and this record will be written to the file. Enter the rest of the records, and then press ESC to end the program and see information similar to the following:

```
Creating JAPANESE.DOC file.

Press a key to enter a record, or ESC to quit

The JAPANESE.DOC file has 234 bytes.
The file is closed.
```

Program MAKEFIL2 uses a WRITE # statement to write one record, consisting of two fields, to the file. The statement

```
WRITE #1, FieldA$, FieldB$
```

tells the computer to write the values of the string variables, *FieldA$* and *FieldB$,* to file 1. The WRITE # statement encloses each string in quotation marks and inserts a comma (,) between the two strings. Therefore, one record consists of the first string enclosed in quotation marks, a comma, the second string enclosed in quotation marks, and the usual two end-of-record characters, CR and LF.

To view the JAPANESE.DOC file, you can use Program READFIL2 or the DOS TYPE command. Either method will display the seven records, as shown here:

```
"Nihon'go","Japanese language"
"Ohayo gozaimasu","Good morning"
"Kon'nichi wa","Hello or Good day"
"Kon'ban wa","Good evening"
"Oyasumi nasai","Good night"
"Jaa, mata ashita","Well, see you again tomorrow"
"Sayonara","Goodbye"
```

Note that each record consists of two fields. Each field is enclosed in quotation marks. A comma separates the fields. For example:

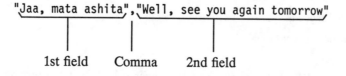

          1st field   Comma   2nd field

If you were studying Japanese or some other language, you might create several files of this type, perhaps one called NOUNS.DOC, another called VERBS.DOC, and so on. In order to append records to any of these files, change the OPEN statement in the CreateFile SUB to the following:

```
OPEN filename$ FOR APPEND AS #1
```

 Opening a file for *output* erases an existing file, if any. Opening a file for *appending* does not erase an existing file. Instead, you may append new records to the end of the file, thus increasing the length of the file. If a file does not already exist, opening for appending creates a new file.

USING THE JAPANESE.DOC FILE FOR SEQUENTIAL PRACTICE

You can use Program 11-6, READFIL3 (Scan a Structured Sequential File), to scan the JAPANESE.DOC file one record at a time, from the first record to the last record. You press a key to display the Japanese word or phrase (*FieldA$*), and then (when ready) you press a key to display the English equivalent (*FieldB$*). Continue pressing keys to display the Japanese and then the English word or phrase. The program begins like this:

```
Scan a sequential file with two fields
Name of file? _
```

> Type: **JAPANESE.DOC**
> and press ENTER

You are prompted to press a key to obtain the first field and then press a key to obtain the second field. Here is the first record after two keypresses:

```
Press a key to see first field
Nihon'go
Press a key to see second field
Japanese language
Press a key to continue
```

Keep pressing keys to see the rest of the records. When the last record is on the screen, pressing a key causes end-of-file information to be printed, as shown by the screen in Figure 11-10.

You can use Program READFIL3 like you would use flash cards to study any subject. Instead of Japanese and English words and phrases, create a file of Spanish and English words and phrases, or English words and definitions, or words and synonyms. Think of *FieldA$* as one side of a flash card and *FieldB$* as the other side.

In perusing the program, note that an INPUT # statement is used to read the two fields that make up one record. The statement

```
INPUT #1, FieldA$, FieldB$
```

```
DECLARE SUB ScanFile (filename$)
REM ** Scan a Structured Sequential File *
' QBasic Made Easy, Chapter 11. Filename: READFIL3.BAS

REM ** Main program **
CLS : PRINT "Scan a sequential file with two fields"
PRINT
INPUT "Name of file"; filename$          'Acquire name of file

REM ** Use the ScanFile SUB procedure to scan the file **
CALL ScanFile (filename$)
END

SUB ScanFile (filename$)
' Scans a sequential file with two string fields
  OPEN filename$ FOR INPUT AS #1

  DO UNTIL EOF(1)
    INPUT #1, FieldA$, FieldB$    'Read 1 record with 2 fields

    CLS
    PRINT "Press a key to see first field"
    kbd$ = INPUT$(1)
    PRINT : PRINT FieldA$

    PRINT : PRINT "Press a key to see second field"
    kbd$ = INPUT$(1)
    PRINT : PRINT FieldB$

    PRINT : PRINT "Press a key to continue"
    kbd$ = INPUT$(1)
  LOOP

  PRINT : PRINT "That's the end of the file."
  CLOSE #1
  PRINT "The "; filename$; "file is closed."

END SUB
```

PROGRAM 11-6. Scan a Structured Sequential File

reads two strings from file 1. The first string is assigned as the value of the string variable *FieldA$*. The second string is assigned as the value of the string variable *FieldB$*. The INPUT # statement acquires information from a

```
Press a key to see first field

Sayonara

Press a key to see second field

Goodbye

Press a key to continue

That's the end of the file.
The JAPANESE.DOC file is closed.
```

FIGURE 11-10. Last record and end-of-file information, JAPANESE.DOC file

file in the same way that the INPUT statement acquires information entered from the keyboard. Both statements recognize a comma (,) as a separator between two items. Also, INPUT # is like using READ and DATA statements where the data is in a file.

The JAPANESE.DOC file was created using a WRITE # statement. Therefore, each field is enclosed in quotation marks, and the two fields are separated by a comma, as shown here.

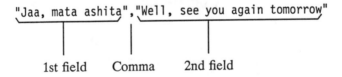

"Jaa, mata ashita","Well, see you again tomorrow"

1st field   Comma   2nd field

Because each field is enclosed in quotation marks, the commas following "Jaa" and "Well" are not recognized as separators by the INPUT # statement. These commas are read as part of the strings in which they occur. However, the INPUT # statement does not read the enclosing quotation marks as part of the string, as does the LINE INPUT # statement. Therefore, as you can see by the screen in Figure 11-10, the information appearing on the screen is not enclosed in quotation marks.

SOME SUGGESTIONS ABOUT FILES

You now know how to create and scan sequential files. You also know how to append new information to the end of an existing file. This section describes additional file management tools and suggests programs for you to write.

Changing a File Name

You can change the name of a file by using the DOS RENAME command or by using QBasic's NAME statement. The NAME statement has the form

```
NAME "oldfilename" AS "newfilename"
```

where *oldfilename* is the current name of the file and *newfilename* is the new name to be given to the file. Note that both file names must be enclosed in quotation marks. For example, to change the name of the JAPANESE.DOC file to NIHONGO.DOC, use the following statement:

```
NAME "JAPANESE.DOC" AS "NIHONGO.DOC"
```

After a file's name has been changed, the file still exists on the same disk drive and in the same place on the disk as before; the only difference is that the file has a new name.

A Program for You to Write

Write a program to copy and edit a sequential file. It might begin like this:

```
Copy and edit a sequential file

Old file name? JAPANESE.DOC

New file name? NIHONGO.DOC
```

You can't copy a file onto itself on the same disk. You can't copy JAPANESE.DOC to JAPANESE.DOC on the same disk or directory. You can copy a file to differently named files on the same disk. Then, after completion of the copying and editing process, you can delete the old file and rename the new file.

You can copy a file from one disk to another, using the same name. For example:

```
Copy and edit a sequential file

Old file name? A:JAPANESE.DOC

New file name? B:JAPANESE.DOC
```

Your program should read one record at a time from the old file and then let you choose whether to copy it to the new file. This way, you can copy only selected records from the old to the new file. If you wish, add an option to insert a new record from the keyboard at any time during the copy and edit process. Write your program as a main program and a set of SUB procedures to perform selected tasks. Start with a simple program, make it work, and then expand it as you think of more ways to manage your files.

Keep a list of your files and a brief description of each. You will find such a list especially useful as you create more and more files. Use the NAME statement to change the name of a file.

SUMMARY

You now know how to create and use both program files and data files. There are two types of data files: sequential files and random-access files.

The records in a sequential file must be accessed in order: record 1, record 2, record 3, and so on. The records in a random-access file can be accessed in any order: record 344, record 3, record 11, record 102, and so on. This chapter presented both unstructured and structured sequential files. An unstructured sequential file is one in which each record is a single string. A structured sequential file contains records that have two or more fields.

To create a sequential file, you open the file, write records to it, and, finally, close the file. To access the records in a sequential file, you open the file, and the records are read from the file. When all the records have been accessed, the file is closed.

chapter 12

RANDOM-ACCESS FILES

In this chapter, you will learn about the differences between random-access and sequential files, as well as how to use random-access files. In particular, you will

- Learn how information is stored in sequential and random-access files

- Learn to create a random-access file

- Learn to use the TYPE ... END TYPE structure to define a random-access file structure

- Learn to open a random-access file

- Learn to write (PUT) records to a random-access file

- Learn to access (GET) records from a random-access file

SEQUENTIAL AND RANDOM-ACCESS FILES

As you learned in Chapter 11, a sequential file is one in which the records must be accessed in the order in which they occur in the file. To access record 3, you must first access record 1 and then record 2. A random-access file, in contrast, is one in which the records can be accessed in a random order. You can access record 5, then record 72, then record 1, then record 11, and so on. You can obtain any record directly and quickly without first reading any other record. If you wish to access record 237, you can read it immediately, without first reading the previous 236 records in the file.

Random-access files are highly structured, *fixed-length files.* This means that all records in a random-access file are the same length, as are all the fields within a record. When you open a random-access file, you set the record length of that file; if you do not specify a record length, QBasic assigns a default record length of 128 bytes.

Random-access records are divided into fields. Each record in a random-access file has the same fields, in the same order; each field within a record has a fixed length. That is, corresponding fields in different records are the same length.

Random-access files have several advantages over sequential files: You can access any record very quickly; you can modify a record without having to rewrite the entire file; you can insert or delete records more easily than in sequential files; and you can sort them more easily than sequential files.

Random-access files also have some disadvantages. Data is often not stored efficiently; because random-access files have fixed-length fields and fixed-length records, the same number of bytes is used regardless of the number of characters being stored. In addition, a random-access file must be designed in advance. The length of each field must allow enough space for any data that might possibly be stored in that field.

Sequential and random-access files store information somewhat differently. Although they both have fields, the fields in a sequential file can be variable-length, but the fields in a random-access file must be of fixed length. Also, numbers are stored differently in the two types of files.

Sequential Files

In a sequential file, each character in a string is stored as 1 byte and each digit in a number is stored as 1 byte. For example, the string "abc" is stored as 3 bytes, the number 123 is stored as 3 bytes, −123 is stored as 4 bytes,

1.234 is stored as 5 bytes, and the floating-point number 1.234567E+13 is stored as 12 bytes. Each complete record is followed by two end-of-record characters, CR (carriage return) and LF (line feed).

Sequential files have variable-length records and can be either unstructured or structured. An unstructured sequential file is one in which one string is one record. Structured sequential files have at least two variable-length fields. In Chapter 11, you created and used two sequential data files called NOTES.DOC and JAPANESE.DOC, described here:

- **NOTES.DOC** This file is an unstructured sequential file. Each record is one string of variable length.

- **JAPANESE.DOC** This is a structured sequential file. Each record consists of two variable-length fields.

Figure 12-1 shows the JAPANESE.DOC file as it would appear if displayed in the View window. Each character in this file appears in Figure 12-1, except the two end-of-record characters (CR and LF) that follow each

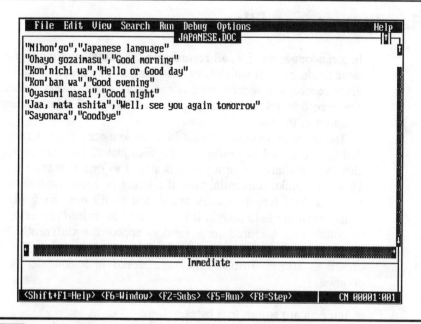

FIGURE 12-1.   JAPANESE.DOC file displayed in View window

record. Notice that the fields in this file vary in length. Each field is enclosed in quotation marks, and the fields are separated by commas. The records shown vary in length from 22 to 51 characters. For example, the first record is 32 bytes long, as shown here:

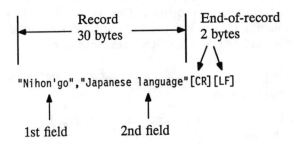

The JAPANESE.DOC file, as shown in Figure 12-1, has seven records. The shortest record is stored as 22 bytes, and the longest record is stored as 51 bytes. The file has seven records with a total length of 234 bytes. Therefore, the *average* record length is 234 divided by 7, or about 33 bytes.

Random-access Files

In a random-access file, all records are the same length; every record has the same fields, each of which is of fixed length. The first field is the same size in every record, the second field is the same size in every record, and so on. The record length and field lengths must be specified before any information is stored in the file.

There are two kinds of fields in a random-access file: string and numeric. Strings are stored in random-access files just as they are in sequential files; that is, one character in a string is stored as one character in a string field. However, unlike sequential files, if a string in a random-access file is shorter than the field length, spaces are added to fill out the field. If a string is longer than the field length, it is truncated to fit into the field.

Numbers are stored in a random-access file differently from the way they're stored in a sequential file. In a random-access file, they are not stored as strings. Instead, they are stored in a compact binary form, as follows:

- Integers are stored in 2 bytes.
- Long integers are stored in 4 bytes.

Record Number	First Field (Phrase.Japanese)	Second Field (Phrase.English)
1	Nihon'go	Japanese language
2	Ohayo gozaimasu	Good morning
3	Kon'nichi wa	Hello or Good day
4	Kon'ban wa	Good evening
5	Oyasumi nasai	Good night
6	Jaa, mata ashita	Well, see you again tomorrow
7	Sayonara	Goodbye

TABLE 12-1.   Records to Enter into the JAPANESE.RAN File

- Single-precision numbers are stored in 4 bytes.

- Double-precision numbers are stored in 8 bytes.

In this chapter, you will create and use two random-access files. The file JAPANESE.RAN is a random-access version of the JAPANESE.DOC file used in Chapter 11; this file has two string fields. CAMPING.CAT is a random-access file containing data about camping equipment; it has three string fields and three numeric fields.

CREATING JAPANESE.RAN, A RANDOM-ACCESS FILE

The JAPANESE.RAN file is a random-access file version of the sequential file JAPANESE.DOC, used in Chapter 11. Each record in the JAPANESE.RAN file has two string fields, and each field is exactly 78 characters long.

You can use Program 12-1, MAKEFIL3 (Create the JAPANESE.RAN Random-access File), to enter the records shown in Table 12-1. These

```
REM ** Create the JAPANESE.RAN Random-access File **
' QBasic Made Easy, Chapter 12.  Filename: MAKEFIL3.BAS

REM ** Set up and acquire name of file to create **
CLS
PRINT "Create a random-access file with two string fields"
PRINT
INPUT "Name of file"; filename$

REM ** Define structure of random-access file record **
TYPE RecordType
   Japanese AS STRING * 78    'String field with 78 characters
   English AS STRING * 78     'String field with 78 characters
END TYPE

REM ** Declare a variable of above type **
DIM Phrase AS RecordType

REM ** Open for random-access input and output **
OPEN filename$ FOR RANDOM AS #1 LEN = LEN(Phrase)

REM ** Enter records from keyboard, write to file **
DO
   CLS : PRINT "Creating "; filename$; " random-access file."
   PRINT : PRINT "Press a key to enter a record, or ESC to quit"
   kbd$ = INPUT$(1): IF kbd$ = CHR$(27) THEN EXIT DO

   PRINT : INPUT "Record number"; RecordNmbr

   PRINT : PRINT "Enter Japanese word or phrase"
   PRINT : LINE INPUT ">"; Phrase.Japanese

   PRINT : PRINT "Enter English equivalent"
   PRINT : LINE INPUT ">"; Phrase.English

   PUT #1, RecordNmbr, Phrase       'Put this record into file
LOOP

REM ** Print length of file, close file, end program **
PRINT
PRINT filename$; " has"; RecordNmbr; "record(s),"; LOF(1); "bytes."
CLOSE #1: END
```

═══════ **PROGRAM 12-1.**   Create the JAPANESE.RAN Random-access File

records are the same as those entered into the JAPANESE.DOC sequential file in Chapter 11. The program begins like this:

```
Create a random-access file with two string fields

Name of file? _
```

> Type: **JAPANESE.RAN**
> and press ENTER

The program then prompts you as follows:

```
Creating JAPANESE.RAN random-access file.

Press a key to enter a record, or ESC to quit
```

Press a key other than ESC to signal that you want to enter a record. You are asked for the record number:

```
Record number? _
```

> Type: **1**
> and press ENTER

Now enter record 1—first the Japanese word or phrase and then the English equivalent. After you type this information, but before you press ENTER, you should see this on the screen:

```
Record Number? 1

Enter Japanese word or phrase

>Nihon'go

Enter English equivalent

>Japanese language_
```

Press ENTER and this record is written to the file as record 1. Again you see

```
Creating JAPANESE.RAN random-access file.

Press a key to enter a record, or ESC to quit
```

The JAPANESE.RAN file now has one record. Do not enter another record. Instead

> Press: ESC

Pressing ESC ends the file creation process. You should see the following on the screen:

```
Creating JAPANESE.RAN random-access file.

Press a key to enter a record, or ESC to quit

JAPANESE.RAN has 1 record(s), 156 bytes.
```

The file now has one record, and this record is 156 bytes long. The record consists of two fields, each 78 bytes long, as follows:

First field: *Nihon'go* followed by 70 spaces

Second field: *Japanese language* followed by 61 spaces

In the next section, you will learn how Program MAKEFIL3 works. But first, press a key to return to the View window, run the program again, and enter records 2 through 7. For example, enter record 2 like this:

```
Record number? 2

Enter Japanese word or phrase

>Ohayo gozaimasu

Enter English equivalent

>Good morning_
```

Press ENTER and this record is written to the file as record 2. Continue entering records: record 3, record 4, and so on, to record 7. After you have entered record 7, end the file creation process:

Press: ESC

You will see this information on the screen:

```
Creating JAPANESE.RAN random-access file.

Press a key to enter a record, or ESC to quit

JAPANESE.RAN has 7 record(s), 1092 bytes.
```

The JAPANESE.DOC sequential file and the JAPANESE.RAN random-access file contain essentially the same information. However, the JAPANESE.RAN file is much larger than the JAPANESE.DOC file, as shown here:

• The JAPANESE.DOC file has 234 bytes.
• The JAPANESE.RAN file has 1092 bytes.

This size difference results from their different file structures. JAPANESE .DOC is a sequential file with seven *variable-length* records, and JAPANESE.RAN is a random-access file with seven *fixed-length* records. Each record in JAPANESE.RAN is 156 bytes long. You can calculate the record length like this:

```
Length of record = length of file/number of records
                 = 1092/7
                 = 156
```

Program MAKEFIL3 Explained

When creating a random-access file, you must first define the record structure. The following program block does this:

```
REM **  Define structure of random-access file record **
TYPE RecordType
   Japanese AS STRING * 78    'String field with 78 characters
   English AS STRING * 78     'String field with 78 characters
END TYPE
```

The TYPE...END TYPE structure defines *RecordType* as a kind of variable with two fields, called *Japanese* and *English*. The names *RecordType, Japanese,* and *English* were chosen to be descriptive of this file; all type names must conform to the conventions for QBasic variables. Once a TYPE structure has been defined, you must declare a variable to be of this type. This variable is then used whenever you assign data to this type. The following block declares the variable *Phrase* as type *RecordType*:

```
REM ** Declare a variable of above type  **
DIM Phrase AS RecordType
```

The variable *Phrase* is now of the type defined by the TYPE...END TYPE structure. You will use the variable *Phrase* to write to or read from the JAPANESE.RAN file. Associated with *Phrase* are two string field variables, as follows:

- *Phrase.Japanese* is a string field variable with a length of 78 characters.

- *Phrase.English* is a string field variable with a length of 78 characters.

Next, open the file for random access as file 1, like this:

```
REM ** Open for random-access input and output **
OPEN filename$ FOR RANDOM AS #1 LEN = LEN(Phrase)
```

When you open a random-access file, it is open for both input and output. You can write information to the file or read information from the file. You should also specify the record length (the default is 128 bytes). In the preceding OPEN statement, the record length is calculated by the clause LEN = LEN(Phrase). This specifies the record length as the length of *Phrase,* which is 156 bytes long.

Now the program is ready to acquire records entered from the keyboard. You do this by means of a DO ... LOOP. Inside the DO ... LOOP, the following program lines control entry of a record:

```
PRINT : INPUT "Record number"; RecordNmbr

PRINT : PRINT "Enter Japanese word or phrase"
PRINT : LINE INPUT ">"; Phrase.Japanese

PRINT : PRINT "Enter English equivalent"
PRINT : LINE INPUT ">"; Phrase.English

PUT #1, RecordNmbr, Phrase       'Put this record into file
```

Records in a random-access file are numbered 1, 2, 3, and so on. Record 1 is the first record in the file, record 2 is the second record, and so on. When a record is accessed in a random-access file, it is accessed by its record number. To create a random-access file, you can enter record 1, then record 2, and so on. The following statement acquires the record number and assigns it as the value of *RecordNmbr*:

```
INPUT "Record number"; RecordNmbr
```

Next, the value of *Phrase.Japanese* is acquired by the statement

```
LINE INPUT ">"; Phrase.Japanese
```

If the value entered has fewer than 78 characters, spaces are added to make a total of 78 characters in *Phrase.Japanese.* If the value entered is exactly 78 characters long, then it exactly matches the length of *Phrase.Japanese* and no spaces are added. If you enter a value that has more than 78 characters, it is truncated. The first 78 characters (from the left) are assigned as the value of *Phrase.Japanese*.

In a similar way, the value of *Phrase.English* is acquired by the statement

```
LINE INPUT ">"; Phrase.English
```

Together, *Phrase.Japanese* and *Phrase.English* make up one record, called *Phrase*. The statement

```
PUT #1, RecordNmbr, Phrase
```

writes (PUTs) the entire record (*Phrase*) to file 1 as record number *Record-Nmbr*. Note that, once you have entered a record, you can change it easily — just use its record number again, and then enter the new values of *Phrase.Japanese* and *Phrase.English*.

To exit the DO...LOOP, you press ESC at the appropriate time. The following program block prints information about the file, closes the file, and ends the program.

```
REM ** Print length of file, close file, end program **
PRINT
PRINT filename$; " has"; RecordNmbr; "record(s),"; LOF(1); "bytes."
CLOSE #1: END
```

Note that opening a file for random access does not erase any existing information. You can use Program MAKEFIL3 to append to an existing file. Just begin with a record number that is one more than the last record number in the existing file. You can also use the program to change any record in the file, by supplying the number of the record and entering the new information.

Scanning the JAPANESE.RAN File

After creating any new file, it is a good idea to proofread it. You can use Program 12-2, READFIL4 (Scan the JAPANESE.RAN Random-access File), to display records from the JAPANESE.RAN file on the Output screen, thus allowing you to examine it.

```
REM ** Scan the JAPANESE.RAN Random-access File **
' QBasic Made Easy, Chapter 12.  Filename: READFIL4.BAS

REM ** Set up and acquire name of file to create **
CLS
PRINT "Scan a random-access file with two string fields"
PRINT
INPUT "Name of file"; filename$

REM ** Define structure of random-access file record **
TYPE RecordType
   Japanese AS STRING * 78    'String field with 78 characters
   English AS STRING * 78     'String field with 78 characters
END TYPE

REM ** Declare a variable of above type **
DIM Phrase AS RecordType

REM ** Open for random-access input and output **
OPEN filename$ FOR RANDOM AS #1 LEN = LEN(Phrase)

REM ** Tell what to do **
CLS : PRINT "Scan "; filename$; " random-access file."

REM ** Start at first record in file **
RecordNmbr = 1

REM ** Get records from file and print to screen **
DO UNTIL EOF(1)
   PRINT : PRINT "Press a key to get a record, or ESC to quit"
   kbd$ = INPUT$(1): IF kbd$ = CHR$(27) THEN EXIT DO
   GET #1, RecordNmbr, Phrase
   PRINT : PRINT "Record number:"; RecordNmbr
   PRINT Phrase.Japanese
   PRINT Phrase.English
   RecordNmbr = RecordNmbr + 1
LOOP

REM ** Close the file and print end of program message **
IF EOF(1) THEN PRINT "End of file"
CLOSE #1
PRINT : PRINT "The "; filename$; " file is closed."
END
```

PROGRAM 12-2. Scan the JAPANESE.RAN Random-access File

```
Scan JAPANESE.RAN random-access file.

Press a key to get a record, or ESC to quit

Record number: 1
Nihon'go
Japanese language

Press a key to get a record, or ESC to quit

Record number: 2
Ohayo gozaimasu
Good morning

Press a key to get a record, or ESC to quit

The JAPANESE.RAN file is closed.
```

FIGURE 12-2. The first two records of the JAPANESE.RAN file

Run program READFIL4 and enter **JAPANESE.RAN** as the name of the file to scan. You can press a key other than ESC to see a record or press ESC to quit. Figure 12-2 shows the output after a scan of the first two records. ESC was pressed to end this run.

If you keep pressing a key, you will reach the end of the file, and the program ends as shown in Figure 12-3. Because the JAPANESE.RAN file has only seven records, an attempt to get record 8 causes an end-of-file condition.

Program READFIL4 reads records from the file in record number order; first record 1, then record 2, and so on. The records are read and printed to the screen by this DO ... LOOP:

```
DO UNTIL EOF(1)
  PRINT : PRINT "Press a key to get a record, or ESC to quit"
  kbd$ = INPUT$(1): IF kbd$ = CHR$(27) THEN EXIT DO
  GET #1, RecordNmbr, Phrase
  PRINT : PRINT "Record number:"; RecordNmbr
  PRINT Phrase.Japanese
  PRINT Phrase.English
  RecordNmbr = RecordNmbr + 1
LOOP
```

You use a GET statement to read a record from a random-access file. The statement

```
GET #1, RecordNmbr, Phrase
```

reads the record specified by the value of *RecordNmbr* and assigns this record as the value of *Phrase*. Each record has two fields: the first field is *Phrase.Japanese;* the second field is *Phrase.English.* In reading a record from the file, the GET statement assigns values to these two variables that were previously defined by a TYPE ... END structure and the DIM *Phrase* AS *RecordType* statement. These values are printed by the statements

```
PRINT Phrase.Japanese
PRINT Phrase.English
```

After the values of *Phrase.Japanese* and *Phrase.English* are printed, the value of *RecordNmbr* is increased by 1, as follows:

```
RecordNmbr = RecordNmbr + 1
```

Each time you press a key other than ESC, the DO ... LOOP retrieves and prints the next consecutively numbered record. The DO ... LOOP ends when you press ESC, or when the end-of-file is reached. End-of-program information is printed by the program block shown next:

```
REM ** Close the file and print end of program message **
IF EOF(1) THEN PRINT "End of file"
CLOSE #1
PRINT : PRINT "The "; filename$; " file is closed."
END
```

```
Press a key to get a record, or ESC to quit

Record number: 7
Sayonara
Goodbye

Press a key to get a record, or ESC to quit

Record number: 8


End of file

The JAPANESE.RAN file is closed.
```

FIGURE 12-3. End of file in scanning the JAPANESE.RAN file

The statement

```
IF EOF(1) THEN PRINT "End of file"
```

checks the end-of-file condition. If the DO . . . LOOP ended because the end-of-file was reached, the message "End of file" is printed. If you press ESC before reaching the end of the file, this message is not printed. In either case, the program closes file 1, tells you the file is closed, and ends.

Using the JAPANESE.RAN File for Random Practice

In Chapter 10, you used Program FLSHCD04 for random practice with data read from DATA statements into arrays. You can use the JAPANESE.RAN file for random practice without first reading it into arrays in memory. Program 12-3, FLSHCD05 (Random Flash Card with Random-access File), provides this capability. This program reads a randomly selected record, displays "side A," delays 3 seconds, and then displays "side B." You can press ESC to quit or another key to see another flash card. There is one chance in seven of seeing the record shown here:

```
Random practice with JAPANESE.RAN random-access file.
The file has 7 records.

Kon'ban wa

Good evening

Press a key for another, or ESC to quit
```

```
DECLARE SUB Delay (seconds!)
DECLARE SUB ShowSides (SideA$, SideB$)
REM ** Random Flash Card with Random-access File **
' QBasic Made Easy, Chapter 12.  Filename: FLSHCD05.BAS

REM ** Set up **
DEF FNran (n) = INT(n * RND) + 1    'Random integer function
RANDOMIZE TIMER

REM ** Acquire name of file **
CLS : PRINT "Random practice with a random-access file"
PRINT : INPUT "Name of file"; filename$
```

PROGRAM 12-3. Random Flash Card with Random-access File

```
REM ** Define structure of random-access file record **
TYPE RecordType
  SideA AS STRING * 78      'String field with 78 characters
  SideB AS STRING * 78      'String field with 78 characters
END TYPE

REM ** Declare a variable of above type **
DIM FlashCard AS RecordType

REM ** Open for random-access & compute number of records **
OPEN filename$ FOR RANDOM AS #1 LEN = LEN(FlashCard)
NmbrRcrds = LOF(1) / LEN(FlashCard)

REM ** Random practice -- press ESC to quit **
DO
  CLS
  PRINT "Random practice with "; filename$; " random-access file."
  PRINT "The file has"; NmbrRcrds; "records."

  ' Get a random flash card (record) & show sides
  CardNmbr = FNran(NmbrRcrds)
  GET #1, CardNmbr, FlashCard
  CALL ShowSides(FlashCard.SideA, FlashCard.SideB)

  PRINT : PRINT "Press a key for another, or ESC to quit"
  kbd$ = INPUT$(1): IF kbd$ = CHR$(27) THEN EXIT DO
LOOP

REM ** End of program stuff **
CLOSE #1
PRINT : PRINT "The "; filename$; " file is closed."
END

SUB Delay (seconds!)
  start! = TIMER: DO WHILE TIMER < start! + seconds!: LOOP
END SUB

SUB ShowSides (SideA$, SideB$)
  PRINT : PRINT SideA$         'Show side A
  CALL Delay(3)                'Call time delay SUB (3 seconds)
  PRINT : PRINT SideB$         'Show side B
END SUB
```

═══════ **PROGRAM 12-3.**   Random Flash Card with Random-access File
(continued)

Each time you press a key other than ESC, you will see another randomly selected record. When you tire of practicing, press ESC and you will see the end-of-program message, along with the last record viewed, perhaps as shown here:

```
Jaa, mata ashita

Well, see you again tomorrow

Press a key for another, or ESC to quit

The JAPANESE.RAN file is closed.
```

Program FLSHCD05 defines the record structure by means of the following program block:

```
REM ** Define structure of random-access file record **
TYPE RecordType
  SideA AS STRING * 78      'String field with 78 characters
  SideB AS STRING * 78      'String field with 78 characters
END TYPE
```

Next, it declares a record variable named *FlashCard*:

```
REM ** Declare a variable of above type **
DIM FlashCard AS RecordType
```

Together, these two program blocks define the variables *FlashCard.SideA* and *FlashCard.SideB*.

The file is opened and the number of records in the file is computed by the following block:

```
REM ** Open for random-access & compute number of records **
OPEN filename$ FOR RANDOM AS #1 LEN = LEN(FlashCard)
NmbrRcrds = LOF(1) / LEN(FlashCard)
```

The statement

```
NmbrRcrds = LOF(1) / LEN(FlashCard)
```

computes the number of records in file 1 and assigns it as the value of *NmbrRcrds*. This is done by dividing the length of the entire file (LOF) by the length of one record (LEN(*FlashCard*)). The value of *NmbrRcrds* is used later in the program to obtain a random record number.

This completes the preliminaries, and random practice begins, controlled by a DO...LOOP. Inside the DO...LOOP, the following block gets a randomly selected record and then calls the ShowSides SUB procedure to display the flash card on the screen:

```
' Get a random flash card (record) & show sides
CardNmbr = FNran(NmbrRcrds)
GET #1, CardNmbr, FlashCard
CALL ShowSides(FlashCard.SideA, FlashCard.SideB)
```

The statement

```
CardNmbr = FNran(NmbrRcrds)
```

computes a random record number and assigns it as the value of *CardNmbr.* This value is a random integer in the range 1 to the value of *NmbrRcrds.* The function *FNran* is defined in the program's setup block.

The GET statement gets the randomly selected record from the file, thus obtaining the values of *FlashCard.SideA* and *FlashCard.SideB.* These values are passed to the ShowSides SUB procedure by the following statement:

```
CALL ShowSides(FlashCard.SideA, FlashCard.SideB)
```

The ShowSides SUB procedure is shown here:

```
SUB ShowSides (SideA$, SideB$)
   PRINT : PRINT SideA$          'Show side A
   CALL Delay(3)                 'Call time delay SUB (3 seconds)
   PRINT : PRINT SideB$          'Show side B
END SUB
```

The CALL statement passes the value of *FlashCard.SideA* as the value of the SUB procedure variable *SideA$* and passes the value of *FlashCard.SideB* as the value of the SUB procedure variable *SideB$.* The procedure then displays the value of *SideA$,* calls the Delay SUB procedure to obtain a 3-second delay, and then displays the value of *SideB$.*

For the JAPANESE.RAN file, the Japanese word or phrase is displayed first, and then the English equivalent. You can reverse this order to display first English and then Japanese by writing the CALL statement like this:

```
CALL ShowSides(FlashCard.SideB, FlashCard.SideA)
```

This CALL statement passes the value of *FlashCard.SideB* to the variable *SideA$* and passes the value of *FlashCard.SideA* to the variable *SideB$*. You could even randomly select between the two possibilities by replacing the CALL statement with the following IF . . . THEN structure:

```
IF FNran(2) = 1 THEN
  CALL ShowSides(FlashCard.SideA, FlashCard.SideB)
ELSE
  CALL ShowSides(FlashCard.SideB, FlashCard.SideA)
END IF
```

SOME PROGRAM SUGGESTIONS The JAPANESE.RAN file shown here is very short. The authors have several long files for studying Japanese and other subjects. Here are some suggestions for programming projects you can do.

Write a program to use a file for sequential practice, with an option to save for later review any item for which your response is incorrect. You might call this file OOPS.RAN. Later, you can use the OOPS.RAN file for further study.

Write a program to use a file for random practice. Initially, each record has the same probability of being chosen as any other record. After making your mental response and viewing the correct response, press the C key to indicate "correct" or the N key to indicate "not correct." Have your program then increase the probability of choosing any record on which you make an incorrect response.

A PERSONAL CAMPING EQUIPMENT FILE

If you are a catalog browser, you might find the next program useful. It is designed to store and retrieve information from various camping equipment catalogs. If you aren't interested in camping, you can use this program to store information on other topics by making minor changes to the program.

Perhaps the main advantage of random-access files over sequential files is the ability to PUT or GET any record by using its record number. You can use Program 12-4, CAMPCAT (PUT or GET Records, CAMPING.CAT File), to create the CAMPING.CAT file, append records to the file, change existing records, and display existing records.

```
DECLARE SUB GetRecord ()
DECLARE SUB PutRecord ()
REM ** PUT or GET Records, CAMPING.CAT File **
' QBasic Made Easy, Chapter 12.  Filename: CAMPCAT.BAS

    CLS                              'Clear the Output screen

REM ** Define structure of CAMPING.CAT file **
TYPE FileStructure
    Catalog AS STRING * 20      'String field, name of catalog
    Item AS STRING * 72         'String field, item description
    CatNum AS STRING * 12       'String field, catalog number
    Page AS INTEGER             'Numeric field, page number
    Price AS SINGLE             'Numeric field, price each
    Ounces AS SINGLE            'Numeric field, weight in ounces
END TYPE

REM ** Declare a record variable of above type **
DIM Camping AS FileStructure

REM ** Open the file **
OPEN "CAMPING.CAT" FOR RANDOM AS #1 LEN = LEN(Camping)

REM ** PUT or GET records, or quit (Esc) **
DO
    ' Find out what to do
    CLS : PRINT "PUT or GET individual records, CAMPING.CAT file."
    NmbrRcrds% = LOF(1) \ LEN(Camping)
    PRINT : PRINT "CAMPING.CAT has"; NmbrRcrds%; "records."
    PRINT : PRINT "Press P to PUT, G to GET, or ESC to quit: ";
    DO
      BEEP: kbd$ = UCASE$(INPUT$(1))
    LOOP UNTIL kbd$ = "P" OR kbd$ = "G" OR kbd$ = CHR$(27)
    PorGorEsc$ = kbd$: PRINT PorGorEsc$

    ' Perform requested operation, PUT (P) or GET (G) or ESC
    SELECT CASE PorGorEsc$
      CASE CHR$(27)                   'Esc to quit
        EXIT DO
      CASE "P"                        'P to PUT
        CALL PutRecord
```

───────── **PROGRAM 12-4.** PUT or GET Records, CAMPING.CAT File

```
      CASE "G"                           'G to GET
          CALL GetRecord
      END SELECT
LOOP

REM ** End of program stuff **
CLOSE #1
PRINT : PRINT "The CAMPING.CAT file is closed."
END

SUB GetRecord
    ' Declare Camping as record defined in main program
    DIM Camping AS FileStructure
    PRINT : INPUT "Record number"; RcrdNmbr
    GET #1, RcrdNmbr, Camping
    PRINT : PRINT "Name of Catalog: "; Camping.Catalog
    PRINT : PRINT "Page number:"; Camping.Page
    PRINT : PRINT "Description of item: ": PRINT Camping.Item
    PRINT : PRINT "Catalog number: "; Camping.CatNum
    PRINT : PRINT "Price each:"; Camping.Price
    PRINT : PRINT "Weight in ounces:"; Camping.Ounces
    PRINT : PRINT "Press a key to continue"
    kbd$ = INPUT$(1)
END SUB

SUB PutRecord
    ' Declare Camping as record defined in main program
    DIM Camping AS FileStructure
    PRINT : INPUT "Record number"; RcrdNmbr
    PRINT : LINE INPUT "Name of catalog? "; Camping.Catalog
    PRINT : INPUT "Page number"; Camping.Page
    PRINT : PRINT "Description of item:"
    PRINT : LINE INPUT "? "; Camping.Item
    PRINT : LINE INPUT "Catalog number? "; Camping.CatNum
    PRINT : INPUT "Price each"; Camping.Price
    PRINT : INPUT "Weight in ounces"; Camping.Ounces
    PUT #1, RcrdNmbr, Camping
    PRINT : PRINT "Press a key to continue"
    kbd$ = INPUT$(1)
END SUB
```

═══════ **PROGRAM 12-4.** PUT or GET Records, CAMPING.CAT File
                          (continued)

Program CAMPCAT consists of a main program and two SUB procedures: GetRecord and PutRecord. These are described in the sections that follow.

The CAMPCAT Main Program

Figure 12-4 shows the main program of Program CAMPCAT. It begins by defining the record structure of the CAMPING.CAT random-access file as shown next. The record type name *FileStructure* is intentionally chosen to be different from the record type name *RecordType* used in other programs in this chapter. This is done to remind you that you can use any record type name you want, as long as it conforms to the conventions for naming QBasic variables.

```
REM ** Define structure of CAMPING.CAT file **
TYPE FileStructure
   Catalog AS STRING * 20      'String field, name of catalog
   Item AS STRING * 72         'String field, item description
   CatNum AS STRING * 12       'String field, catalog number
   Page AS INTEGER             'Numeric field, page number
   Price AS SINGLE             'Numeric field, price each
   Ounces AS SINGLE            'Numeric field, weight in ounces
END TYPE
```

This TYPE...END TYPE structure defines a record that has three string fields and three numeric fields. The storage requirements for these fields and the total for the entire record are shown in Table 12-2.

The structure of the records in the CAMPING.CAT file has now been defined. Next, a variable is declared that represents the entire record. Again, any name that conforms to QBasic's naming conventions is fine. *Camping* is declared a *FileStructure* type by the following program block:

```
REM ** Declare a record variable of above type **
DIM Camping AS FileStructure
```

Camping has now been defined as the name of an entire record, 114 bytes long. Associated with the record name are three string variables and three numeric variables, as shown in Table 12-3.

Once the file has been defined, it can be opened.

```
REM ** Open the file **
OPEN "CAMPING.CAT" FOR RANDOM AS #1 LEN = LEN(Camping)
```

```
DECLARE SUB GetRecord ()
DECLARE SUB PutRecord ()
REM ** PUT or GET Records, CAMPING.CAT File **
' QBasic Made Easy, Chapter 12.  Filename: CAMPCAT.BAS

REM ** Define structure of CAMPING.CAT file **
TYPE FileStructure
  Catalog AS STRING * 20        'String field, name of catalog
  Item AS STRING * 72           'String field, item description
  CatNum AS STRING * 12         'String field, catalog number
  Page AS INTEGER               'Numeric field, page number
  Price AS SINGLE               'Numeric field, price each
  Ounces AS SINGLE              'Numeric field, weight in ounces
END TYPE

REM ** Declare a record variable of above type **
DIM Camping AS FileStructure

REM ** Open the file **
OPEN "CAMPING.CAT" FOR RANDOM AS #1 LEN = LEN(Camping)

REM ** PUT or GET records, or quit (Esc) **
DO
   ' Find out what to do
   CLS : PRINT "PUT or GET individual records, CAMPING.CAT file."
   NmbrRcrds% = LOF(1) \ LEN(Camping)
   PRINT : PRINT "CAMPING.CAT has"; NmbrRcrds%; "records."
   PRINT : PRINT "Press P to PUT, G to GET, or ESC to quit: ";
   DO
      BEEP: kbd$ = UCASE$(INPUT$(1))
   LOOP UNTIL kbd$ = "P" OR kbd$ = "G" OR kbd$ = CHR$(27)
   PorGorEsc$ = kbd$: PRINT PorGorEsc$

   ' Perform requested operation, PUT (P) or GET (G) or ESC
   SELECT CASE PorGorEsc$
      CASE CHR$(27)                'Esc to quit
         EXIT DO
      CASE "P"                     'P to PUT
         CALL PutRecord
      CASE "G"                     'G to GET
         CALL GetRecord
   END SELECT
LOOP

REM ** End of program stuff **
CLOSE #1
PRINT : PRINT "The CAMPING.CAT file is closed."
END
```

FIGURE 12-4. Main program of Program CAMPCAT

Name of Field	Type of Field	Bytes Required
Catalog	string	20
Item	string	72
CatNum	string	12
Page	numeric, integer	2
Price	numeric, single-precision	4
Ounces	numeric, single-precision	4
	Total bytes required	114

TABLE 12-2. CAMPING.CAT Record Storage Requirements

Now the file exists in name only but has no records. A DO . . . LOOP allows you to PUT records into the file or to GET and display records that you have entered. The top part of the DO . . . LOOP is shown here:

```
' Find out what to do
CLS : PRINT "PUT or GET individual records, CAMPING.CAT file."
NmbrRcrds% = LOF(1) \ LEN(Camping)
PRINT : PRINT "CAMPING.CAT has"; NmbrRcrds%; "records."
PRINT : PRINT "Press P to PUT, G to GET, or ESC to quit: ";
DO
  BEEP: kbd$ = UCASE$(INPUT$(1))
LOOP UNTIL kbd$ = "P" OR kbd$ = "G" OR kbd$ = CHR$(27)
PorGorEsc$ = kbd$: PRINT PorGorEsc$
```

Variable Name	Variable Type
Camping.Catalog	string
Camping.Item	string
Camping.CatNum	string
Camping.Page	numeric, integer
Camping.Price	numeric, single-precision
Camping.Ounces	numeric, single-precision

TABLE 12-3. Field Variables in *Camping* Record

This block prints information on what to do, including the number of records in the file, and then waits for someone to press P or G or ESC. No other keys are accepted—if you press another key, you will hear a beep. When you press one of the three acceptable keys, the key it is assigned as the value of *PorGorEsc$* to be used in the SELECT CASE structure, shown here.

```
' Perform requested operation, PUT (P) or GET (G) or ESC
SELECT CASE PorGorEsc$
   CASE CHR$(27)                    'Esc to quit
      EXIT DO
   CASE "P"                         'P to PUT
      CALL PutRecord
   CASE "G"                         'G to GET
      CALL GetRecord
END SELECT
```

This SELECT CASE structure selects one of three possibilities. If the value of *PorGorEsc$* is the ESC key, an exit is made from the DO . . . LOOP and the program ends. If the value of *PorGorEsc$* is P, the PutRecord SUB procedure is called so you can enter a record to the file. If the value of *PorGorEsc$* is G, the GetRecord SUB procedure is called to get a record and display it on the Output screen. The PutRecord and GetRecord SUB procedures are described in the next two sections.

The PutRecord SUB Procedure

Figure 12-5 shows the PutRecord SUB procedure. It begins by defining *Camping* as the record variable defined by the TYPE . . . END TYPE structure in the main program, as follows:

```
DIM Camping AS FileStructure
```

The TYPE . . . END TYPE structure cannot be used in a SUB or FUNCTION procedure. It must appear in the main program, or *main module,* as it is also called in QBasic. You must include the preceding DIM statement in order to use the variables defined by *FileStructure,* such as *Camping.Catalog, Camping.Item,* and so on.

```
SUB PutRecord
   ' Declare Camping as record defined in main program
   DIM Camping AS FileStructure
   PRINT : INPUT "Record number"; RcrdNmbr
   PRINT : LINE INPUT "Name of catalog? "; Camping.Catalog
   PRINT : INPUT "Page number"; Camping.Page
   PRINT : PRINT "Description of item:"
   PRINT : LINE INPUT "? "; Camping.Item
   PRINT : LINE INPUT "Catalog number? "; Camping.CatNum
   PRINT : INPUT "Price each"; Camping.Price
   PRINT : INPUT "Weight in ounces"; Camping.Ounces
   PUT #1, RcrdNmbr, Camping
   PRINT : PRINT "Press a key to continue"
   kbd$ = INPUT$(1)
END SUB
```

FIGURE 12-5. The PutRecord SUB procedure

The rest of the procedure acquires the record number and the information to be put into the file and then PUTs the record to the file. Figure 12-6 shows a sample first record entered from the keyboard. Near the top of the screen, notice that the CAMPING.CAT file had 0 records prior to entry of this record.

Figure 12-7 shows entry of record 2. When you press a key to continue the program, you will see the following:

```
PUT or GET individual records, CAMPING.CAT file.

CAMPING.CAT has 2 records.

Press P to PUT, G to GET, or ESC to quit:
```

The CAMPING.CAT file now has two records. If you wish, press P and enter record 3. Or go on to the next section and learn about the GetRecord SUB procedure.

The GetRecord SUB Procedure

Figure 12-8 shows the GetRecord SUB procedure. It begins by defining *Camping* as the record variable defined by the TYPE ... END TYPE structure in the main program, as follows:

PUT or GET individual records, CAMPING.CAT file.

CAMPING.CAT has 0 records.

Press P to PUT, G to GET, or ESC to quit: P

Record number? 1

Name of catalog? Real Good Gear

Page number? 37

Description of item:

? Slobbovian army knife

Catalog number? SAK-1234

Price each? 9.95

Weight in ounces? 3

Press a key to continue

FIGURE 12-6. First record entered into CAMPING.CAT file

```
DIM Camping AS FileStructure
```

The rest of the procedure acquires the record number of the desired record, gets the record, and prints the information in the record to the screen. Figure 12-9 shows record 2 as it is displayed on the screen.

Pressing ESC to End the CAMPCAT Program

You can continue pressing P to PUT a new record or change an existing record or continue pressing G to GET and display an existing record. When you are finished,

Press: ESC

PUT or GET individual records, CAMPING.CAT file.

CAMPING.CAT has 1 records.

Press P to PUT, G to GET, or ESC to quit: P

Record number? 2

Name of catalog? Vagabond Outfitters

Page number? 6

Description of item:

? Slumberbum sleeping bag

Catalog number? zzzzz007

Price each? 69.95

Weight in ounces? 53

Press a key to continue

FIGURE 12-7. Second record entered into CAMPING.CAT file

```
SUB GetRecord
  ' Declare Camping as record defined in main program
  DIM Camping AS FileStructure
  PRINT : INPUT "Record number"; RcrdNmbr
  GET #1, RcrdNmbr, Camping
  PRINT : PRINT "Name of Catalog: "; Camping.Catalog
  PRINT : PRINT "Page number:"; Camping.Page
  PRINT : PRINT "Description of item: ": PRINT Camping.Item
  PRINT : PRINT "Catalog number: "; Camping.CatNum
  PRINT : PRINT "Price each:"; Camping.Price
  PRINT : PRINT "Weight in ounces:"; Camping.Ounces
  PRINT : PRINT "Press a key to continue"
  kbd$ = INPUT$(1)
END SUB
```

FIGURE 12-8. The GetRecord SUB procedure

```
PUT or GET individual records, CAMPING.CAT file.

CAMPING.CAT has 2 records.

Press P to PUT, G to GET, or ESC to quit: G

Record number? 2

Name of Catalog: Vagabond Outfitters

Page number: 6

Description of item:
Slumberbum sleeping bag

Catalog number: zzzzz007

Price each: 69.95

Weight in ounces: 53

Press a key to continue
```

══════ **FIGURE 12-9.** Second record of CAMPING.CAT retrieved and
displayed

This ends the program. You will see the following, or something similar, on
the screen:

```
PUT or GET individual records, CAMPING.CAT file.

CAMPING.CAT has 2 records.

Press P to PUT, G to GET, or ESC to quit:

The CAMPING.CAT file is closed.
```

SUMMARY

Random-access files are files in which any record can be accessed at any
time. They store information less efficiently than sequential files, but, unlike

sequential files, you can access and modify any record without having to rewrite the entire file.

The TYPE . . . END TYPE structure is used to define the structure of a random-access file. A TYPE . . . END TYPE structure is given a name and is declared as a variable. That variable name is then used when assigning or accessing the fields defined in the TYPE . . . END TYPE structure.

The records in a random-access file are accessed by record number. Use the GET keyword to read a record from a random-access file; use the PUT keyword to write a record to a random-access file.

chapter 13

YOUR QBASIC
BACKPACK

In Chapters 1 through 12 of this book, you learned how to use many elements of QBasic. You now know how to use the QBasic keywords listed in Table 13-1.

This chapter poses problems for you to solve by applying your QBasic skills. If you would like some solution hints, send a self-addressed, stamped envelope to: Your QBasic Backpack, P.O. Box 1635, Sebastopol CA 95473.

NUMBER CRUNCHING

When BASIC came into use in 1964, it was a number-crunching language, used primarily for numerical calculations. The ability to handle strings was added later. Here are some number-crunching exercises for your enjoyment.

The Million Factory

In the Million Factory, the raw materials are

* The decimal digits: 0, 1, 2, 3, 4, 5, 6, 7, 8, 9

- The QBasic operations: addition (+), subtraction (−), multiplication (*), division (/), and exponentiation (^)

- Parentheses ( )

ABS	EOF	LOOP	SINGLE
AND	EXIT	LPRINT	SOUND
APPEND	FIX	MID$	SPACE$
AS	FN	MOD	SQR
ASC	FOR	NAME	STEP
BASE	FUNCTION	NEXT	STR$
BEEP	GET	OPEN	STRING
CALL	GOTO	OPTION	STRING$
CASE	IF	OR	SUB
CHR$	INKEY$	OUTPUT	TAB
CIRCLE	INPUT	PAINT	THEN
CLOSE	INPUT$	PRINT	TIME$
CLS	INSTR	PSET	TIMER
COLOR	INT	PUT	TO
DATA	INTEGER	RANDOM	TYPE
DATE$	IS	RANDOMIZE	UBOUND
DECLARE	KILL	READ	UCASE$
DEF	LBOUND	REM	UNTIL
DIM	LCASE$	RESTORE	USING
DO	LEFT$	RIGHT$	VAL
DOUBLE	LEN	RND	VIEW
DRAW	LINE	SCREEN	WEND
ELSE	LOCATE	SELECT	WHILE
ELSEIF	LOF	SGN	WIDTH
END	LONG	SHARED	WRITE

TABLE 13-1. QBasic Keywords

The finished product is the number 1 million, shown on the screen or printed as 1000000.

You are the million maker. Complete the following program by writing a QBasic numerical expression the value of which is exactly 1,000,000.

```
REM ** The Million Factory **
' QBasic Made Easy, Chapter 13.  Filename: MILLION.BAS

CLS

Million = _____

PRINT "One million:"; Million
```

In your numerical expression for one million,

- Use every decimal digit, 0 through 9, once and only once.

- Use only these QBasic operations:

    + − * / ^

- Use them as many times as you want.

- Use parentheses ( ) as many times as you want.

Here is an easy, but not very interesting, solution:

```
Million = 10 ^ 6 + (2 + 3 - 5) * (4 + 7 + 8 + 9)
```

Try to make your solutions more interesting than the one just shown. Here are some ideas:

- Use each operation (+, −, *, /, ^) at least once.

- Use each operation (+, −, *, /, ^) exactly once.

- Use the digits 0 to 9 in ascending order.

- Use the digits 9 to 0 in descending order.

- Surprise everyone by your clever use of digits, operations, and parentheses.

The Digit Factory

In the Digit Factory, the raw materials are

- The numbers 1, 2, 3, 4, and 5
- The QBasic operations: addition (+), subtraction (−), multiplication (*), and division (/)
- Parentheses ( )

The finished products are the decimal digits 0, 1, 2, 3, 4, 5, 6, 7, 8, and 9.

You are the digit maker. For each decimal digit, 0 through 9, write a QBasic numerical expression the value of which is equal to the digit. In any such expression,

- Use each number (1, 2, 3, 4, 5) once and only once.
- Use each BASIC operation (+, −, *, /) once and only once.
- No other QBasic operations may be used, except parentheses.
- Use as many parentheses as you wish.

For example, here are three BASIC expressions for the digit 5. Each expression is equal to 5.

```
2 * 3 / 1 + 4 - 5
(3 + 2 - 1) * 5 / 4
(3 + 2) / (1 * 5 - 4)
```

Write one or more BASIC expressions for *each* digit, 0 through 9. Try to write expressions in which one or more of the following is true:

- The numbers 1, 2, 3, 4, 5 are in ascending order.
- The numbers are in descending order (5, 4, 3, 2, 1).
- The operations appear in the order +, −, *, /.
- The operations appear in the order /, *, −, +.

Write a program using the Digit Factory rules to compute and display all ten digits. Your program might include a block like the one shown here to print the results of previous computations:

```
PRINT "Zero:", zero
PRINT "One:", one
PRINT "Two:", two
PRINT "Three:", three
PRINT "Four:", four
PRINT "Five:", five
PRINT "Six:", six
PRINT "Seven:", seven
PRINT "Eight:", eight
PRINT "Nine:", nine
```

The World's Most Expensive Checkbook Balancer

If you would rather use your $1000 computer than your $10 solar-powered calculator, here is a problem for you. Write a program to help you balance your checkbook. A run of this program might begin like this:

```
World's Most Expensive Checkbook Balancer

    Enter a check as a negative number and press ENTER
    For example: -14.95 [ENTER]

    Enter a deposit without + or - and press ENTER
    For example: 123.45 [ENTER]

    To quit, enter zero (0) and press ENTER

May the Force keep all your balances positive
```

Having printed the instructions, the program is ready to receive the old balance and any number of checks and deposits. For example:

```
Old balance (type number and press ENTER)? 567.89

Check (-) or deposit? -14.95
The new balance is        552.94

Check (-) or deposit? 123.45
The new balance is        676.39

Check (-) or deposit? _
```

Enter as many checks and deposits as you want. The new balance is printed after each entry. To quit, enter **0**, and the computer will print the old balance, the total values of checks and deposits that you entered, and the new balance, perhaps like this:

```
Old balance:            567.89
Total checks entered:   -14.95
Total deposits entered: 123.45
New balance:            676.39
```

If you enter lots of checks and/or deposits, the instructions will scroll upward and off the screen. To prevent this, you can locate the instructions in the bottom part of the screen and then lock them in with a VIEW PRINT statement. The instructions will then remain fixed while other information is allowed to scroll.

Perhaps you would like to print all information to the printer. To do so, change all PRINT statements to LPRINT. Also add statements to LPRINT the old balance and the values of checks and deposits that are entered from the keyboard. You may want to line up checks (negative numbers) and deposits (positive numbers) in separate columns by judicious use of PRINT USING and TAB.

How Many Ways to Lose the Lottery?

In a typical lottery game, you pick a set of numbers, all different, from a larger set of numbers. For example, in one lottery you choose six numbers in the range 1 to 49.

In how many ways can you pick k different numbers from a set of n numbers? Try a small example: In how many ways can you pick two different numbers from the numbers 1, 2, 3, and 4? In this case, it is easy to list the possible choices, as shown here:

1 and 2
1 and 3
1 and 4
2 and 3
2 and 4
3 and 4

There are only six choices. Remember, choosing 2 and 1 is the same as choosing 1 and 2; choosing 1 and 3 is the same as choosing 3 and 1, and so on.

Try listing the ways in which you can choose two different numbers from the numbers 1, 2, 3, 4, and 5. There are ten ways. Also list the ways you can choose three different numbers from the numbers 1, 2, 3, 4, and 5. Again, there are ten ways.

Write a program to compute the number of ways you can choose k numbers from a set of n numbers. Here is a sample run of a program using 5 as the value of n and 2 as the value of k:

```
Number of ways to pick k different numbers from n numbers

How many numbers to pick from? 5
How many numbers do you pick ? 2

Number of ways: 10
```

Here is another run, showing the number of ways to pick six different numbers from the numbers 1 to 49.

```
Number of ways to pick k different numbers from n numbers

How many numbers to pick from? 49
How many numbers do you pick ? 6

Number of ways: 13983816
```

If you have one set of six numbers in the 6-49 lottery game, you have one chance to win and 13,983,815 ways to lose.

The Binary Blues

People use *decimal numbers* to do arithmetic. A $10 solar-powered calculator does decimal arithmetic correctly. Let's do some simple decimal arithmetic.

Suppose that the local sales tax is 6%. To compute the sales tax, multiply the amount of the sale by .06. For example:

Amount of sale: 100
Sales tax: 100 × .06 = 6

Amount of sale: 10000
Sales tax: 10000 × .06 = 600

Amount of sale: 1000000
Sales tax: 1000000 × .06 = 60000

Now do it in QBasic. Enter and run the following program:

```
CLS
TaxRate = .06
PRINT 100 * TaxRate
PRINT 10000 * TaxRate
PRINT 1000000 * TaxRate
```

You will see these results on the screen:

```
6
600
59999.99865889549
```

Oops! 6 and 600 are okay, but how about the third answer? It is supposed to be *exactly* 60,000. It's only off a little, less than a penny, but that's bothersome. After all, your $10 calculator has no problem with this calculation.

This error occurs because QBasic uses *binary numbers* to represent numbers and do arithmetic, thus introducing tiny errors in some numbers. The decimal numbers you type into the computer are converted to binary numbers. That's okay for integers, but commonly used decimal fractions, such as .06, cannot be exactly represented as binary computer numbers.

QBasic's binary numbers are close enough to the real thing for most purposes, but keep in mind that a tiny error can exist. When in doubt, use double-precision numbers, which are more precise. That is, the error in converting from decimal to binary is less for double-precision numbers than for single-precision numbers. Run the following tiny program, which uses double-precision numbers (.06# and 1000000#) and a double-precision variable (*TaxRate#*):

```
CLS
TaxRate# = .06#
PRINT 1000000# * TaxRate#
```

When you run this program, the computer will print 60000 as the result, which seems to be correct. However, inside the computer, the result is still not quite exact. You can verify this by running the following program:

```
CLS
TaxRate# = .06#
PRINT 1000000# * TaxRate# - 60000
```

If the value of 1000000# * *TaxRate#* is exactly correct (equal to 60,000), then the value of 1000000# * *TaxRate#* − 60000 should be 0. Instead, this is the value you see:

```
-2.2204460492503130-12
```

As you can see, there is still a tiny error, about 2 in the 12th decimal place. This error is much smaller than the error that occurred using single-precision arithmetic.

The error, if any, in a double-precision number is quite small. However, if you add a bunch of numbers with tiny errors, they accumulate. The next program assigns the double-precision value .1# to the double-precision variable *x#* and then computes the double-precision value of *sum#* by adding *x#* 10,000 times to the previous value of *sum#*. This program also prints the value of TIMER before and after it does the work so that you can see how long it took.

```
CLS
x# = .1#
sum# = 0
PRINT TIMER
FOR k = 1 TO 10000
  sum# = sum# + x#
NEXT k
PRINT TIMER, sum#
```

Here is a run. You can see that it took about 14 seconds. You can also see the accumulated error on the right end of the value of *sum#*.

```
31234.26
31247.82        1000.000000000159
```

What might happen if you change *x#* to a single-precision variable in both places where it occurs in the program? Try it and find out.

Be careful about using a decimal fraction as the STEP value in a FOR statement. You might accumulate errors. For example:

```
CLS
sum = 0
FOR x = 0 TO 10 STEP .1
  sum = sum + x
NEXT x
PRINT sum
```

The correct result is 505, exactly. However, this program produces a result of 494.9998, a rather large error. Rewrite the program, this time using double-precision variables and numbers to see a better approximation to the true result. Whenever possible, avoid using a STEP value that cannot be represented exactly as a QBasic binary number.

Minimum or Maximum of Two Numbers

Design a FUNCTION procedure called Min that returns the minimum of two numbers. Here is a main program to test your procedure:

```
CLS
DO
  INPUT "First number "; first
  INPUT "Second number"; second
  PRINT "The minimum is "; Min(first, second)
  PRINT
LOOP
```

The FUNCTION procedure is called by the program line

```
PRINT "The minimum is "; Min(first, second)
```

Here is a sample run:

```
First number ? 7
Second number? 3
The minimum is  3

First number ? -1
Second number? 0
The minimum is -1
```

```
First number ? 3.14
Second number? 3.14
The minimum is  3.14
```

Begin your FUNCTION procedure like this:

```
FUNCTION Min(n1, n2)
```

After you get your Min procedure working, you can modify it easily to get another FUNCTION procedure, called Max, that returns the maximum of two numbers. Or write a SUB procedure that returns both the minimum and the maximum. This SUB procedure might begin like this:

```
SUB MinMax(n1, n2, Min, Max)
```

Use the following main program to check out your MinMax SUB procedure:

```
CLS
DO
  INPUT "First number "; first
  INPUT "Second number"; second
  CALL MinMax(first, second, minimum, maximum)
  PRINT "The minimum is "; minimum
  PRINT "The maximum is "; maximum
  PRINT
LOOP
```

STRING MUNCHING

QBasic has an excellent assortment of string-manipulation tools. You can add more tools by constructing FUNCTION and SUB procedures to do tasks not included in QBasic's list of keywords.

Counting the Spaces in a String

Counting the spaces in a string gives you a rough idea of the number of words in the string. Design a FUNCTION procedure called CountSpaces%. Note that CountSpaces% is an integer FUNCTION. The value of

CountSpaces%(*strng$*) is the number of spaces in the value of *strng$*. Test your procedure in a program that counts and prints the number of spaces in a string entered from the keyboard. A sample run might look like this:

```
String? This string has some spaces.
Number of spaces is 4

String? Thisstringhasnospaces.
Number of spaces is 0

String? This string, as you can see, has commas.
Number of spaces is 7

String? This string has    lots    of    spaces!
Number of spaces is 17
```

In your main program, use a LINE INPUT statement to acquire the string so that the string can include commas.

In writing the CountSpaces% procedure, you might find QBasic's INSTR function useful. INSTR is available in two forms. In its simplest form, INSTR is a numeric function of two string arguments. INSTR returns a numeric value that depends on whether the second argument is a substring of the first argument. If not, the value of INSTR is 0; if there is a match, the value of INSTR is the position in the first argument where the second argument matches. Table 13-2 shows values of INSTR for several pairs of arguments.

You will probably find INSTR's second form more useful in your CountSpaces% procedure. In this form, INSTR has one numeric and two string arguments. An example is shown here:

```
INSTR(start%, strng$, substrng$)
```

The first argument (*start%*) is numeric, an integer variable. It tells where to begin looking in *strng$* for a match with *substrng$*. If the value of *start%* is 1, the search begins at the first character in *strng$*. If the value of *start%* is 10, the search begins at the tenth character of *strng$*.

In your FUNCTION procedure, you might use an INSTR function that looks like one of these:

```
INST(start%, strng$, " ")
INST(start%, strng$, CHR$(32))      (CHR$(32) is a space)
INST(start%, strng$, SPACE$(1))     (SPACE$(1) is one space)
```

INSTR Function	Value	Result
INSTR("abc","a")	1	Match at position 1 of first argument
INSTR("abc","b")	2	Match at position 2 of first argument
INSTR("abc","c")	3	Match at position 3 of first argument
INSTR("abc","*")	0	No match; no asterisk in first argument
INSTR("abc","A")	0	No match; no *A* in first argument
INSTR("abc","ab")	1	Match at position 1 of first argument
INSTR("abc","bc")	2	Match at position 2 of first argument
INSTR("abc","abc")	1	Match at position 1 of first argument
INSTR("ab","abc")	0	No match; *abc* is not in first argument

TABLE 13-2. Values of INSTR for Several Pairs of Arguments

You might use INSTR within a DO . . . LOOP. With *start%* = 1, you will find the first space and count it. The value of INSTR will be the character position in the string where the space was found. The next search should start one place to the right, and so on to the end of the string. Good hunting!

String Squeezer

Design and write a FUNCTION procedure called Squeezer to squeeze the spaces out of a string. For example,

Value of *strng$*	Value of Squeezer(*strng$*)
North Dakota	NorthDakota
2 / 3	2/3
3 D 6	3D6
Never Odd or Even	NeverOddOrEven

Also write a main program to test your Squeezer FUNCTION. A sample run might go something like the one shown in Figure 13-1.

```
String, please? North Dakota

Original string: North Dakota
Squeezed string: NorthDakota

String, please? 2   /   3

Original string: 2   /   3
Squeezed string: 2/3

String, please? S q u e e z e , p l e a s e

Original string: S q u e e z e , p l e a s e
Squeezed string: Squeeze,please
```

═══ **FIGURE 13-1.** Sample run to test Squeezer FUNCTION

Making Your Own Anagrams

An anagram is a scrambling of the letters in a word or phrase. Write a program to scramble a word and print scrambled words that are, as you can see, anagrams of the original word. Here is a sample run of one program:

```
Your word? anagram
How many anagrams shall I print? 10

nmaarga     aagmarn     gaaramn     nagmaar     armnaga
agnmara     gaanmar     nrgaama     nmargaa     gnramaa
```

There are many ways to write this program. You might first put the letters of the word in a string array, one letter per array element, and then scramble the array and assemble the letters into an anagram. To do this, you might find QBasic's SWAP statement useful.

The statement

```
SWAP strng1$, strng2$
```

tells the computer to swap the values of *strng1$* and *strng2$*. In your program, suppose the array containing letters of the word is called *Letter$( )*. You might use a SWAP statement similar to this one:

```
SWAP Letter$(k), Letter$(RandomSubscript)
```

This SWAP statement swaps the letter in position *k* with the letter in position *RandomSubscript,* a previously computed random subscript. If your program does this for k = 1, then k = 2, then k = 3, and so on, to the end of the *Letter$( )* array, this should scramble the array quite nicely.

CALENDAR PROBLEMS

Many applications require calendar computations. Is the year a common year with 365 days, or a leap year with 366 days? What day of the year is April 15? What is the date of the 200th day of the year? How many days between March 13 and August 20? Try your hand at these calendar problems.

Common Year or Leap Year?

A common year has 365 days. A leap year has 366 days. Leap years are years that are multiples of 4, except the centurial years. Centurial years are years that are multiples of 100. A centurial year is a leap year only if it is a multiple of 400.

- 1987 was a common year.

- 1988 was a leap year.

- 1900 was a common year.

- 2000 will be a leap year, if we are still using the Gregorian calendar adopted in 1582.

Write a FUNCTION procedure to determine if a year is a common year or a leap year. Call it Leap%. The value of Leap% is −1 or 0. For example:

- 1990 was a common year, so Leap%(1990) is 0.

- 1988 was a leap year, so Leap%(1988) is −1.

These values are chosen so that, when used as a condition, Leap% will be true for a leap year and false for a common year. Use the following main program to test your FUNCTION:

```
CLS
DO
  INPUT "Year"; year%
  IF Leap%(year%) THEN
    PRINT "Leap year"
  ELSE
    PRINT "Common year"
  END IF
  PRINT
LOOP
```

Here is a sample run:

```
Year? 1990
Common year

Year? 1988
Leap year

Year? 2000
Leap year

Year? 1900
Common year
```

Day of the Year for a Given Date

Number the days of the year 1 to 365 for a common year or 1 to 366 for a leap year. Table 13-3 shows the day of the year and the corresponding dates for both common and leap years.

   Design and write a FUNCTION procedure to compute the day of the year for arguments *Month%* (1 to 12), *DayOfMonth%* (1 to 31), and *Year%*. Also write a main program to test the procedure. For March 15, 1990 (a common year), a run might look like this:

Day	Date: Common Year	Date: Leap Year
1	January 1	January 1
31	January 31	January 31
32	February 1	February 1
59	February 28	February 28
60	March 1	February 29
61	March 2	March 1
365	December 31	December 30
366	---	December 31

TABLE 13-3. Day of Year and Dates for Common and Leap Years

```
Month (1 to 12)? 3
Day (1 to 31)  ? 15
Year           ? 1990

Day of the year: 74
```

For March 15, 1988 (a leap year), the result is different, as shown here:

```
Month (1 to 12)? 3
Day (1 to 31)  ? 15
Year           ? 1988

Day of the year: 73
```

Date for a Day of the Year

Number the days of the year 1 to 365 for a common year or 1 to 366 for a leap year. Table 13-3 shows the day of the year and the corresponding dates for both common and leap years.

Design and write a SUB procedure to compute the date for a given day of the year. Your SUB definition might look like this:

```
SUB Date(DayOfYear%, Year%, Month%, DayofMonth%)
```

You supply the values of *DayOfYear%* and *Year%*. Your SUB procedure returns the values of *Month%* and *DayOfMonth%*. A program to test the function might produce results like the following for the 60th day of 1990, a common year:

```
Day of year (1 to 366)? 60
Year                   ? 1990

Month: 3
Day:   1
```

For a leap year, the result is different, as shown here:

```
Day of year (1 to 366)? 60
Year                   ? 1988

Month: 2
Day:   29
```

REARRANGING AN ARRAY

You can use arrays to store lists of information and perform calculations. You can also use arrays to rearrange information. For example, you can use arrays to sort lists of numbers or names into some desired sequence, such as least to greatest or greatest to least. You can even use arrays to scramble information into random patterns.

Scrambling an Array of Numbers

Sometimes, especially when creating computer simulations or games, you may want to scramble a list, or array, of numbers. For example, you can use an array of numbers 1 to 52 to represent the 52 cards in a deck of cards and then "shuffle the deck" by scrambling the array.

Write a program to scramble an array of integers from 1 to *NmbrElements,* where you enter the value of *NmbrElements.* Figure 13-2 shows a sample run for a list of seven numbers, 1 through 7. Since there are 5040 different ways to arrange the integers 1 through 7, you are likely to see a different arrangement when you run the program and ask for seven numbers.

```
Scramble an array of numbers

How many numbers shall I scramble? 7

Here are the unscrambled numbers:

1            2            3            4            5
6            7

Here are the scrambled numbers:

5            4            1            6            2
7            3
```

FIGURE 13-2. Sample run of Scramble an Array Program

You generate the original, unscrambled array by assigning 1 to *array(1)*, 2 to *array(2)*, 3 to *array(3)*, and so on. If *NmbrElements* is 7, the unscrambled array will contain the values shown here:

Array Element	Value
array(1)	1
array(2)	2
array(3)	3
array(4)	4
array(5)	5
array(6)	6
array(7)	7

You can use a FOR . . . NEXT loop to generate the array, like this:

```
FOR k = 1 TO NmbrElements
   array(k) = k
NEXT k
```

You can use another FOR . . . NEXT loop to scramble the array. One way to do this is to swap each array element with a randomly selected array element. Use a SWAP statement to do so. After scrambling the array, print the scrambled array, as shown in Figure 13-2.

Scrambling and Sorting an Array of Numbers

The converse of scrambling an array is sorting an array. Write a program to generate an array of numbers, scramble the array, print the scrambled numbers, sort the array, and print the sorted numbers. A sample run is shown in Figure 13-3.

One of the simplest ways to sort an array is by means of a *bubble sort*. Suppose that the array has four elements, scrambled as shown here:

Array Element	Value
array(1)	2
array(2)	4
array(3)	1
array(4)	3

A bubble sort would compare the value of *array(1)* with the other array elements and swap values whenever a smaller value was found, thus "bubbling up" the value 1 to occupy *array(1)*. This would leave 2 elsewhere in

---

```
Scramble and sort an array of numbers

How many numbers shall I scramble? 7

Here are the scrambled numbers:

3          1          7          4          6
5          2

Here are the sorted numbers:

1          2          3          4          5
6          7
```

FIGURE 13-3. Sample of program to scramble and sort an array of numbers

the array. Then, by a similar process, 2 is "bubbled up" to occupy *array(2)*, and so on, until the array is sorted. The process is shown here:

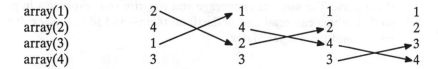

When an entire array is in reverse order, it will require the most swaps to sort it. In fact, there will be exactly $(n-1) * (n-2)$ swaps, where n is the number of elements in the array. The sorting process for an array of four elements in reverse order is shown next. For this array, $n = 4$, and the number of swaps required is $(4-1) * (4-2) = 6$.

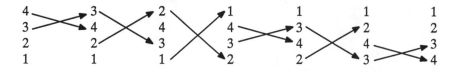

The bubble sort is simple, but slow. When you get your program working properly, add program lines to print the value of TIMER before and after the sort. Then run your program for, say, a number of elements equal to 100, 200, 500, or even 1000.

SUMMARY

You now know a great deal about QBasic. You can use QBasic to tell the computer what to do and how to do it, the way you want it done.

This chapter posed several problems that you can solve by applying your QBasic skills. You can continue learning about QBasic from books about QuickBASIC as well as from books about QBasic. In particular, you might want to consult the following Osborne/McGraw-Hill books:

- *QuickBASIC Made Easy* by Bob Albrecht, Wenden Wiegand, and Dean Brown

- *Using QuickBASIC* by Don Inman and Bob Albrecht

- *QuickBASIC: The Complete Reference* by Steven Nameroff

QBasic is also the major theme in "Hands on BASIC" by Bob Albrecht and George Firedrake, a monthly column in *PC Hands On* magazine.

The best way to learn more about QBasic is to write programs and make them work. The authors encourage you to write your programs in good style so that others can read and understand them—and so that *you* can read and understand them a year later.

THE QBASIC
SURVIVAL GUIDE

From the opening screen, shown in Figure A-1, you can access the Survival Guide by pressing the ENTER key. The Survival Guide contains information on using QBasic and directions for obtaining help. When you press the ENTER key from the opening screen, a Help window appears. The Help window is displayed at the top of the screen, and the View window and Immediate window are compressed to make room for the help information.

Figure A-2 shows the Help window with instructions for using QBasic at the top of the window and directions for browsing the QBasic help system below. Notice that the help system is divided into three parts: Index, Contents, and Using Help. The cursor is located at the first option, Index. Start by exploring the help system. To do so, choose the third option, Using Help, by pressing the ↓ key twice. Then,

Press: ENTER

The screen in Figure A-3 appears when you select the Using Help option and press the ENTER key. Directions are displayed for using the help system from QBasic. When you have read the directions, follow the directions of the next-to-last item:

Press: PGDN

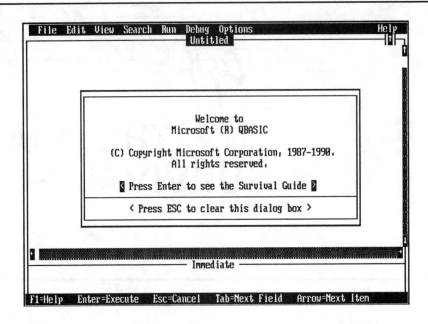

FIGURE A-1. Opening screen

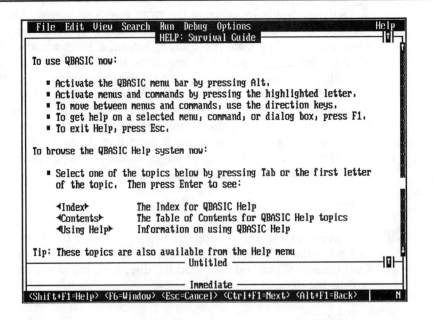

FIGURE A-2. Help Window instructions

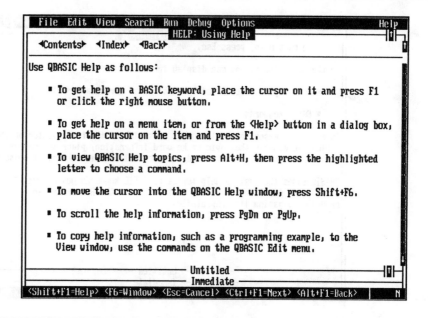

```
 File  Edit  View  Search  Run  Debug  Options                    Help
                          HELP: Using Help                         ▲
 ◄Contents► ◄Index► ◄Back►                                         ▲
 ──────────────────────────────────────────────────────────────────
 Use QBASIC Help as follows:

    ▪ To get help on a BASIC keyword, place the cursor on it and press F1
      or click the right mouse button.

    ▪ To get help on a menu item, or from the <Help> button in a dialog box,
      place the cursor on the item and press F1.

    ▪ To view QBASIC Help topics, press Alt+H, then press the highlighted
      letter to choose a command.

    ▪ To move the cursor into the QBASIC Help window, press Shift+F6.

    ▪ To scroll the help information, press PgDn or PgUp.

    ▪ To copy help information, such as a programming example, to the
      View window, use the commands on the QBASIC Edit menu.
                                                                   ▼
 ──────────────────────── Untitled ───────────────────────────────
 ──────────────────────── Immediate ──────────────────────────────
 <Shift+F1=Help> <F6=Window> <Esc=Cancel> <Ctrl+F1=Next> <Alt+F1=Back>    N
```

═══ **FIGURE A-3.**   Using Help, page 1

This scrolls more Using Help information into the Help window, as shown in Figure A-4. Read this information, and then scan the status bar at the bottom of the screen. Notice the last two items: CTRL+F1=Next and ALT+F1=Back. You can use these two key combinations to move forward or backward through the Survival Guide. For now,

Press: CTRL-F1

to move to the next screen. The Survival Guide Table of Contents is displayed, as shown in Figure A-5. The Table of Contents is divided into four categories: Orientation, Keys, Using QBASIC, and Quick Reference. You can select any item from any of the four categories by moving the cursor to the item with the TAB and arrow keys and then pressing ENTER. Notice, at the top of the screen, that you can move to Contents, Index, or Back by selecting one of the three options. While the cursor is at the Index option,

Press: ENTER

Help Index appears in the Help window, as shown in Figure A-6. At the top are directions for using this index. The QBasic keywords are listed alphabetically, with the groups of keywords beginning with A and B visible in the

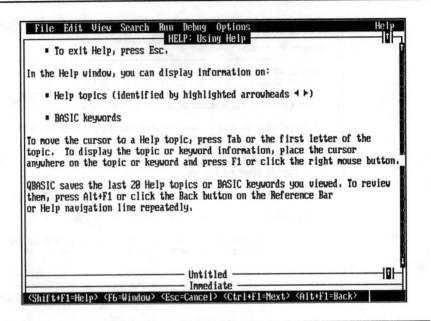

FIGURE A-4. Using Help, page 2

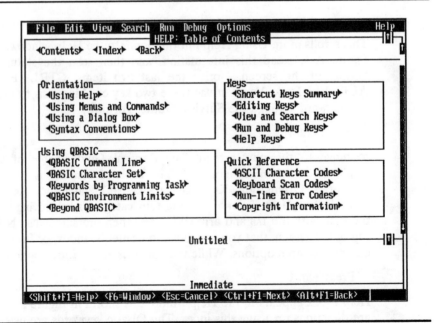

FIGURE A-5. Help Table of Contents

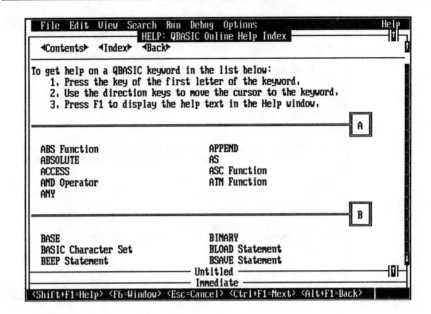

═══ **FIGURE A-6.** Help Index

Help window. You can move between pages of keywords by pressing PGDN and PGUP, or you can select a keyword by following the three instructions at the top of this window. As an example, to select the keyword ASC,

Press: A

Use the arrow (direction) keys to move the cursor to ASC Function. Then,

Press: F1

A description of the ASC and CHR$ functions is displayed, as shown by the screen in Figure A-7. These two functions are described together because of the close relationship of the tasks they perform. Notice the note at the bottom of the Help window:

See Also   ◄ ASCII Character Codes ►

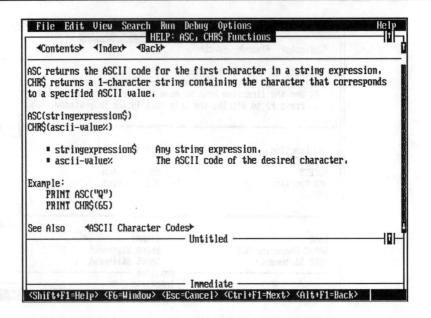

FIGURE A-7. Description of ASC and CHR$ functions

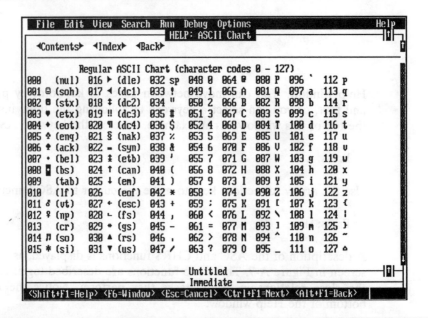

FIGURE A-8. ASCII codes 0-127

```
 File  Edit  View  Search  Run  Debug  Options                    Help
                        ┌ HELP: ASCII Chart ┐
                Extended ASCII Chart (character codes 128 - 255)
 128 Ç    144 É    160 á    176 ▓    192 └    208 ╨    224 α    240 ≡
 129 ü    145 æ    161 í    177 ▓    193 ┴    209 ╤    225 ß    241 ±
 130 é    146 Æ    162 ó    178 ▓    194 ┬    210 ╥    226 Γ    242 ≥
 131 â    147 ô    163 ú    179 │    195 ├    211 ╙    227 π    243 ≤
 132 ä    148 ö    164 ñ    180 ┤    196 ─    212 ╘    228 Σ    244 ⌠
 133 à    149 ò    165 Ñ    181 ╡    197 ┼    213 ╒    229 σ    245 ⌡
 134 å    150 û    166 ª    182 ╢    198 ╞    214 ╓    230 µ    246 ÷
 135 ç    151 ù    167 º    183 ╖    199 ╟    215 ╫    231 τ    247 ≈
 136 ê    152 ÿ    168 ¿    184 ╕    200 ╚    216 ╪    232 Φ    248 °
 137 ë    153 Ö    169 ⌐    185 ╣    201 ╔    217 ┘    233 Θ    249 ·
 138 è    154 Ü    170 ¬    186 ║    202 ╩    218 ┌    234 Ω    250 ·
 139 ï    155 ¢    171 ½    187 ╗    203 ╦    219 █    235 δ    251 √
 140 î    156 £    172 ¼    188 ╝    204 ╠    220 ▄    236 ∞    252 ⁿ
 141 ì    157 ¥    173 ¡    189 ╜    205 ═    221 ▌    237 ø    253 ²
 142 Ä    158 ₧    174 «    190 ╛    206 ╬    222 ▐    238 ε    254 ■
 143 Å    159 ƒ    175 »    191 ┐    207 ╧    223 ▀    239 ∩    255

 ├────────────────────────── Untitled ──────────────────────────┤
 ├────────────────────────── Immediate ─────────────────────────┤
 <Shift+F1=Help> <F6=Window> <Esc=Cancel> <Ctrl+F1=Next> <Alt+F1=Back>
```

FIGURE A-9.   ASCII codes 128-255

To see this item, move the cursor to a character between the markers
◄ and ►, such as the A of ASCII. Then,

Press: ENTER

The ASCII codes 0-127 are displayed along with their functions and the printed characters (where they are available) that they return, as shown by the screen in Figure A-8.
   To see the ASCII codes 128-255,

Press: PGDN

The codes and characters for 128-255 are displayed, as shown in Figure A-9.
   You can leave the Survival Guide at any time by pressing the ESC key. Before you do so, spend some time exploring the help system.

ASCII CODES

This appendix lists the ASCII codes for characters.

Decimal Value	Character	Decimal Value	Character
0	Null	10	Line-feed
1	☺	11	Cursor home
2	☻	12	Form-feed
3	♥	13	Enter
4	♦	14	♫
5	♣	15	☼
6	♠	16	►
7	Beep	17	◄
8	◘	18	↕
9	Tab	19	‼

Decimal Value	Character	Decimal Value	Character
20	¶	46	.
21	§	47	/
22	▬	48	0
23	↕	49	1
24	↑	50	2
25	↓	51	3
26	→	52	4
27	←	53	5
28	Curor right	54	6
29	Cursor left	55	7
30	Cursor up	56	8
31	Cursor down	57	9
32	Space	58	:
33	!	59	;
34	"	60	<
35	#	61	=
36	$	62	>
37	%	63	?
38	&	64	@
39	'	65	A
40	(	66	B
41	)	67	C
42	*	68	D
43	+	69	E
44	,	70	F
45	-	71	G

Decimal Value	Character	Decimal Value	Character
72	H	98	b
73	I	99	c
74	J	100	d
75	K	101	e
76	L	102	f
77	M	103	g
78	N	104	h
79	O	105	i
80	P	106	j
81	Q	107	k
82	R	108	l
83	S	109	m
84	T	110	n
85	U	111	o
86	V	112	p
87	W	113	q
88	X	114	r
89	Y	115	s
90	Z	116	t
91	[	117	u
92	\	118	v
93	]	119	w
94	^	120	x
95	—	121	y
96	`	122	z
97	a	123	{

Decimal Value	Character	Decimal Value	Character
124	¦	150	û
125	}	151	ù
126	~	152	ÿ
127	⌂	153	Ö
128	Ç	154	Ü
129	ü	155	¢
130	é	156	£
131	â	157	¥
132	ä	158	Pt
133	à	159	ƒ
134	å	160	á
135	ç	161	í
136	ê	162	ó
137	ë	163	ú
138	è	164	ñ
139	ï	165	Ñ
140	î	166	ª
141	ì	167	º
142	Ä	168	¿
143	Å	169	⌐
144	É	170	¬
145	æ	171	½
146	Æ	172	¼
147	ô	173	¡
148	ö	174	«
149	ò	175	»

Decimal Value	Character	Decimal Value	Character
176	░	202	╩
177	▒	203	╦
178	▓	204	╠
179	│	205	═
180	┤	206	╬
181	╡	207	╧
182	╢	208	╨
183	╖	209	╤
184	╕	210	╥
185	╣	211	╙
186	║	212	╘
187	╗	213	╒
188	╝	214	╓
189	╜	215	╫
190	╛	216	╪
191	┐	217	┘
192	└	218	┌
193	┴	219	█
194	┬	220	▄
195	├	221	▌
196	─	222	▐
197	┼	223	▀
198	╞	224	α
199	╟	225	β
200	╚	226	Γ
201	╔	227	π

Decimal Value	Character		Decimal Value	Character
228	Σ		242	≥
229	σ		243	≤
230	μ		244	⌠
231	τ		245	⌡
232	φ		246	÷
233	Θ		247	≈
234	Ω		248	°
235	δ		249	•
236	∞		250	·
237	Ø		251	√
238	ε		252	n
239	∩		253	2
240	≡		254	■
241	±		255	(blank)

QBASIC KEYWORDS

ABS	CLNG	DEFSTR
ACCESS	CLOSE	DIM
ALIAS	CLS	DO
AND	COLOR	DOUBLE
ANY	COM	DRAW
APPEND	COMMAND$	ELSE
AS	COMMON	ELSEIF
ASC	CONST	END
ATN	COS	ENDIF
BASE	CSNG	ENVIRON
BEEP	CSRLIN	ENVIRON$
BINARY	CVD	EOF
BLOAD	CVDMBF	EQV
BSAVE	CVI	ERASE
BYVAL	CVL	ERDEV
CALL	CVS	ERDEV$
CALLS	CVSMBF	ERL
CASE	DATA	ERR
CDBL	DATE$	ERROR
CHAIN	DECLARE	EXIT
CHDIR	DEF	EXP
CHR$	DEFDBL	FIELD
CINT	DEFINT	FILEATTR
CIRCLE	DEFLNG	FILES
CLEAR	DEFSNG	FIX

411

FN	MKDIR	RSET
FOR	MKDMBF$	RTRIM$
FRE	MKI$	RUN
FREEFILE	MKL$	SADD
FUNCTION	MKS$	SCREEN
GET	MKSMBF$	SEEK
GOSUB	MOD	SEG
GOTO	NAME	SELECT
HEX$	NEXT	SGN
IF	NOT	SHARED
IMP	OCT$	SHELL
INKEY$	OFF	SIGNAL
INP	ON	SIN
INPUT	OPEN	SINGLE
INPUT$	OPTION	SLEEP
INSTR	OR	SOUND
INT	OUT	SPACE$
INTEGER	OUTPUT	SPC
IOCTL	PAINT	SQR
IOCTL$	PALETTE	STATIC
IS	PCOPY	STEP
KEY	PEEK	STICK
KILL	PEN	STOP
LBOUND	PLAY	STR$
LCASE$	PMAP	STRIG
LEFT$	POINT	STRING
LEN	POKE	STRING$
LET	POS	SUB
LINE	PRESET	SWAP
LIST	PRINT	SYSTEM
LOC	PSET	TAB
LOCAL	PUT	TAN
LOCATE	RANDOM	THEN
LOCK	RANDOMIZE	TIME$
LOF	READ	TIMER
LOG	REDIM	TO
LONG	REM	TROFF
LOOP	RESET	TRON
LPOS	RESTORE	TYPE
LPRINT	RESUME	UBOUND
LSET	RETURN	UCASE$
LTRIM$	RIGHT$	UEVENT
MID$	RMDIR	UNLOCK
MKD$	RND	UNTIL

USING	VIEW	WIDTH
VAL	WAIT	WINDOW
VARPTR	WEND	WRITE
VARPTR$	WHILE	XOR
VARSEG		

INDEX

The manuscript for this book was prepared and submitted to Osborne/McGraw-Hill in electronic form. The acquisitions editor for this project was Jeff Pepper, the technical reviewer was Ramon Zamora, and the project editor was Madhu Prasher.

This book was designed by Stefany Otis, using Times Roman for text body and Helvetica for display.

Cover art by Bay Graphics Design, Inc. The color separation and cover supplier was Phoenix Color Corporation. Screens were produced with InSet, from InSet Systems, Inc. This book was printed and bound by R.R. Donnelley & Sons Company, Crawfordsville, Indiana.